Social W

Social W

Yearbook 2

Still available

Social Work and Social Welfare Yearbook 1

Contents

Social Work and Social Welfare Yearbook 2

1990

Edited by
Pam Carter,
Tony Jeffs and
Mark Smith

Open University Press
Milton Keynes · Philadelphia

Open University Press
Celtic Court
22 Ballmoor
Buckingham MK18 1XW

and
1900 Frost Road, Suite 101
Bristol, PA 19007, USA

First Published 1990

British Library Cataloguing in Publication Data

Social work and social welfare yearbook
  1. Great Britain. Welfare work
  361.3′0941

  ISBN 0–335–09424–4
  ISBN 0–335–09423–6 Pbk

Library of Congress Catalog number available

Typeset by Scarborough Typesetting Services
Printed in Great Britain by
Biddles Ltd, Guildford and Kings Lynn

Contents

Notes on editors
and contributors

Ruth Allan — Former Probation Officer; Research Assistant to Barry Sheerman, MP, Labour Party Home Affairs Spokesperson.

John Baker — Lecturer, Department of Politics, University College, Dublin.

Caroline Ball — Barrister, Lecturer in Social Work Law, University of East Anglia.

Sarah Banks — Tutor in Community and Youth Work, Department of Adult and Continuing Education, Durham University.

Eric Blyth — Lecturer, School of Human and Health Studies, Huddersfield Polytechnic.

Pam Carter — is at the Centre for Social Welfare Studies, Newcastle upon Tyne Polytechnic.

Angela Everitt — Reader, Centre for Social Welfare Studies, Newcastle upon Tyne Polytechnic.

Ahmed Gurnah — Sheffield Education Department.

David Howe — Lecturer, Social Work Department, University of East Anglia.

Tony Jeffs — is at the Centre for Social Welfare Studies, Newcastle upon Tyne Polytechnic.

Sandra Leventon — Carer; Editor *The Carer*, journal of the Carers' National Association.

Jenny Lumley — Independent Consultant.

Nano McCaughan — Consultant, The Children's Society.

Peter Malpass — Lecturer in Housing Studies, Bristol Polytechnic.

Phyllida Parsloe — Pro-Vice Chancellor and Professor of Social Work, University of Bristol.

Andy Pithouse   Lecturer, School of Social and Administrative Studies,
                         University of Wales, Cardiff.
Mark Smith   Tutor at the Centre for Professional Studies in Informal
                         Education, YMCA National College London.
Liz Stanley   Lecturer, Sociology Department, University of Man-
                         chester.
Alan Stanton   Co-ordinator of Participatory Research Exchange.
Anthea Tinker   Professor of Gerontology and Director of the Age
                         Concern Institute of Gerontology, King's College,
                         London.
Sue Wise   Lecturer in Social Work, Department of Social Admin-
                         istration, University of Lancaster.

The views expressed are those of the contributors and should in no way be taken to represent those of their employers or other agencies with which they are connected.

In the last edition we incorrectly described Christopher Turner as being employed at the University of Edinburgh. He is in fact Professor of Sociology and Social Policy and Deputy Principal at Stirling University.

Introduction

In editing this the second volume of the *Social Work and Social Welfare Yearbook* we have again sought not to provide a mere review of the year or a catalogue of administrative detail. As before we have attempted to bring together a collection which will help readers to understand better the direction and nature of social work and social welfare practice. Material which:

1 updates and reviews current and potential practice developments, policy changes and research;
2 allows readers to gain or maintain a broad perspective on social welfare so that discussions about specialisms are better informed;
3 facilitates critical debate.

The Yearbook occupies a position somewhere between the weekly magazines which can carry only limited analysis, substantive works which take sometime to appear, and journals which are either more specialist or diverse in coverage.

There appears to be little merit in offering a summation of the contributions that follow. The titles and the opening paragraphs of each one will give the reader a clear indication of their content. Instead we would like to use this space to respond to a number of enquiries regarding how content is determined. Although as most of you will have guessed all volumes such as this contain the 'wild card' article which dropped unexpectedly on to the doormat, overall intelligence has been at work here. We try to operate according to a rolling programme which seeks to give space to the questions of the moment. However, we don't allow these to sweep aside other concerns and debates which require continuous exploration. The principle behind the rolling programme is a recognition that within one edition only a proportion of the relevant questions may be included. The important task is to acquire balance between and over editions. This will, of course, never be achieved in totality.

Although largely content driven we do endeavour to offer potential contributors the chance to follow an idea. The working list is influenced by our interests; reading; the concerns of students, friends and colleagues; and the interplay of ideas between ourselves and contributors. Chapters are not commissioned in one fell swoop. This is a recognition that debates wax and wane, major issues irrupt and opportunities to present long-standing debates in a fresh light and context emerge during the process of producing any one of the *Yearbooks*. Consequently while some contributors may have eighteen months to prepare a chapter, others will have only a few weeks. All this must be placed in the context of a tight and unyielding series of deadlines. These enable the publisher to achieve the remarkable turnround for an academic text of less than five months.

Perhaps as a result of the pace contributors have been known to mysteriously disappear; break their legs; travel abroad; get new jobs; become bored with the subject; fall out with the editors; or any combination of these. The majority, however, stay with us throughout, producing to deadlines that must impose considerable strain upon their working and domestic lives. It would be difficult to convey our appreciation of their commitment. Similarly recognition has to be afforded to the publishers, typesetters and printers, who also have to work within a tight schedule. To all these our thanks. Not least because their efforts help to make the process immensely enjoyable and stimulating for us.

Pam Carter
Tony Jeffs
Mark Smith

1
The Children Act 1989: origins, aims and current concerns

Caroline Ball

The Children Act 1989 is a major and long-overdue piece of legislation which, for the first time, brings together almost all the so-called private and public law relating to children, in a single coherent statute. Such is the complexity of the subject matter, and the mass of yet-to-be drafted rules, regulations and transitional provisions needed to effect its implementation, that the new law is unlikely to come into force until some time in 1991. When it is fully implemented, however, the effect of the Act will be that, whatever the nature of the proceedings, the same remedies, mostly applied according to identical principles and reached on the basis of the welfare criteria of the child's interest being paramount, will be available whenever judicial decisions are made about the care and upbringing of children. This will apply whether the decisions are being made in private proceedings between adult parties such as divorce or guardianship, or in public law cases in which the state is intervening to protect children and make arrangements for them on a voluntary or compulsory basis when their families by fault or default fail to do so.

This chapter seeks, within the limitations of its length, to trace the origins of the new legislation by reviewing the wide-ranging evidence of professional concern about existing legal provisions and the unsatisfactory court system in which those provisions are administered; considering the process by which the proposals for the reform of the separate strands were formulated and eventually came together; and identifying issues which illustrate concern about the balance achieved in the Act.

Historically the private and the public law provisions relating to children have been contained in separate statutes and administered in different proceedings from the public law. The private law has never been in quite the parlous state of the public law although it is full of inconsistencies and anomalies which result in its often making little sense to children and families.

The pressures for, and process of, reform of each strand were correspondingly diverse and it was almost a matter of chance that they eventually came together in a single statute (Hoggett 1989a).

Reform of the public law

The public law relating to children involves profound public policy issues. These concern both the rights of parents to bring up their children free from interruption by the state, and those of children to be brought up within their families with the safeguard that the state will intervene on their behalf to exercise parental responsibility and make short- or long-term provision for them should their parents fail to do so, or abuse them in the process. The relationship between the two is both delicate and crucial. At its most simplistic, if the balance is not achieved, either too many children will be deprived of an up-bringing within their own families (and the state in the form of local authority care often fails to provide a truly satisfactory substitute for family life), or too many will be left vulnerable to neglect or abuse by their parents without the state's having power to protect them and make, where appropriate, secure long-term plans for their future. The practice of social work with children and their families can be helped or frustrated by the statutory framework within which it takes place.

The dilemma for legislators is that of maintaining the delicate balance between respect for the personal rights of parents to bring up their children without unnecessary interference from authority, and the rights of children to be protected from abuse. Given that the balance is such a difficult one to achieve, and that failure in one direction or the other arouses such intense public reaction, it is perhaps not surprising that the law relating to state provision for, and the protection of, children is peculiarly vulnerable to shifts in political and ideological thinking. Child care legislation during the last twenty years demonstrates that such swings provide statutory licence for practice which not only may defeat the best intentions of the legislators, but also will eventually require further statutory reform which may also fail to achieve the desired balance. As will be discussed below there are real concerns that aspects of the Children Act 1989 illustrate this phenomenon.

The public law of child care is further complicated by the fact that its roots lie in separate, originally clearly identifiable, though recently more closely entangled, strands of state provision for children. One strand, with its origins in Poor Law relief for the destitute, is currently contained in the Child Care Act 1980, a consolidating statute which brought together remnants of the Children Act 1948, the Children and Young Persons Act 1963 and parts of the Children Act 1975. The other strand contains the quasi-criminal provisions for the protection or control of abused or unruly children, currently contained in the much amended and partially repealed Children and Young Persons Acts 1933 and 1969. The significance of the consequence of these separate strands of development is beyond the scope of this chapter, however, the extent to which they have contributed to the current complexity of the law and the unsatisfactory nature of many of the legal proceedings should not be underestimated (RCCL 1985).

The Children Act 1975 was the last major piece of reforming child care legislation, though there have been several important subsequent statutory amendments. That Act, which sought to reform the law in three particular areas, started life as a high-profile private members' Bill introduced by Dr David Owen in response to media-aroused public concern about several 'tug-of-love' cases in which natural parents appeared to reclaim children who were well and happily settled in foster homes. The tragic death of Maria Colwell at the hands of her stepfather and mother to whom she had been returned from care, although under a supervision order, both against her own wishes and those of her foster parents fuelled demand for reform. The fact that the juvenile court making the decision to discharge the care order had no opportunity to hear Maria's view of the planned move, because there was no mechanism for the appointment of a child care expert independent of the local authority, to consider Maria's wishes and feelings and make a report to the court on their view of the child's welfare, was a key factor in the case (Field-Fisher 1974).

In view of its origins it is not surprising that the 1975 Act has a certain 'rag-bag' quality. Not only did it introduce improvements to care proceedings following the Maria Colwell inquiry, but also, largely as a result of research findings about children drifting in care (Rowe and Lambert 1973), measures designed to ensure that long-term plans could be made by local authorities for children who had spent long periods in their care. In addition it introduced the major changes to adoption law recommended by the Houghton Committee, including the concept of freeing children for adoption before adopters were involved, and the 'half-way house' of custodianship for children needing security with their carers, but for whom adoption was not appropriate (Stockdale 1972).

Despite its multifarious aims the basic thrust of the 1975 Act was to require local authorities to consider children's wishes and feelings when making decisions about their future and empower them to intervene to make, and implement, long-term plans. Sadly the often-delayed and piecemeal implementation of the Act, which dragged on for over a decade, together with the way in which its accompanying regulations were framed, allowed local authorities to make too great a shift towards routine use of compulsory measures including wardship. Parents' rights were in many cases seriously undermined or ignored. The resulting steady stream of appeals to the Court of Human Rights over issues such as local authority assumption of parental rights and access to children in care, together with the evidence emerging from research studies, started the pendulum swinging back towards parents and away from local authorities (Douglas 1988).

During the period when the 1975 Act was partially implemented attempts were made by means of the consolidating statutes, the Adoption Act 1976 and the Child Care Act 1980, to rationalize child care law by bringing outstanding earlier provisions together with some of those in the 1975 Act, both implemented and not, grouped in single statutes. Although the measures were intended to rationalize existing legislation they 'succeeded only in highlighting their confusion and inadequacy' (Rowe 1989).

When the House of Commons Social Services Committee on children in care, chaired by Mrs Renee Short, heard evidence in the 1982/83 parliamentary session it was clear that the general view was that the state of the law and the courts was such that it was frustrating, rather than helping, good child care practice. The committee's chosen topic for the session was 'children in care', and the weight of the evidence given by those involved in all aspects of child care of the extent to which they felt children and families were disadvantaged by the unsatisfactory state of the law and the courts administering it was both unexpected and compelling. Witnesses did not mince their words. In the committee's report (the Short Report; House of Commons 1984: para 118) evidence from a group of lawyers and social workers is quoted:

> The present state of children's legislation can only be described as complex, confusing and unsatisfactory. . . . The effect and implication of this on children is diverse with far-reaching consequences for their welfare.

and the committee commented:

> The time has arrived – indeed it arrived some time ago – for a thorough-going review of the body of statute law, regulations and judicial decisions relating to children, with a view to the production of a simplified and coherent body of law comprehensible not only to those operating it but also to those affected by its operation.
>
> (para 119)

The practitioners and politicians were not alone: they had the sympathy and support of the judiciary. In 1983 Lord Ormrod, addressing the annual meeting of the British Association of Adoption and Fostering (BAAF), said:

> I am sure my perspective on the present state of child care law is shared in the broadest sense by everyone who has anything to do with its administration. It is in a state of confusion which is unparalleled in any other branch of the law now or at any other time in the past.
>
> (Ormrod 1983)

Students of literature and history will notice that the eminent former Family Division judge and Lord of Appeal did not exclude nineteenth-century Chancery law and procedure, when making his sweeping condemnation. More recently Mr Justice Waite struck a chord in the hearts of many professionals struggling to make sense of and administer the existing tangle of overlapping, partially implemented and much amended provisions when he referred to them as a 'legislative thicket through which even the most practised members of the legal and social work professions had to struggle' (Waite 1987).

Pressure for reform of the law, and for a court system with a unified jurisdiction for its administration, came from the whole spectrum of professionals rightly concerned about the complexity and lack of clarity of the substantive law and the inadequacy of the courts, as well as from organizations representing children and families most disadvantaged by its worst manifestations, and from academics. The published findings of substantial DHSS- and ESRC-funded research into all aspects of social work decision-making in relation to children, taking place within that legal framework, also added considerable weight to generalized demands for reform (DHSS 1985). These studies, which altogether involved a large number of local authorities, identified a fairly depressing level of poor practice (Fisher *et al.* 1986); defensive ill-planned crisis intervention in families already well-known to departments, with over-use of statutory provisions, particularly place-of-safety orders rather than voluntary care (Packman 1986); and the lack of active work to maintain links between children in care and meaningful relatives which led to lengthy care episodes and to children losing all contact with their families (Millham *et al.* 1986).

Most child abuse cases which come to public attention concern children whom social workers are perceived to have failed to protect. Public awareness of some of the problems caused by the inadequacy and complexity of the statutory provisions and social workers' failure to understand the legal framework of their practice, had also been spasmodically aroused by media coverage of the tragic lives and deaths of children such as Jasmine Beckford, Tyra Henry and Kimberley Carlile. These children and others were neglected, tortured and eventually killed by their carers when either in the care of, or known about by, local authority social services departments. In his reports on the public inquiries into the deaths of Jasmine Beckford and Kimberley Carlile, Blom-Cooper made specific and, in the latter case in relation to the protection of children in an emergency, very detailed recommendations for changes in the law as well as practice (Blom-Cooper 1985; 1987).

Earlier than this, in urgent response to the recommendation in the Short Report (House of Commons 1984) an inter-departmental working party with Law Commission support was set up as a matter of urgency by the government with a very tight timetable, to 'frame proposals for changes to child care law which will provide a framework for developing the best child practice and meeting more effectively the needs of children and their families' (para 1). The working party's Review of Child Care Law was published only just over a year after work started, during which time twelve detailed working papers had been circulated to professionally concerned organizations and individuals, and their comment invited and considered (RCCL 1985).

The government accepted many but not all of the recommendations of the working party, and in January 1987 published its proposals, introduced in the following terms, for wide-ranging reform of the public law in a White Paper, *The Law on Child Care and Family Services*:

In bringing forward these proposals for change the intention has been to achieve greater clarity and consistency so as to help parents and children who may be affected by the law and those who have to work professionally within it – lawyers, social workers and others. The other prime objective has been to seek improvements in the law so as to offer a fairer deal both to children and parents, especially in the legal processes when compulsory state intervention is necessary to protect and promote the interests of the child.

(DHSS 1987: para 4)

Following publication of the White Paper, which attracted much professional interest and considerable support, public concern about another aspect of the unsatisfactory state of the law and its administration was aroused by media reaction both to the inappropriate use of the draconian powers of local authorities to separate children from their parents under place of safety orders, and the inability of the local juvenile court and the guardian *ad litem* panel to cope with lengthy and complex sexual abuse related care proceedings in Cleveland in 1987. The government ordered a statutory inquiry and appointed Mrs Justice Butler-Sloss (as she then was) to undertake it. The setting up of that inquiry meant that legislation to reform the public law of child care, originally hoped for in the 1987/88 parliamentary session, was delayed until after publication of the report of the inquiry and consideration of its recommendations (Butler-Sloss 1988).

The private law relating to children

In 1984 the Law Commission alongside their work on illegitimacy (Law Commission 1979; 1982; 1986a) began a detailed review of the private law, that is to say the 'rules of common law and statute under which responsibility for bringing up or looking after a child is allocated to particular individuals usually his parents'. The Commissioners' declared aim was to make the law 'clearer simpler and . . . fairer for families and children alike' (Law Commission 1988: 1). With research support and a less politically pressured timetable than that imposed on the public child care law working party, they published, between 1985 and 1988, working papers on Guardianship (Law Commission 1985), Custody (Law Commission 1986b), Care, Supervision and Interim Orders in Custody Proceedings (Law Commission 1987a) and Wardship (Law Commission 1987b). These papers, which provide an exhaustive review of the current state of the law together with proposals for reform, were followed in 1988 by a report containing a draft Bill for reform of the private law which left spaces for the insertion of public law clauses. This gave the first indication that the two strands of the law relating to children might be brought together in a coherent whole (Law Commission 1988).

Professor Hoggett, the Law Commissioner chiefly responsible for the private law provisions in the Act, suggests that it was only the chance delay to the long-awaited reform of the public law caused by events in Cleveland that allowed the previously separated strands of the public and private law relating to children to come together in a single statute. Had that inquiry not happened it is likely that there would have been a Child Care Bill in the 1987/88 parliamentary session, followed at a later date by a measure to reform the private law (Hoggett 1989a). Had that enabled greater consideration to have been given to the implications of some of the provisions in the Act many of those concerned about the mass of important detail being rushed through the legislative process without sufficient debate would probably feel that to have been the preferred option.

Reform of the courts

A family court with a unified jurisdiction was recommended by the Finer Committee in its report on one-parent families before the Children Act 1975 reached the statute book (Finer 1974) but, as with so many of the other recommendations of that seminal report, no action was taken. The Short Committee, having heard a considerable body of compelling evidence about the unsatisfactory nature of the court system, and in particular about the inadequacies of many juvenile courts hearing complex care proceedings, recommended that 'the Government now provide the House with a detailed and fully costed scheme for the establishment of family courts (House of Commons 1984: para 93). Although many of those responding to the working party on child care law's working papers suggested that reform of the law without a concurrent reform of the court system was not viable, the view was taken that the working party's terms of reference precluded their considering reform of the courts, and that in any event the state of the substantive law was a matter of such urgency that its reform could not wait for the completion of the necessarily slow process of replacing the court system. The Children Act does, however, provide for two tentative steps towards the establishment of a family court.

Although the transfer of care proceedings at the magistrates' level from the juvenile court with its criminal connotations to the magistrates' domestic court may be seen as somewhat cosmetic, the fact that care proceedings will become straightforward civil proceedings instead of quasi criminal in nature is of fundamental importance (Ball 1989b). Until implementation of the Act only the wholly lay forum of the magistrates' juvenile court has jurisdiction to hear care proceedings, however complex or lengthy. This has resulted in many local authorities choosing to use the expensive route of wardship in the high court to which they have exclusive access in care cases, as a means of getting a care order. Under the Act the magistrates' domestic, the county and the high court will have concurrent jurisdiction, with cases being able to be allocated, by means of a system (the details of which are not yet available) to the most suitable forum for the complexity of the proceedings. At the same time local authorities will lose their recourse to wardship if they are seeking a care order.

Most professionals working in the child care field hope that one day all family matters will be dealt with in a specialist court staffed by laypeople and professional judges, all of whom will have received appropriate training, with a unified jurisdiction to allow easy transfer of cases from one level to another and its own independent social work service to provide court welfare and guardian *ad litem* reports as well as a conciliation service. At the time of writing that seems a somewhat unrealistic dream.

The provisions of the Act

Any detailed account of the provisions in a massive statute containing over seventy sections and nine schedules is clearly beyond a single chapter, and in any event a welter of informed commentaries on the Act will provide this information. The legislators' aims, and the basic principles which underlie what Lord Mackay has referred to as a 'single rationalised system', were helpfully explained by Professor Hoggett in an address to an early conference on the Bill (Hoggett 1989b). The principles she draws attention to are those of parental responsibility, all orders being available in all proceedings, the law providing a minimum threshold which has to be established before courts can justify the removal of a child from home or the imposition of compulsory supervision, and a single welfare principle being applied to all decisions regarding a child's upbringing, income or property.

If the principles which inform the Act, most of its private and many of its public law provisions, are largely uncontentious and have been generally welcomed, the same cannot be said about a few of the public law provisions. These provisions provide almost an extreme example of the tendency for any new legislation in this field to swing the pendulum that needs to be so carefully balanced as between children, their parents and the state too far in one direction or another. As a leading child care expert, whose work influenced many of the provisions of the last major child care Act, has said:

> It is right and proper that new legislation has a new emphasis but neither the public nor the law makers should put so much emphasis on Cleveland and the infringement of parents' rights that Maria Colwell and her tragic successors are forgotten.
>
> (Rowe 1989: 30)

The last major piece of reforming child care legislation, the Children Act 1975 referred to above, produced a shift away from up-holding parents' rights by giving local authorities more administrative and legal control to make long-term plans for children in care. The political will to achieve this change followed the harrowing details of the inquiry into the death of Maria Colwell (Field-Fisher 1974), which followed several well-publicized 'tug of love' cases in the late 1960s and early 1970s, and damning research evidence of the plight of children allowed to drift in care because local authorities were powerless to make and implement long-term plans for them (Rowe and Lambert 1973). The 1989 Act appears, in a way which concerns many individuals and organizations, to allow the pendulum to swing back again to the up-holding of parents' rights by diminishing local authorities' powers in relation to children for whom they provide accommodation on a voluntary basis.

Voluntary arrangements between parents and local authorities

Under the Child Care Act 1980 s2, local authorities have very wide discretionary powers to receive children whose parents are unable to look after them on a short- or long-term basis into care. While these children are in care the local authority may make any decisions it considers necessary about accommodation, education and contacts, although parents may request the return of their children at any time. After children have been in care for six months parents or guardians must give 28 days' notice to the local authority of their intention to remove them from care, and it is an offence for anyone to take a child during that time without consent. This allows either for a planned and phased return home of children who may have become well settled in a foster home, or, until the new Act is implemented, if grounds exist under s3 of the Act, the local authority may, either before the parents give notice of their intention to remove the child or during the 28 days, assume parental rights in order to prevent the child's leaving care (Hoggett 1987).

While children are in care, regardless of whether they have entered care under a voluntary arrangement under s2 or by a compulsory route, the local authority has a statutory responsibility to review the child's case on a regular basis and when reaching any decision to give

> first consideration to the need to safeguard and promote the welfare of the child throughout his childhood; and ... so far as is practicable to ascertain the wishes and feelings of the child regarding the decision and give due consideration to them, having regard to his age and under-standing.
>
> (Child Care Act 1980 s18(1))

Local authorities are also, however, responsible for providing accommodation for many children, mainly mentally or physically handicapped, who are placed away from their homes by local authorities under health legislation. These children can become very isolated and it has long been a matter of concern that local authorities have no statutory responsibility to have regard to their welfare as individuals or consult their wishes and feelings. As a result of evidence presented by numerous voluntary organizations to the Short Committee on children in care (House of Commons 1984), the inter-departmental working party set up to review child care law proposed that in future support for children at home and the provision of accommodation on a voluntary basis would be based on the assumption that local authorities would have the same responsibility for all children regardless of the reasons for their need for local authority support, and that that responsibility should be to promote the up-bringing of children within their own families and where this is not possible, having consulted the child's wishes and feelings and given due consideration to them, to provide other accommodation (RCCL 1985).

The problems long associated with voluntary care under the Child Care Act 1980 s2 and its predecessor, in terms of uncertainties about responsibilities, the powerlessness of parents and the potentially stigmatizing nature of the care status, were acknowledged and addressed by the working party, who proposed an imaginative dual system of 'shared' and 'respite' care. Continuation of the requirement for notice to be given after the child had been in care for some time was also recommended (RCCL 1985). The government in their subsequent White Paper, *The Law on Child Care and Family Services*, accepted the need to unify child care and the health and welfare legislation but rejected the dual system as being overly complex, and the retention of the 28 days' notice as being damaging to the concept of a truly voluntary arrangement between parents and the local authority (DHSS 1987), despite research evidence that local authorities on the whole made sensible and sensitive use of the provision (Stevenson and Smith unpublished).

This somewhat doctrinaire approach is reflected in Part III of the Act, which replaced voluntary care with a much wider general power to provide assistance, including accommodation, for children in need. Where children are accommodated there will be no statutory requirement to give notice however long the child has been in that accommodation. These provisions represent a reaction, or possibly an over-reaction to the existing imbal..nce of power towards local authorities and against parents. They will mean that unless another order has been obtained to secure the child in the foster home parents will be free to remove children, who may be very deeply attached to their carers, without any preparation or any duty to consider their wishes and feelings. Although in some cases such an act might be grounds for care proceedings this will not always be the case. Many of those representing the whole range of concerned organizations such as BASW, BAAF, Family Rights Group and the Children's Legal Centre, as well as informed individual child care experts of great knowledge and experience, suggest that the provisions represent a swing of the pendulum too far towards parents, not all of whom are able to act in their children's best interests.

Jane Rowe voiced this general concern when she suggested that the ending of the status of voluntary care and its replacement with the provision of accommodation by the local authority (referred to elsewhere as 'having echoes . . . of what is done with lodgers and parcels' – Hammond 1989: 27) will leave some children very vulnerable either to drift or to the inappropriate use of compulsory measures, when trying a voluntary arrangement might have been the preferred option but would be seen as too risky (Rowe 1989). The only government concession at the time of writing is that written agreements setting out agreed arrangements will be required, though it does not appear that there will be any mechanism for enforcing them.

The protection of children in an emergency

If problems inherent in framing voluntary arrangements for the care of children illustrates part of the difficulty of achieving the delicate balance between parents' rights and state intervention already referred to, statutory provisions for the protection of children in an emergency provide an even more extreme example and one which clearly demonstrates the extent to which social work practice and the legal framework within which that practice takes place are inextricably interwoven. Such measures, that is to say place-of-safety orders and warrants, currently contained in the Children and Young Persons Acts 1933 and 1969 are 'at the cross roads of competing social policies – personal rights and the interests of children' (Blom-Cooper 1987), and came dramatically to the attention of the public in 1987 at one extreme through the case of Kimberley Carlile, who dies at the hands of her stepfather partly as a result of perceived lack of powers to protect her, as well as of ignorance of provisions that could have allowed intervention, and at the other as a result of abuse of place-of-safety orders in Cleveland.

In this area the dilemma for those seeking to legislate is to strike the necessary delicate balance between provisions that are sufficiently widely drafted to ensure that there are no circumstances in which children in immediate danger would have to be left at risk for want of the existence of adequate legal powers to secure their protection, while at the same time ensuring that such powers can be used only where the need for protection is real and immediate, and open to challenge at the earliest practicable opportunity. Whether Emergency Protection Orders under the Children Act 1989 will strike the right balance, only time and research will show.

The areas of concern regarding place-of-safety orders are well known, having been the subject of adverse comment in the Short Report (House of Commons 1984), the Review of Child Care Law (RCCL 1985), as well as by Louis Blom-Cooper in his reports on the circumstances surrounding the deaths of Jasmine Beckford, in which he made trenchant comment although place-of-safety orders were not in issue, and Kimberley Carlile, in which they were (Blom-Cooper 1985; 1987), and in the Cleveland Report (Butler-Sloss 1988). All the evidence makes it clear that place-of-safety orders under the 1969 Act may be, and are, applied for in circumstances well outside the need to protect the child from immediate harm or danger (Ball 1989a).

The report into the death of Kimberley Carlile also published in 1987 directed attention to another shortcoming in existing legislation about which practitioners were acutely aware but the general public had little knowledge. This is the lack of an adequate power to deal with the situation where there is real concern about a child but no evidence of neglect or physical abuse because social workers have been denied access, or the child is never at home when they call. With hindsight in Kimberley's case, there is little doubt that very poor legal advice was given to the social worker in that in the circumstances as they existed a magistrate would have been most unlikely to refuse a place-of-safety order and also no one appeared to have mentioned the existence of the power to request the police to get a warrant to search for the child under the 1933 Act s40.

In his report on this inquiry, *A Child in Mind*, Blom-Cooper advocated both an appealable emergency protection order obtainable for a maximum of 8 days, rather than the 28 days of a place-of-safety order, and available only on evidence of immediate harm or likely harm to the child, and also a new child assessment order which would require the production of a child to whom access had been requested but not achieved, at a clinic for examination. The latter order would not itself authorize retention of the child, which would depend on a further application for an emergency protection order. Such an order would, he suggests, enable the child to be seen without emergency protection powers which authorize removal of the child having to be interpreted in such a way as to defeat the intention of providing strict criteria for their use (Blom-Cooper 1987).

The grounds for an emergency protection order under the Act provide for a considerable shift of emphasis towards a fairer balance between the powers of the applicants and the rights of parents to challenge orders; much shorter orders; and clarification of rights and responsibilities during an order with new recourse to the courts for parents to challenge local authorities. The government has been reluctant, however, to accept the need for an assessment order and at the time of writing it is unclear as to whether they will introduce an amendment to provide some form of lesser order or will open up the originally tightly drafted grounds for an emergency protection order to cover cases where only suspicion but no proof exists.

Conclusion

The Children Act 1989 is a massive and in many respects, far-sighted, piece of legislation. The provisions relating to voluntary arrangements and of the protection of children in an emergency provide examples of the extent to which achieving the necessary delicate balance between the rights of parents to bring up their children free from interference, and the power of the state to intervene to protect children from abuse, is fraught with difficulty and vulnerable to the failure of legislators to accept detached and informed advice, or to recognize the delicacy of the balance they should strive to achieve.

References

Ball, C. (1989a) 'The current and future context of emergency protection', *Adoption and Fostering* 13, 2: 38–42.
—— (1989b) *Law for Social Workers: An Introduction*, Aldershot: Wildwood House.
Blom-Cooper, L. (1985) *A Child in Trust: The Report of the Panel of Inquiry into the Circumstances Surrounding the Death of Jasmine Beckford*, London: Borough of Brent.
—— (1987) *A Child in Mind: The Report of the Commission of Inquiry into the Circumstances Surrounding the Death of Kimberley Carlile*, London: Borough of Greenwich.
Butler-Sloss, E. (1988) *Report of the Inquiry into Child Abuse in Cleveland 1987*, Cm 412, London: HMSO.
DHSS (1985) *Social Work Decisions in Child Care: Recent Research Findings and their Implications*, London: HMSO.
—— (1987) *The Law on Child Care and Family Services*, Cm 62, London: HMSO.
Douglas, G. (1988) 'The family and the state under the European Convention on Human Rights', *International Journal of Law and the Family* 2, 1: 76–105.
Field-Fisher, T. G. (1974) *Report of the Committee of Inquiry into the Care and Supervision Provided in Relation to Maria Colwell*, London: HMSO.
Finer, M. (1974) *Report of the Committee on One-Parent Families*, Cmnd 5629, London: HMSO.
Fisher, M., Marsh, P. and Phillips, D. with Sainsbury, E. (1986) *In and Out of Care – The Experiences of Children, Parents and Social Workers*, London: Batsford.
Hammond, C. (1989) 'The Children Bill: key issues for practitioners', *Adoption and Fostering* 13, 1: 24–9.
Hoggett, B. (1987) *Parents and Children: The Law of Parental Responsibility*, London: Sweet & Maxwell.
—— (1989a) 'Family Law in the 1990s', *Family Law* 19: 169–208.
—— (1989b) 'The Children Bill: the aim', *Family Law* 19: 209–48.

House of Commons (1984) *Second Report from the Social Services Committee Session 1983/4: Children in Care,* HC 360, London: HMSO.
Law Commission (1979) *Illegitimacy,* Working paper no. 74, London: HMSO.
—— (1982) *Report on Illegitimacy,* Law Commission, no. 118, London: HMSO.
—— (1985) *Review of Child Law: Guardianship,* Working Paper no. 91, London: HMSO.
—— (1986a) *Illegitimacy: Second Report,* Law Commission no. 157, London: HMSO.
—— (1986b) *Review of Child Law: Custody,* Working Paper no. 96, London: HMSO.
—— (1987a) *Review of Child Law: Care, Supervision and Interim Orders in Custody Proceedings,* Working Paper no. 100, London: HMSO.
—— (1987b) *Review of Child Law: Wards of Court,* Working Paper no. 101, London: HMSO.
—— (1988) *Law Commission Family Law Review of Child Law: Guardianship and Custody,* London: HMSO.
Millham, S., Bullock, R., Hosie, K. and Haak, M. (1986) *Lost in Care,* Aldershot: Gower.
Ormrod, R. (1983) 'Child Care Law: a personal perspective', *Adoption and Fostering* 7, 4: 10.
Packman, J. (1986) *Who Needs Care? Social Work Decisions About Children,* Oxford: Blackwell.
RCCL (1985) *Review of Child Care Law: Report to Ministers of an Inter-Departmental Working Party,* London: HMSO.
Rowe, J. (1989) 'Caring concern', *Guardian,* 2 June.
Rowe, J. and Lambert, L. (1973) *Children Who Wait,* London: Association of British Adoption Agencies.
Stevenson, O. and Smith, J. (unpublished) 'The implementation of s56 of the Children Act 1975', University of Nottingham.
Stockdale, F. A. (1972) *Report of the Departmental Committee on the Adoption of Children,* Cmnd 5107, London: HMSO.
Waite, Mr Justice (1987) Rv Corby Juvenile Court ex parte M. [1987] IFLR p. 490.

2
Sexual harassment, sexual conduct and gender in social work settings

Sue Wise and Liz Stanley

People have become increasingly accustomed to hearing about 'sexual harassment' and a range of images are conjured up by the term: a woman crossing a shop-floor and being subject to – or rather the object of – a stream of sexual abuse; another woman, a secretary or office junior, fending off the physical advances of her male boss; or women manual workers going to the work's stores to be confronted by pornographic pictures of women. In these images, 'sexual harassment' is seen as a problem of 'over-sexed men', more to be found in manual trades and 'working-class' jobs than in white-collar or professional occupations. And the problem is usually portrayed as being associated with a power imbalance resulting from the different hierarchical position of women and men within organizations.

What is sexual harassment?

Whatever the general validity of such a view (we think it is a comforting gloss which shields people from a more disturbing reality), in relation to social work the situation is very different, and a considerably more complex set of theoretical and analytical tools are required to understand the interweavings of 'sexual harassment' with occupational cultures and ideologies. However, before discussing this argument in more detail, it is important to establish at the outset just how serious a problem sexual harassment is.

Many attempts have been made to establish the scale of sexual harassment. For example, late 1970s and early 1980s surveys by NALGO and NUPE in Britain emphasized that sexual harassment at work was experienced by a large minority of women, and a smaller group of men. However, such attempts at 'mapping' the phenomenon have been largely unsuccessful, mainly because of definitional problems. That is, whether 'sexual harassment' has taken place is a matter of interpretation and judgement, for the 'same' behaviour done by different men with different intentionality can be experienced quite differently by a woman. Moreover, the way that unions and others have defined sexual harassment (as inappropriate sexual behaviour in the work-place) has set it apart from most women's experiences of those persistent, annoying intrusions which are the everyday experience of sexual harassment.

Recent interest in the problem by British women's magazines have revived incidence surveys. One published in *Living* (a supermarket-sold magazine, September 1989 issue) treats the problem in considerably broader terms than the usual work-place definitions. This survey covered women's experience of a number of sexual harassment problems, like obscene telephone calls, 'flashing' and 'groping'. The results are fairly staggering: over the previous five years around 13 million women in Britain experienced these 'minor' sexual assaults, which are in fact criminal behaviours, although only a tiny minority of these offences were ever reported to the police, and of those that were few came to court.

This broad approach to defining the problem is a useful one. Indeed, in an earlier discussion of sexual harassment in everyday life (Wise and Stanley 1987) we argued that focusing on sexual harassment as extreme sexual behaviour in the work-place (a kind of sexual incontinence) means that the sexual political nature of sexual harassment as sexism (all-intrusive male behaviour), as a constituent feature of everyday life – both in and out of paid work – is lost sight of. Although the medium through which sexual harassment gets done is often 'sex', actually its essence is power rather than sexuality (although, as we shall discuss later, it does raise uncomfortable questions concerning the relationship between sex and power in heterosexual relationships more generally). That is, sex may be used as the *means* for effecting power over others; but both its intention and its *end*, its product, is power.

The term 'sexual harassment' came to be defined and analysed by a group of American feminists in the 1960s who were concerned with the forms that sexism in paid employment took, and particularly with the use of sexual means to effect sexual political ends. Effectively, they saw sexual harassment as *the* means of perpetuating gender inequalities in paid employment (see also Farley 1978 for an account of these early discussions). Sexual harassment of women in their places of paid employment is obviously an important phenomenon, one that requires research, analysis and theorizing because it needs to be stopped through whatever means are most effective. However, it is equally important not to lose sight of the fact that 'sexual harassment' does not occur in a vacuum, but is connected to conventional definitions and practices associated with sexual behaviours and feelings ('sexual conduct') between women and men ('heterosexuality' as the assumed mode of interaction between all women and all men). It is also connected to constructions of masculinity and femininity ('gender') that assign to women and girls 'inferior' attributes and characteristics which then justify the inequality, exploitation and oppression of women ('sexual politics'). In other words, it is important to locate an analysis and understanding of sexual harassment within a more general feminist analysis of sexism.

One reason why this is important is that the form in which sexual harassment is understood and related to by trade unions (in Britain) and by trade unions and constitutional law (in the USA; see also MacKinnon 1979) is in fact highly atypical of most women's experiences of it. First, it is presented as a clearly sexual behaviour; second, as extreme and unmistakable. However, in life, as distinct from union guidelines, most sexual harassment is any unsought and enforced intrusion by a man or men upon a woman or women; and taking a 'sexual' form is only one among a range of ways harassment is carried out. Moreover, most sexual harassment is not of the 'sledgehammer' variety, of obscenities and physical assaults. Rather, it is *ambiguously* expressed behaviour by men which, by virtue of its ambiguities, often renders women complicit within it before they realize what its intent is; and it happens so many times that its effect can be described as a 'dripping tap' to which one becomes accustomed as the ordinary condition of everyday life.

We have written elsewhere about the most extreme and incontrovertible sexual harassments women may experience, in the form of obscene telephone calls, street violence, rape and sexual murder; however, it is the more mundane expressions which are the most difficult to relate to. Obscene telephone calls, assaults, rapes and murders are incontrovertible sexism, unquestionably appalling and terrible. Most of us very clearly know where we stand in relation to such things. But how do we feel about 'compliments', about 'flattery', about 'jokes', about persistent slighting remarks about women's minds, behaviours and bodies, about men's demands for time and attention? For most of us, the response is 'Well, it all depends . . .'.

Our particular concern (Wise and Stanley 1987) was in understanding the interactional dynamics by which this latter form of sexual harassment is, more often than not, named as something very different, and women's negative responses treated as unreasonable and inappropriate. However, in this present discussion we are specifically concerned with the sexual framework within which sexual harassment and sexism is done.

This framework constitutes a 'meta-narrative' of heterosexuality, which depicts it as synonymous with a drive reduction model of male sexuality as a 'spermatic economy', but also treats it as synonymous with not merely power but power over, and even against, women. Such a framework is so taken-for-granted that it is rarely problematized or seen as a *social construction* with *sexual political* consequences. And yet understanding its dynamic is crucial to understanding the ways in which organizations in general, and 'social work' organizations in particular, systematically respond to or ignore particular 'sexual' behaviours.

In examining the relationship of sexual conduct in general to sexual harassment in particular, we address a number of analytic topics:

1 There are consequences of a narrow definition of sexual harassment as *specific, sexual* and *extreme* behaviours. One of these is that the taken-for-grantedness of a 'drive reduction' model of male sexuality as biologically based, penetrative and unstoppable once aroused is never questioned nor conceived as a key element in legitimizing a range of male sexual intrusions;

2 'Organizations' and 'sex' are treated as separate unless and until women are present, such that the endemic nature of sexual behaviour at work is actually rendered organizationally invisible apart from in certain taboo forms which are associated with women and not men;
3 Structural position and power, and interactional power, are sometimes mutually reinforcing, sometimes run in opposite directions. A considerably more complex analysis of power is necessary to a proper understanding of the implicit legitimizing of much organizational sexuality with reference to drive reductionist ideas and thus, relatedly, to an understanding of the contested territory that is 'sexual harassment'.

These are our analytic concerns, addressed in the three following sections of this paper: first, looking at recently developed ideas concerning organizational structure and its cultural and subcultural life; second, continuing our introductory remarks about sexual conduct and its relationship to organizational life; and third, applying some of these ideas to field social work.

A new view of 'the organization'

The sociology of organizations has gained a new lease of life in recent years (Mills 1989). First, there is an increasing awareness of the importance of 'organizational culture'. That is, that 'the organization' is a complex social grouping which develops a sometimes very overt and up-front organizational ethos, and which may be internally organized in such ways that employees at multiple levels within it necessarily (at least in public) subscribe to it. And here work on the so-called 'Pepsi wars' has been a powerful influence, although earlier work such as that of Donald Roy (1973) has pointed up the existence within organizational culture of 'subcultures' which may be specific to particular groups of workers in specific enclaves within an organization. Second, there has been a rediscovery of the crucial importance of the culture and rules of the informal to the operation of the formal structure. Indeed, following Strauss *et al.*'s (1973) influential research, the informal is seen as symbiotically related and necessary to the formal, such that they cannot be separated without the formal organization's ceasing to function.

Third, and most importantly for this present discussion, there has been a growing awareness on the part of feminist and pro-feminist researchers that 'the organization' and 'sexuality' are linked in complex and consequential ways (examples of which are Gutek and Dunwoody 1987; Haavio-Mannila *et al.* 1988; Hearn and Parkin 1987; Hearn *et al.* 1989). Many of these writers draw upon the subcultural ideas referred to previously, although others make use of feminist-generated analyses of 'the public' and its relationship to 'the private' (for example, Parkin 1989 and in a different way Pringle 1989).

The traditional view of the organization sees it as having a formal pyramidical hierarchical structure, supported by a systematic set of rules which specify the relationship between subordinates and superordinates at all points in the hierarchy. 'Organization' is thus seen as having specific, defined and clearly set out organizational purposes to which all internal activity is oriented. It is also seen as sexless, as a physical but also a social space with its 'appropriate' set of activities devoted to specialist, and decidedly neither everyday nor mundane purposes, and from which 'personal' relationships and ways of operating have been deliberately stripped.

Much of the force of recent organizational sociology has been devoted to deconstructing such a view, pointing out its one-dimensionality. Around the work of Goffman (1961), Roy (1973), Strauss *et al.* (1973), Bittner (1973), and in Britain through the synthesizing work of Salaman and Thompson (1973), 'the organization' has been reconstructed in more subtle and sophisticated analytic terms. Alongside the level of the formal organization – which may approximate more, or sometimes much less, to the model described above – is seen to lie an equally complex informal structure inhabited by cross-cutting subgroups with their own 'cultures' or systems of beliefs, assumptions and rules, and which are concerned with interactional events and interactionally defined purposes as well as with those formally specified.

One of these informal 'purposes' and ways of interacting is the realm of the sexual: sexual jokes and remarks, sexual banter, flirtations, affairs, and cohabitations and marriages; but also sexual harassment ranging from mild intrusions to direct physical assaults and sometimes rapes and worse.

Organizations are seen as sexless; they are also, particularly regarding their managerial roles and sometimes also manual grades, seen as archetypically male. A social setting which includes men only and is devoted to some specific and defined purpose is treated as, by definition, sexless. Gay male readers may well be surprised to hear this; but of course the point is that an assumption of universal heterosexuality underpins such views. Moreover this cannot be separated from a highly particular view of the relationship between sexless purposeful organizational men and the women who are deemed to staff organizations.

It has become a truism in feminist sociology that a male researcher will open the door, look in on a group of men and see *people*; but look in on a group of women and see *women*, something separate from the universality of people/ men. Similarly women in organizations tend to be seen as the bearers of sex into them; and if problems ensue then they are (1) caused by women, for (2) by their presence they signal sexuality and to which (heterosexual) men cannot but respond on some level. This argument, however, presupposes an originally all-male organization to which women are admitted to occupy certain minority (in both senses of the word) positions within it; and clearly social work cannot be described in such terms.

Organizations inhabit physical as well as social space; and different grades and levels of people have differential access to particular kinds of physical spaces: executive toilets (almost invariably for men only) and dining areas, 'works' toilets and canteens, workshops and shop-floors, offices and conference rooms. Because men and women tend to occupy different occupational positions within organizations (which are typically categorized by their vertical and horizontal segregation of the work-force by gender), these physical spaces are also gendered and, because they are gendered, they are also sexed by virtue of women's presence where it occurs or is permitted.

In a way, then, simply by being present women are assumed (but by whom is the crucial question) to be available sexually on some level or another.

However, the sexual harassment literature with few exceptions treats sexual harassment as different in kind from the 'pleasurable' aspect of flirtations, conveniently ignoring the fact that if women are seen as 'available' then this is likely to be subject to many different interpretations by men. 'Men', after all, is no unitary group but an aggregate term for different individual men, some of whom at least do not accept, or are not interested in, the 'availability' ethos surrounding women's organizational presence. Moreover, even those that are will not all respond to it in the same way: responses can vary from being warned off by redoubtable women to the frisson of making gentlemanly eyes at someone, to joking banter, to bottom feeling, to trapping someone on the back-stairs and attempting an assault, and others, like for example the conduct of licit and illicit consensual sexual relationships.

Organizational life, then, is a very complex business. However, what can be said with some certainty is that the formal structure and rules and the formal organizational culture are cross-cut and also underpinned and made to work by the informal structure, rules and enclave cultures generated by particular work groups.

One simple example of this is depicted in the *Cagney and Lacey* television detective series: Christine and Mary Beth work within the formal structure and, at formal levels, adhere to its rules, hierarchies and procedures; yet they also form a 'subculture' of women within a particular work-space (the precinct) whose maleness they subvert by using that space taboo to men, the women's toilet. Moreover, they also operate outside of the boundaried part of the organization – in the public – in ways which are seen to be different from that of their male colleagues. They treat people, but people also respond to them, differently from male police officers; and this is sometimes enabling and constructive, but also sometimes it hinders, confines and subscribes the possibilities for them.

Organizations inhabit physical space which thereby becomes private or semi-private space as well. They may not be completely sealed from 'the public', for many people have different kinds of access to them. However, they do have private 'behind the scenes' places to which outsiders do not have easy access; and more often than not it is women who constitute the gatekeepers who are situated in a semi-public/semi-private space between these inner areas and the public space outside. These women – telephonists, secretaries, 'personal assistants' and the like – are thus continually managing people, often men, who want access but are policed before being allowed to have it ('I'm sorry, he's not in his office today', 'I'm afraid you can't see Mr Bloggs without an appointment', and so on). A highly ironic instance of this occurred when we tried to obtain information on whatever sexual harassment guidelines NAPO (National Association of Probation Officers) might have: on a number of occasions we were unable to speak to the relevant official because, as the telephonist relaying a message from him to us explained, 'But he doesn't know you'. It was almost as difficult to establish that BASW (British Association of Social Workers) has no such guidelines but has set up a 'Gender Issues Advisory Panel' (members of which, unlike BASW staff themselves, were incredibly helpful). Any woman seeking to rely on formalized means of dealing with sexual harassment in social work, it seems to us, will receive little assistance or even information from these two key professional organizations.

Women 'gatekeepers' constitute a relatively powerless group, in formal organizational terms, but their role is to manage access to the relatively powerful. They carry out the same function in relation to other organizational subordinates who want access to organizational superordinates. It is no wonder that women in such roles are so often subject to or object of a range of sexually harassing and otherwise offensive behaviours, for in effect a part of their job is to take the brunt of the wounded and bruised egos of subordinate men, but who can always make themselves (in their own eyes at least) superior to these damned *women*.

Considering the public and the private in such interactional, and sexual political, terms provides a very powerful analytic tool for teasing out some of the complex dynamics of organisational sexuality. It also reveals some of the sites at which sexual harassment and ordinary (hetero)sexuality meet and overlap.

Sex is seen to be disruptive of the 'real' (read formal) purposes of an organization; the disruption is seen to derive from the presence of women, to whom men cannot 'biologically' help but respond in a variety of sexual ways; for organizations are seen as, by definition, both unsexed and male. At the same time, sexual harassment is treated as aberrant, different in kind and not just degree from the ordinary and acceptable sexual encounters typified in looks, innuendoes, banter, flirtations, touching, affairs. However, it is instructive to note that 'sexual harassment' and 'ordinary sexual encounters' follow more or less exactly the same levels of expression and telling them apart is sometimes – even for the women, and perhaps also for the men, involved – extraordinarily difficult. For instance, we know of a mature graduate student who 'gave way' to the persistent sexually harassing looks, remarks and so forth of her male supervisor and had an affair with him as a means of ending the harassment and so the amount of time and energy it took up; and a young gay male friend who ended up having a sexual relationship with a man he really didn't want to be involved with as the price of (the man clearly implied) organizational silence about his sexuality. How are we to understand 'consent' in such situations?

Theorizing 'sexual conduct'

Many people who see, for example, 'intelligence' and 'delinquency' as the product of social interaction in micro-political contexts leave their social constructionist convictions behind when it comes to thinking about 'sex'. The most usual way of thinking about sex is to see it as 'natural', something we know about for supposedly 'innate' reasons connected with human biology. What this actually amounts to is a view of 'sex' as actually (indeed literally potentially) procreative behaviours, in the form of penetrational heterosexual genital contact. Of course many people who think this on one level may well also accept that there are other legitimate forms of sexual contact, like oral-genital sex, which can lead to orgasm; but none the less there is often still a residual conviction that 'real', fundamental sex involves a penis in a vagina.

There are consequences of such an understanding of 'sex', from the assumption that this is what 'everyone' does, that this is the 'it' ('Have you done "it" yet?') we all swapped references to as adolescents, to the implication that anyone who doesn't do 'it' doesn't really have 'sex' but a substitute, rather like wearing Asda-brand jeans instead of Levi 501s. There are additional consequences as well.

Within sociology 'sexual conduct' (a term which encompasses both sexual behaviour and sexual thoughts, fantasies and feelings) has been analysed and theorized using a social constructionist framework (Gagnon and Simon 1973; Barker-Benfield 1976; Plummer 1975; Strong 1974; Faraday 1981). The view of 'everyday' understandings of sex sketched above is one known as the 'drive reduction model', in which sex is seen as an innate biologically founded 'drive' or 'force' which men experience in much more powerful ways than women, whose role is to act as a 'stimulus' to which men produce a 'response'. Indeed, some social scientists have argued that contemporary ideas about sex locate it within a 'spermatic economy'; that is, that sex is actually *male* and women are receptors of 'it', male sexuality, which is pentrational and indeed totally penile in its nature.

Of course this is not to say that all people actually 100 per cent believe this: but it is certainly very difficult for both gay and heterosexual men who neither do, nor want to, experience their sexuality in such terms to say so, particularly when they think that their actual or prospective sexual partners *are* likely to believe it. One of the most interesting features of sex, in social science terms, is that it is a complex interactional set of behaviours but which are more often than not – and unlike almost every other aspect of human social behaviour – carried out in near-silence. Touch, small movements, non-speech sound, have to serve the same purposes that complex vocal interactions play for carrying out much less complex behaviours – like having a conversation about the weather, for instance. The result is a high degree of uncertainty, trepidation and even fear in initial sexual encounters; and also omissions, misrepresentations and downright lies in what is said to other people about past sexual encounters.

And this is particularly likely to be so for men. It is men in the terms of the drive reduction model who are supposed to initiate and guide sexual encounters and not women, from the initial phrases of 'getting off' with someone to its termination at the point of ejaculation; it is men rather than women, and boys rather than girls, who are seen as having more sexual knowledge, experience and desire. And so a boy or man without sexual knowledge, and/or experience, and/or desire, is hardly likely to articulate this, particularly not to other boys/men, for he has 'face' to maintain.

One product is that many men end up knowing actually very little about sexual possibilities, have very narrow experience, and only very specific desires, because their need to maintain face and be a 'real man' cuts them off from learning about other ways of being sexual, other ways of expressing need and desire. Another is that 'women' are seen as in a sense 'for men', as the passive objects of an active (and presumed to be heterosexual) male desire. And yet another raises further complications, for drive reductionist thinking presupposes that women are subordinate in a number of ways to the superordinacy of men. That is, this view of heterosexuality as pentrational sex defined by men's needs and wants and imposed on women's bodies (willing, or of course sometimes very unwilling) is a key element in the construction and maintenance of sexual politics.

We now bring the discussion of sexual conduct and sexual politics back to a consideration of the interrelationship of these within organizations and in sexual harassment. We do so in relation to social work, where one of us has been a residential worker as well as a field social worker, and both of us are involved in various voluntary groups.

Sexual harassment in social work settings

There are three analytically different, although in practice often complexly linked, 'levels' at which sexual harassment becomes an issue within social work.

First, sexual harassment is conventionally seen as a product of the male dominance of organizations: originally all male and now open to women who occupy minority places within them. Consequently some men use and misuse their relatively superior hierarchical positions. Supervisors, line managers, office bosses, union organizers, all feature in the literature as key sources of sexual harassment. However, seeing 'position' as the *source* of sexual harassment is clearly problematic given the history of social work. Numerically women still predominate, as in nursing and teaching, yet this has not prevented sexual harassment happening since the inception of these professions and long before men achieved the managerial dominance they presently have in social work. Of course sexual harassment of women from hierarchical male superiors does happen in social work and of course it is a serious problem; however, this is by no means its exclusive or even predominant form.

Second, women workers (both field and residential) report sexually harassing behaviours happening as much or more so from their supposed equals. Social work offices decorated with soft porn; co-workers openly contemptuous of anything 'women's libby' (aimed at anyone differentiating herself from a doormat, as Rebecca West noted); open opposition to raising the issue of the sexual abuse of children (including by co-workers). 'Kincora' – where male residential workers operated a vice ring using boys and young men to supply sexual services and which involved among others top-level officials and politicians in Northern Ireland (*Community Care* 6 February1986: 5; 13 February 1986: 1–3; 4 December 1986: 15–17; 12 February 1987: 1) – and 'Birmingham' – where a series of sexual scandals erupted into public view (*Community Care* 13 August 1987: 3; 25 August 1988: 2; 8 September 1988: 1; 22 September 1988: 2; 6 October 1988: 3) – will both be familiar memory-joggers to social worker readers, and constitute the tip of an iceberg, a problem that spreads far beyond these two places.

Third, women field and residential workers commonly experience sexual harassment, sometimes complexly mixed with open violence. The reaffirmation of their masculinity/power specifically in sexual terms, is one of the most important means by which organizationally de-powered male clients re-empower themselves. Social workers we know report the daily expression of anger, tirades, sexually and otherwise abusive remarks from some male clients, as well as open 'chatting up' coupled with a refusal to 'hear' any social work talk from these women workers, as well as staring, laughs and whispering amongst men in groups. These problems are greatly increased for women residential workers, for often they find themselves working at a very close and indeed intimate level of contact with men of various ages. As Wendy Parkin (1989) has noted, this makes the management of 'interactional troubles' incredibly difficult. She suggests that the complexities are compounded when the worker experiences sexual or emotional feelings about residents. While we would agree, it seems to us that acting upon such feelings for as long as the institutional basis of the relationship remains is *always* an abuse of trust and of power.

In the rest of this section, the argument laid out in the previous three paragraphs is related to the complexities of sexual conduct and organizational sexuality.

The view of 'the organization' implicit in even recent work is of something *boundaried*, both spatially and socially, by the precise physical space or spaces that it occupies, and by the organizationally specified hierarchical relations of super- and subordination that all employees operate within. However, certainly field social work is actually not like this: in what ways can be usefully shown by saying something about women in nursing and teaching as well as in residential and field social work.

In a discussion of the practical ethics of both nursing and nursing research by Ann Williams (1989), herself a trained nurse as well as a social scientist, an incident on a ward whereby a male patient 'sexually' touched and felt a female nurse is used to raise a number of points concerning the professional ideology, or culture, of nursing. She points out that on one level, that which guided their behaviour regarding male patients, nurses subscribed to a 'Well, he's ill, it might help him get better, I'm here to help him get better' view of it. However, on another and more personal level, articulated in training discussions with her and other nurses, all nurses present spoke of their deep resentment about such behaviour and a shared feeling that 'It's not right'. A personal and related example concerns one of us lecturing to some hundreds of first-year students about domestic labour and 'the household', to hear the drumming of male heels on the floor in protest accompanied by sexually aggressive remarks.

These examples raise in a direct way one of the crucial similarities between social work, nursing and teaching, and which mark out their difference from, say, working on a production line. Nurses and teachers, together with social workers, are located in organizations with strong professional cultures, each concerned with an ideal of service and of helping others. Moreover, each are precisely *service-providing* occupations, the members of which are brought into daily and close, not to say personal, contact with members of their client groups. Both male patients on hospital wards and male students, and male clients of social work, are men in important ways de-powered, rendered *dependent, subordinate*, although obviously in somewhat different ways and by different means.

However, central to each is the loss of their control not only of themselves but also of these social situations to the women professionals involved. Obviously not all men find this problematic; however, some do and these often use 'sexual' means to re-assert their maleness, and thus their superordinate status, to those who are 'naturally' subordinate to male sexuality. And it should also be noted that in each of these situations 'sex' expressed as synonymous with low-key violence was used as a weapon against women as organizational superiors.

There is a further complexity here which it is worth noting, concerned with the complexities of organizational and sexual political power. Although women in each of these three examples are typically to be found at, or near, the bottom of particular organizational hierarchies, and are thus in formal organizational terms relatively subordinate, none the less in relation to each client group these women professionals have large amounts of both formal (and in the case of social workers, sometimes also statutory) and discretionary power. Formal power then is clearly not an absolute and it can – as any black person of no matter how high a professional status can testify – be undermined, denied, challenged and subverted; if the person concerned is a woman and/or black, the means of doing so are to be found in conventional and indeed stereotypical (white, male) ways of responding to members of these 'inferior' social groups.

In discussing the 'sexual' aspects of social work and organizations, it is of course important not to conflate the two. This is not least because the essentially private setting of residential work offers systematic possibilities for confining and limiting women officers on grounds of gender (whether made explicit or not) not only by co-workers but also by officers in charge (Fogarty 1987). Precisely the same thing may happen – and particularly the more that management levels become increasingly male – in social work offices. However, field social workers spend a good deal of their time in the interactionally very different public setting of 'the field', people's homes, as well as in the social work related organizational settings of, for example, play groups and nurseries, hospitals, housing management offices and so forth.

A recent survey of sexual harassment of American social workers at work (Maypole 1986) found that about one-third of female and one-seventh of male social workers had been sexually harassed not only by co-workers but also by clients. Asked 'cold', similar proportions of people in social work offices known to us confirm this. However, once 'sexual harassment' is defined in the broad terms we prefer, nearly all women field and residential workers we know report having experienced this kind of harassment as a daily part of their working lives.

The essentially non-sexual purposes of such male behaviour is revealed once individual cases are looked at in detail, as Fogarty (1987) did with six women social workers. Interestingly, one of the black women workers interviewed reported sexual harassment as worse than racism. This was in part because racism has become 'an issue' which people know at some level is wrong while sexism remains a joke among most men. It was also in part because her black male co-workers systematically and deliberately used sexual harassment as a means of confining her professional activities to the extent that she felt forced to leave the job. Other women social workers interviewed had experienced a lack of comprehension let alone support, from line managers when they were the subject/object of the harassing behaviours of the 'office lads'. They also felt that the supervisory role of these 'lads' made their work virtually impossible.

An argument in the 'new organizational theory' suggests that where women are very few in number (and so not a threat) or many in number (such that an organization is numerically at least female-dominated and men in it are a self-selecting group) sexual behaviour of all forms will be low-key and minimal in their occurrence (Haavio-Mannila *et al.* 1988). For example, Gutek and Dunwoody's (1987) analysis of sexual harassment sees it as a product of 'sex role spillover': in certain organizational structures all forms of sexual behaviour will be found to a higher degree than in others simply because the mixture of women and men encourages this. However, the argument does not hold for social work.

Field social work remains numerically dominated by women, although increasingly management positions are occupied by men, the higher ones being almost exclusively male jobs (see Everitt in this volume, Chapter 11). However, even though women workers no longer form much of a threat to the increasing male dominance of senior hierarchical positions, sexual harassment from male co-workers and managers remains a serious problem. And it does not need us to remind field social workers of the murder of Frances Bettridge to emphasize the fact that harassment from male clients can be extreme and violent, often takes 'sexual' forms, and can be almost impossible to deal with.

Certainly the position of women residential workers – and also women probation officers – more closely fits the argument. However, it is important to note that residential work is not a single and unitary 'thing'. It comprises many residential settings which ensures that the situation with regard to 'sex' can vary greatly, even where the *numbers* of men and women workers are similar.

The sex composition of a work-force must not be seen as somehow deterministic of social or even sexual behaviour on the part of men any more than women. There are other dynamics at work, which have to do with formal occupational cultures, rules and norms, in particular work-groups; the role of those in charge in supporting or undermining 'lads' and their culture and behaviour; the convictions, assumptions and prejudices of men; the assumptions, beliefs and convictions of women; and the un/readiness to challenge offensive or intrusive behaviour.

Where now?

There is an urgent need to move away from the earlier trade-union-influenced model of sexual harassment, that is, inappropriate sexual and extreme work-place behaviours, not least because this is accompanied by a general conviction, even on the part of many women union activists, that it is unrelated to flirtations, sexual joking and 'getting off' at work, which are not merely 'OK' but to be desired. As we have argued, and has been amply corroborated by the work of other researchers looking at organizational sexuality, all sexual harassment and 'sexual' behaviours are closely linked, for the culture that supports and permits the one is also the source and support of the other.

Conventional models of heterosexuality, to which the majority of people feel constrained to adhere at least in their verbal statements in public, centrally define women as passive objects subordinate to the needs and requirements of active and biologically determined male sexuality. In the long term sexual harassment can be removed only through the dismantling of the current sexual political system in which gender, (hetero)sexuality and power are mutually reinforcing of women's oppression. However, for most of us that's far too long to wait! In the shorter term there are other approaches that can be tried, and of which formal union-backed grievance procedures are one (although we think largely unsuccessful).

Everyone who feels that sexual harassment is offensive and wrong needs to think about their own position with regard to ideas, talk and behaviour, about sexual conduct more generally. All of us, men too, also need to take responsibility for what happens around us, not just leave it up to the particular person who has become object to intrusive behaviours. Making such behaviours public to an entire work-group by not helping to maintain silence and privacy for the offender, is a very specific activity that can often cut short such behaviours. The multiple over-layering of 'public' and 'private' thoughts and behaviours is the key to understanding, and acting, with regard to not only sexual harassment but also all other sexisms.

Men as managers often subscribe, through their silence if nothing else, to the 'lads culture' that drives sexual harassment. Managers need to be made aware of the interconnectedness of their silence and complicity with not only offensive but also sometimes criminal behaviours. They need to be made aware that sexism is as offensive, as political, and as important, as racism. And black and white women need to stop subscribing to any political culture that prioritizes one form of oppression above others.

Unofficially and informally, one way women survive sexual harassment and other sexisms is through sharing knowledge of what has happened, and passing on information about who has done it and who supports it. This needs to become a formalized part of work-place cultures: and men need to become aware that the equivalent of Cagney and Lacey's private conversations happen, and that sexual harassment and other intrusions are on the agenda for publicizing. Additionally, men who find deeply offensive the sexual harassing behaviours of other men similarly need to say this as loud and as often as they can. They may find that they too then become targets for other forms of harassment, but that is another matter.

Overarching all of these is the prime requirement for change within social work organizations: the need for women, subscribing to a liberationist occupational social work culture, to be employed at all levels of the hierarchy and particularly middle and higher management. Certainly the odd woman director or deputy director of social services will make little impact on the everyday and routine events and ways of working in what are large, complex and multi-layered organizations. However, large numbers of women line managers *could* begin to change the routine ways that area offices and residential settings work. Alongside this, similar grievance procedures to those set up in Birmingham following the scandals referred to earlier need to be established throughout the profession, so that grievances are not heard by workers' own line managers. And of course at least 50 per cent of those who hear the grievances need to be women.

References

Barker-Benfield, G. (1976) *The Horrors of the Half-Known Life: Male Attitudes Toward Women and Sexuality in 19th Century America*, New York: Harper Colophon.

Bittner, E. (1973) 'The concept of organisation', in G. Salaman and K. Thompson (eds) *People and Organisations*, London: Longman.

Community Care (various issues).

Faraday, A. (1981) 'Liberating lesbian research', in K. Plummer (ed.) *The Making of the Modern Homosexual*, London: Hutchinson.

Farley, L. (1978) *Sexual Shakedown*, New York: McGraw-Hill.

Fogarty, M. (1987) 'Women social workers talking . . .' *Social Work Today* 26 October: 13–14.

Gagnon, J. and Simon, W. (1973) *Sexual Conduct: The Social Sources of Human Sexuality*, Chicago, Ill: Aldine.

Goffman, E. (1961) *Asylums*, Harmondsworth: Penguin.

Gutek, B. and Dunwoody, V. (1987) 'Understanding sex in the workplace', in A. Stromberg, L. Larwood and B. Gutek (eds) *Women and Work: An Annual Review*, vol. 2, Beverly Hills, Calif: Sage.

Haavid-Manilla, E., Kauppinen-Toropainen, K. and Kandolin, I. (1988) 'The effect of sex composition of the workplace on friendship, romance, and sex at work', in B. Gutek, A. Stromberg and L. Larwood (eds) (1988) *Women and Work: An Annual Review*, vol. 3, Beverly Hills, Calif: Sage.

Hearn, J. and Parkin, W. (1987) *'Sex' at 'Work': The Power and Paradox of Organisational Sexuality*, Brighton: Wheatsheaf.

Hearn, J., Sheppard, D., Tancred-Sheriff, P. and Burrell, G. (eds) (1989) *The Sexuality of Organisations*, London: Sage.

Hopkins, J. (1987) 'The sexual harassment of social workers', *Social Work Today* 26 October: 13.

Living (1989) September.

MacKinnon, C. (1979) *Sexual Harassment of Working Women*, New Haven, Conn: Yale University Press.

Maypole, D. (1986) 'Sexual harassment of social workers at work: injustice within?', *Social Work* January–February: 29–34.

Mills, A. (1989) 'Gender, sexuality and organisation theory', in J. Hearn, D. Sheppard, P. Tancred-Sheriff and G. Burrell (eds) *The Sexuality of Organisation*, London: Sage.

NALGO (National Association of Local Government Officers) (1981) *Sexual Harassment is a Trades Union Issue*, London: NALGO.

Parkin, W. (1989) 'Private experiences in the public domain: sexuality and residential care organisations', in J. Hearn, D. Sheppard, P. Tancred-Sheriff and G. Burrell (eds) *The Sexuality of Organisation*, London: Sage.

Plummer, K. (1975) *Sexual Stigma*, London: Routledge & Kegan Paul.

Pringle, R. (1989) 'Bureaucracy, rationality and sexuality: the case of secretaries', in J. Hearn, D. Sheppard, P. Tancred-Sheriff and G. Burrell (eds) *The Sexuality of Organisations*, London: Sage.

Roy, D. (1973) 'Banana time: job satisfaction and informal interaction', in G. Salaman, and K. Thompson (eds) *People and Organisations*, London: Longman.

Salaman, G. and Thompson, K. (eds) (1973) *People and Organisations*, London: Longman.

Strauss, A., Schatzman, L., Ehrlich, D., Bucher, R. and Sabshin, M. (1973) 'The hospital and its negotiated order', in G. Salaman and K. Thompson (eds) *People and Organisations*, London: Longman.

Strong, P. (1974) 'Doing sex', Proceedings of the 1974 BSA Annual Conference on Sex and Gender, Aberdeen, April.

Trades Union Congress (1983) *Sexual Harassment At Work*, London: TUC.

Williams, A. (1989) Interpreting an Ethnography of Nursing, unpublished Ph.D thesis, University of Manchester.

Wise, S. and Stanley, L. (1987) *Georgie Porgie: Sexual Harassment in Everyday Life*, London: Pandora Press.

3
Punishment in the community

Ruth Allan

Amidst all the publicity that has surrounded government attacks on the legal and medical professions the assault on the probation service has slipped by attracting little attention. Yet the probation service as we know it is under threat. The government may not be deliberately setting out to destroy it, but is prepared to sacrifice the probation service in pursuit of policies for tackling prison overcrowding. The clear theme that runs through government plans for community service (Home Office 1988a), through the Green Paper *Punishment, Custody and the Community* (Home Office 1988b) and its proposals for secure bail hostels (Home Office 1988c) is that the courts do not have full confidence in the alternatives to custody run by the probation service because they are insufficiently punitive. As a result, offenders are being unnecessarily sentenced to imprisonment and the probation service is being blamed for the crisis in the prisons. This chapter will argue that this analysis is wrong, that the development of more punitive alternatives will not affect the prison population but that it will nevertheless fundamentally change the work of the probation service.

The government's criticism is made quite explicit in its plans for community service and in *Punishment, Custody and the Community*. The covering letter that accompanied the first draft of the new national standards for community service stated at the outset that 'the Home Office is looking at ways of increasing the confidence of the courts in the community service order as an alternative to custody' (Home Office 1988a). The introduction of *Punishment, Custody and the Community* makes it even clearer:

> Imprisonment is not the most effective punishment for most crime. Custody should be reserved as a punishment for very serious offences, especially when the offender is violent and a continuing risk to the public.

But not every sentencer or member of the public has full confidence in the present orders which leave offenders in the community.

(Home Office 1988b: 2)

The rest of this chapter sets out the government's proposals, which aim to increase the court's and the public's confidence in keeping offenders in the community (Hone Office 1988b). The criticism is also implicit in the Green Paper *Private Sector Involvement in the Remand System* which proposes new secure bail hostels run by the private sector (Home Office 1988c). No evidence is produced to support this assertion of lack of confidence. The government chooses to ignore the fact that between 1979 and 1987 the proportion of offenders starting probation who have previously been sentenced to custody has increased from 20 per cent to 30 per cent without any effect on success rates. The government also fails to point out the wide and inequitable discrepancies in court sentencing which show, for example, that in 1986 the percentage of adult males sentenced to imprisonment ranged from 8 per cent at Rotherham Magistrates Court to 39 per cent at Tower Bridge Magistrates Court (NAPO 1988a). These are discrepancies which confirm the view that there are adequate noncustodial disposals available to courts which wish to use them.

The government is choosing to evade the evidence because its approach has been dictated by political necessity. It knows that it has to reduce the prison population which is spiralling out of control at enormous cost to the taxpayer, but it cannot appear to be soft to its own supporters. It is for this reason that it is proposing punishing alternatives in the community. The irony is that it is the government's own law-and-order rhetoric which has done so much to encourage the judiciary and magistrates to impose more and longer prison sentences.

However, its chosen strategy will not work. First, because in proposing punishing alternatives in the community it is feeding into the punitive mentality, the 'culture of severity' which has such a strong influence over sentencing in this country (Garland 1989). Britain now has a higher prison population in absolute numbers than any other member state of the Council of Europe. It has a higher prison population relative to its overall population than any other Council of Europe country except Luxembourg. Great Britain imprisons 98.2 prisoners per 100,000 population. The comparable figures for Turkey are 90.2, for West Germany 86.7, for Spain 69.2, for Greece 42.9 and Holland 36.0 (NACRO 1989). If there is to be any hope of decreasing the prison population this punitive mentality must be confronted not sustained.

The second reason is that the government's major new proposal is yet another 'alternative' to custody: the supervision and restriction order. No evidence is put forward to suggest that this 'alternative' will work any better than the other non-custodial penalties which have been introduced during the last twenty years. Experience indicates that new so-called alternatives are all too frequently used instead of other alternatives, and fail to produce an overall drop in the proportionate use of custody. Both community service orders and suspended sentences, for example, have been used as much to replace other non-custodial penalties as to replace custody (Fitzmaurice and Pease 1986).

Third, the government has failed to recognize that the key factor in reducing the prison population is tackling sentence lengths. Concentrating merely on alternatives is insufficient. Fitzmaurice and Pease show, using 1980 figures, sentencing all adult males who received a prison sentence of six months or less to non-custodial measures would have merely reduced the prison population by fewer than 2,000. However, a 10 per cent reduction in overall sentence length would have produced a greater reduction (Fitzmaurice and Pease 1986).

Finally, the policy is unlikely to succeed in the context of a massive prison-building programme. The government has now committed £1.40 billion to prison building. Yet it is quite clear, particularly from experience in the USA, that if capacity expands and extra prison places are provided they are inevitably filled.

While the government's strategy is bound to fail in its main purpose of reducing the prison population, it will have a devastating effect on the probation service. All the proposals are intended to make the work of the probation service more punitive. The community service order was the first probation-run alternative to come under attack at the beginning of 1988. The first draft of the national standards states that 'Community Service must make tough demands – physical and otherwise – on offenders, including the essential discipline of regular attendance and prompt time-keeping' (Home Office 1988a). This sets the tone for the changes that the government has brought about.

The final version of the new rules and standards were introduced in April 1989 (Home Office 1989a; 1989b). They emphasize physical work in groups. Every person who is made subject to a community service order of not less than sixty hours must perform at least twenty-one hours in a group placement. The rules define work in a group placement as 'work of a manual nature' (Home Office 1989a). Each probation area will have to ensure that placements are available which improve the appearance and amenities of the neighbourhood. The document mentions clearing graffiti, cleaning litter and wastegrounds, erecting litter bins and building adventure playgrounds. The stress, therefore, is on visible physical work.

The rules and standards stipulate that offenders must work a minimum weekly average of five and not more than twenty-one hours in a week. There are proposals about the length of tea and lunch breaks and a detailed formula to deal with time lost due to bad weather. Two proposals seem particularly unreasonable. One specifies that only work done at the time and place specified counts towards the community service order, and that an offender who reports to work without an appointment should not normally be allowed to work. The other states that travelling time, however long, should not count towards completion of the order except when the offender travels under the supervision of a supervisor, for example from a pick-up point. This is very unfair to those living in rural areas. These new rules and standards are bureaucratic and rigid. While greater consistency between different areas of the country is a valuable aim, professional probation officers must be entrusted to use some discretion and allowed some flexibility.

The sections on discipline and breach proceedings also give rise to concern.

They state that offenders have failed to comply with the requirements of an order if they fail to attend a work appointment and provide no acceptable explanation, or if they behave or work unsatisfactorily. Offenders who arrive more than half-an-hour late for work are deemed to have failed to attend and 'unsatisfactory behaviour' is defined in worryingly subjective terms as including behaviour which is 'likely to give offence to members of the public or any person for whose benefit the work is being performed' (Home Office 1989a). After three such failures breach proceedings would normally be started.

These sections are again inflexible, allowing little discretion to probation officers. They are likely to result in fewer recommendations for community service from probation officers worried that disorganized offenders in particular will have difficulty keeping to the requirements. They are also likely to produce more breaches, which will lead to a greater number of people going to prison, while more frequent breaches will tend to weaken the confidence of the courts in the probation service's ability to handle difficult offenders.

The National Association of Probation Officers (NAPO) has neatly highlighted the differences between the new rules and the former guidelines for community service by comparing the new standards with old Home Office Circulars (NAPO 1988b). These state for example that:

> Tasks should be seen to be of benefit to the community at large and work should be rehabilitative rather than punitive . . . on the whole offenders seem to have responded best doing work which they can recognize as being of help to people in need. Breach proceedings should be used only as a last resort.
>
> (Home Office 1974)

There are clearly two different philosophies of community service at issue here. Former practice recognized that community service was basically a retributive alternative to custody, but saw the punishment in the deprivation of time and the necessity to work. The government's more recent rules make it overtly punitive (Allan 1988a).

However, the picture is not in fact quite so gloomy as the above analysis suggests. The standards do contain some positive proposals which should be welcomed. It is clearly stated that community service should be used instead of a prison sentence. Some courts have currently been using short orders as a sentence for less serious offences. Each area is required to ensure that placements are available for all ethnic groups, disabled offenders, women offenders, including those who are pregnant, and offenders with children or other domestic responsibilities. In addition the circular suggests that Probation Committees could pay special expenses such as fees for child-minding. This is important since there is some evidence that black offenders are less likely to be given a community service order, and clear evidence that women are discriminated against. In 1985 only 3 per cent of women compared with 7 per cent of men received sentences of community service. A Home Office study in 1987 analyzed social inquiry reports to discover some reasons for this discrepancy. It found that probation officers were less likely to recommend community service when a woman had the responsibility for young children (Jackson and Smith 1987).

The government has also come under intense pressure from probation organizations since it first floated its new proposals and this lobbying has brought important modifications, many of which are contained not in the rules and standards but in the accompanying Circular (Home Office 1989c). So we now learn, for example, that 'visible' means that the 'result of the work should be visible to the public or well publicized. It is not necessary that offenders should be visible to the public'. The word 'manual' has been qualified. It is defined as involving 'the application of manual skills or effort. Work which only occasionally or incidentally has a manual element would not be appropriate for a group placement'. Demanding work is now defined as 'physically, emotionally and intellectually taxing', whereas originally the emphasis had been on physically demanding work. In other words while the rhetoric and imagery of the new community service is punitive, it may be possible for probation officers to get on quietly with operating some aspects at least of community service in traditional ways.

Proposals to change community service were quickly followed in July 1988 by the Green Paper *Punishment, Custody and the Community* (Home Office 1988b) which has the most profound implications for the probation service. This is made clear in the introduction which states the principles which should underlie non-custodial sanctions. The first principle is 'restrictions on the offenders' freedom of action – as a punishment'. In this one sentence the government is proposing a fundamental change in probation work. In defining supervision in terms of punishment it converts supervision from an attempt to influence constructively the offender's future behaviour into a measure which incorporates restrictions as a form of punishment (NAPO 1988c). For example, day centre programmes which emphasize restrictions on freedom will be very different from current programmes which offer intensive but purposeful social work help.

The Green Paper goes on in Part 2 to consider changes in the work of the probation service that can be achieved now without legislation, and in Part 3 and Part 4 to look to long-term change which will require legislation. Part 2 has been fleshed out by *Tackling Offending: An Action Plan* (Home Office 1988d) which is particularly concerned with young adult offenders. It asks all probation areas to establish local action plans and ten areas to set up Intensive Probation Programmes, to reduce the number of young adult offenders being sentenced to custody.

The proposals for local action plans are couched in punitive terms. The government would like to see more compulsory elements in probation orders, for example conditions to take part in activities and to attend day centres under sections 4A and 4B of the Power of Criminal Courts Acts 1973. They are in favour of tracking and frequent reporting. However, the proposals do have positive aspects. They emphasize targeting work on those young adult offenders most at risk of custody, monitoring outcomes, and evaluating work. They suggest there should be better communication with the courts and they support inter-agency co-operation. Action Plans could be used positively despite the rhetoric if the probation service has the confidence to hold on to its traditional values and to mould the proposals to fit its current way of working.

There is a clear analogy here with the juvenile field and the 1983 DHSS Initiative on Intensive Intermediate Treatment, which made available £15 million for alternatives to custody schemes. The Initiative coincided with a drop in the number of juveniles in the population, but the reduced use of custody for juveniles cannot be explained by demographic change alone. The number of juvenile offenders given custodial sentences has almost halved in seven years from a peak of 7,700 in 1981 to 4,000 in 1987. The fall since 1985 from 6,200 to 4,000 has been particularly sharp. Workers in the juvenile field have been successful in keeping juveniles out of custody, and they have done so by strategically intervening in the juvenile justice system (Jones 1989). Targeting, monitoring and evaluation have been important tools, as have gatekeeping and intervention at the key points of the system, such as the decision to prosecute. Prosecution rates have dropped significantly if unevenly. There has been more effort to communicate with courts. Intensive intermediate treatment schemes could have led to a more punitive orientation placing onerous restrictions on juveniles, which is no doubt what the government had in mind. But, by and large, after initial sorties in that direction this has not occurred. Workers in this sector appear to have based alternative to custody schemes on constructive social work values and to have targeted them on those most at risk of a custodial sentence.

There is a need for caution in assuming that the achievement with juveniles will carry over to the young adult field. Courts may be less sympathetic to older offenders who may have more 'form', and a greater number of young adults are dealt with by Crown Courts. Juvenile schemes have been much less successful in winning the confidence of Crown Courts and research by Inner London Probation Service has illustrated the difficulty of effecting any change in Crown Court practice (ILPS 1988). Nevertheless, the probation service may be able to build on the positives in the Action Plan proposals and retain its values by ensuring that probation orders with additional conditions provide social work help and are used only for those who genuinely risk custody. The probation service will have the advantage of a drop in the number of young adults in the population.

It is hard to assess whether the Action Plans which have been submitted to the Home Office will have this effect. The first overview of the Plans suggest that they have in the main obediently reflected the rhetoric of the Green Paper, while largely representing a continued commitment to existing practice. However, some probation services have been tempted down the punitive road (NAPO 1989). Clearly a great deal will depend on how the plans are implemented and success will require a far more sophisticated approach to probation management than is evident in most probation services at present (Audit Commission 1989). It will also require firm resolve from management; but there are worrying indications that some chief probation officers may be prepared to abandon the social work base of the profession.

There is less chance of the service being able to work positively with intensive probation programmes. *Tackling Offending: An Action Plan* makes it quite clear that they 'should include use of methods which exercise a degree of control over offenders'. The Home Office letter to the ten probation areas invited to set up intensive probation programmes states that 'the programme must be seen to place demands and restrictions on offenders which are commensurate with the harm they have done' (Home Office 1989d). All programmes are to include arrangements for offenders to be either tracked or report frequently to probation officers. The government particularly favours tracking. The term 'tracking' is used to describe a scheme run by West Yorkshire Probation Service in which intensive 'supervision' of young adults is carried out by unqualified staff. The trackers maintain very close contact with offenders by telephone or in person up to three times a day, checking their whereabouts, planning their daily schedule and discussing their activities. The West Yorkshire scheme is the only one for adults in the country, and the Green Paper admits that it has not been centrally evaluated. Tracking is based on surveillance and is an intrusive order which represents a major shift in the image and role of the probation service towards a policing approach (LCCJ 1988). Indeed, intensive probation programmes, as envisaged by the government, seem to be designed to introduce surreptitiously the new punishment in the community proposals contained in Part 3 and Part 4 of the Green Paper. Yet even here the probation service could thwart the government. Some of the ten areas have chosen not to set up tracking schemes, but plan intensive supervision programmes run by probation officers. The content of these programmes will be of critical importance.

Proposals to increase the use of alternatives to custody for black and women offenders are noticeably absent from this section of the Green Paper and from *Tackling Offending: An Action Plan*. Home Office plans for intensive probation programmes, however, do specifically require appropriate and relevant programmes for ethnic minority and women offenders. Discrimination in the criminal justice system requires urgent action. There is a disproportionate number of black people in prisons and that number is rising. Black prisoners have substantially fewer previous convictions than white prisoners (Home Office 1986), and are less likely to be placed on probation (Fowler and Voakes 1989). While a smaller proportion of women are sentenced to immediate imprisonment than men, they too appear to be sent to prison at an earlier point in their criminal career with fewer convictions. A greater percentage of women than men are placed on probation, but they are under-represented as clients of day centres (NAPO 1988d). This discrimination is the result of racist and sexist attitudes which permeate the criminal justice system and the probation service is only one of many agencies which need to address their practice if discrimination is to be stamped out. The probation service can play its part by ensuring that black and women offenders do have equal access to alternatives to custody and that they are not over-represented on the government's more punitive proposals such as the intensive probation programme.

There is no opportunity at all for the probation service to operate the supervision and restriction order, the centrepiece of Part 3 without abandoning its social work role. The proposed supervision and restriction order would enable courts to include a whole range of requirements in a single order. The Green Paper mentions compensation to the victim; community service; residence at a hostel, prescribed activities at a day centre or elsewhere, curfew or house arrest; tracking; and other conditions such as staying away from particular places. The philosophy behind the new order is made quite explicit.

> In the formal requirements of the order there would inevitably be an emphasis on restrictions and on compulsory activity . . . the aim of the order would be to make a sharp initial impact on offenders but perhaps to allow them to progress to less rigorous forms of supervision.
>
> (Home Office 1988b)

Before considering the total impact of the new proposal it is necessary to look at elements within it, and in particular house arrest, which the government may wish to combine with electronic monitoring. Although curfews are already used in our criminal justice system as a condition of bail and, less commonly, as a condition of a supervision order, house arrest as a court order is unknown. The following restrictions imposed by a New York District Court in 1985 encapsulate the nature of house arrest. It ordered a Ms Murphy to remain in her apartment for two years. During the period she was allowed to leave only for medical reasons, employment, religious services and for essential food shopping. The order was supervised by the probation department (Petersilia 1986). By 1986 nearly 10,000 adult offenders had been placed on house arrest in the USA. If house arrest were to be introduced in this country the Green Paper hints that there could be restrictions on the maximum period for which it would run and suggests three months. House arrest would still represent a major restriction on civil liberties, of the type normally associated with totalitarian regimes. It is also unenforceable.

This leads the government on to consider electronic monitoring or tagging, operating in parts of the USA and Canada. There are two main types of monitoring equipment in use in North America. The first requires the probationer to wear a small transmitter around the wrist, ankle or neck. The transmitter emits a radio signal which is picked up by a receiver attached to the probationer's telephone. A computer automatically dials the offender's telephone at random intervals to determine whether the receiver is receiving a signal from the transmitter. If it is not the computer registers a potential violation. The second system uses a passive wristband instead of a transmitter. In this case a computer dials the probationer's home. The probationer then inserts an identification bracelet worn on the wrist into a receiver attached to the phone and the receiver sends a signal back to the computer.

There have been problems with the technology. Inaccuracies have been generated by severe thunderstorms, radio station broadcasts, home appliances, and by the probationer sleeping in a foetal position (Schmidt 1986). There have also been human problems of domestic and child violence where enforced home confinement has exacerbated existing family tensions.

Electronic monitoring in the USA is undertaken by probation departments and by private service corporations who in effect assume the duties of a probation department in supervising offenders. Fees of about 200 dollars a month are charged.

The objections to tagging are on the grounds both of civil liberties and penal policy. Electronic monitoring combined with house arrest gives the state enormous power to control the individual's movement and to intrude on home and privacy. One does not have to invoke an Orwellian future to see the dangers (Allan 1987). During the miner's strike the courts and the police became involved in a political response to problems in the coal industry. The courts imposed severe bail conditions restricting the movement of miners. Had the power of house arrest then been available and utilized on a pre-trial basis grave issues of civil liberties would have been raised. In 1988 at the Conservative Party Conference the Home Secretary announced that tagging was to be introduced in this country as a condition of bail. This decision was made several months before the consultation period on the Green Paper had expired. Three experimental schemes are expected to be operational in 1989.

Supporters of tagging argue that the restrictions imposed are justified as the alternative would be a prison sentence. The critical question, therefore, is whether tagging in combination with house arrest will indeed be used for those who would otherwise go to prison, or if it will be used to widen the net of social control. Ironically an American advocate of tagging has spelled out the likely consequences most clearly. 'Judges will sentence offenders to prison as long as capacity exists, and as capacity expands so may prison commitments. If we begin to regard homes as potential prisons, capacity is, for all practical purposes, unlimited' (Petersilia 1986). Research has shown that none of the programmes in the USA has caused a reduction in prison budgets (Ball *et al.* 1987).

The evidence from the USA also supports the view that many offenders who are unlikely to be imprisoned will be sentenced to house arrest and tagged. It has been used for low-risk, non-violent, well-motivated offenders.

Tagging is the most controversial element in the Green Paper. If the probation service was to undertake electronic monitoring of offenders probation officers would be exercising a purely surveillance role far removed from the traditional description of their work as 'advising, assisting and befriending'. Other new, or relatively new, elements in the supervision and restriction order move probation in the same direction. Tracking has already been discussed. The Green Paper also floats the idea of negative conditions such as staying away from particular places, for example streets, clubs or pubs. Pity the poor probation officer asked to monitor such requirements.

The government proposes that the new order should be judicially supervised. The Green Paper suggests that there should be a supervisory magistrate who would have oversight of the order, and the power to vary it. This is an attempt to control the professional discretion of the probation officer, and a thinly veiled attack on the service. The proposal is particularly ironic since supervision in the form of case committees was finally abandoned only in 1984 as an unnecessary duplication of time and accountability.

One of the unique features of the supervision and restriction order is that it combines so many restrictions in one order. The result is a draconian measure, the full force of which comes over in the examples in the appendix to the Green Paper. It is suggested, for example, that unemployed offenders without accommodation should be subject to six days of activity each week for three months. This would be made up of two days' community service, two days at a day centre, and two days of prescribed activity. Offenders would reside in a probation hostel and be subject to a curfew. For offenders who would not have received a prison sentence these are major restrictions on their liberties. Even those offenders who would have received a custodial sentence do not need to be subject to this degree of control. The Green Paper itself points out that most of those now in prison have not been convicted of violent offences. If released they would not pose such a threat to society to justify this level of containment.

The Green Paper again fails to mention black and women offenders in the section on supervision and restriction orders. Against a background of discrimination there must be real concern that black women and black men will be pushed up the sentencing tariff and will be tagged and placed on supervision and restriction orders rather than being given probation or community service orders.

The new order will transform the work of the probation service. Probation supervision has always worked within a system of court-imposed obligations on the offender. However, the purpose of these constraints has been to provide a framework for supervision within which the emphasis is on constructively helping and influencing the offender (NAPO 1988c). This can be done only by gaining the probationer's trust and confidence. The Green Paper seeks to impose punitive restrictions and to give the probation service a surveillance role. It is hard to envisage trusting relationships being achieved or sustained in these circumstances.

Since the publication of the Green Paper yet another new proposal is rumoured to be circulating amongst and favoured by Home Office officials – a combined probation and community service order. This proposal, too, is fraught with dangers. British courts already have more alternatives to custody available to them than their European counterparts, and the creation of an order combining two existing provisions is likely to confuse an already complex system. Furthermore it is very likely that some offenders will be placed on a combined order rather than on a simple probation order. If they re-offend they will be propelled up the sentencing tariff and into prison, since courts will argue that both probation and community service have been tried and failed.

The final section of the Green Paper deals with the organization of the new order, and brings in another major government theme – privatization. Privatization is usually taken to mean the involvement of private profit-making companies in areas traditionally within the public sector. In the criminal justice system, however, it is often voluntary organizations who are seen as the vehicle of privatization. Both forms are attractive to a government obsessed with breaking up public services and introducing competition. The Green Paper suggests two ways in which the new order could be organized, both of which involve the private and voluntary sectors. It argues that the probation service is best placed to take responsibility for supervising punishment in the community, but that it need not provide all the elements itself. It could contract with private and voluntary organizations to obtain some of the components of punishment in the community. Alternatively, if the probation service is not prepared to take on this central role then a new organization could be set up to organize the order. This organization could either be part of the Home Office or a separate public body. It would provide services through contracts with other organizations including the probation service.

It is hard to envisage a major role for private sector companies in this area with the very important exception of tagging. Numerous companies are said to be interested in developing tagging equipment and could take responsibility for its use. The voluntary sector, on the other hand, could take on many aspects of punishment in the community and there is a precedent in the wide-scale involvement of the voluntary sector in the juvenile field. But the government's motives are suspect. It wants to use the voluntary sector to circumvent probation objections to more punitive work (Ward 1988). Voluntary organizations working to fixed contracts would also be more easily controlled by the Home Office. The threat to the probation service is clear and, indeed, Morris has suggested that the Green Paper can be seen as 'a formal warning to those members of the probation service who might be minded to mount campaigns of passive resistance or non cooperation' (Morris 1988).

That threat is carried over into the Green Paper on *Private Sector Involvement in the Remand System* (Home Office 1988c). The bulk of this document is directed at prisons but a small paragraph relates to bail hostels, and the development of secure bail hostels. These would exert more control over defendants, possibly using twelve-hour curfews and more structured daytime programmes. They would be run by the private sector.

Rumours about plans to privatize aspects of probation work had been circulating for months before the Green Papers as a result of a spate of leaks from Home Office sources (Allan 1988b). These rumours have returned with a vengeance, and there are now clear hints from inside the Home Office that ministers are considering putting out to tender all the tasks of the service and not just the proposals for punishment in the community.

What is ultimately so depressing about all these government proposals is that they are based on a philosophy that many commentators now regard as outdated, flawed and failed (LCCJ 1988). That philosophy sees punishment as the means of controlling crime in society and has the prison at the apex of the system. This carceral model has underpinned the criminal justice system since the nineteenth century. It has patently failed. Everywhere prisons are overcrowded, yet crime remains uncontrolled. The USA is a society with enormously high rates of imprisonment yet it also has an alarming crime problem. At home the experience of the last ten years underlines the failure of punishment. The Thatcher governments have placed great emphasis on law and order and tough sentencing, yet levels of recorded crime have spiralled upwards. The government's response has not been to question the validity of this approach, but to bring the prison out into the community to place restrictions outside the prison walls.

Clearly there is a need to tackle crime in a different way. In the last few years there has been a remarkable convergence of views both in Britain and abroad around crime prevention, not as a peripheral but as a central concept in reducing crime. Mary Tuck, head of the Home Office Research and Planning Unit, has suggested that we are seeing the beginning of a shift away from the whole concept of the carceral society towards crime prevention (Tuck 1987).

Crime prevention encompasses a wide range of activities. It is concerned with physical security in terms of locks and bolts and with designing out crime, for example with adequate street lighting and building modifications, but it extends far beyond this. It recognizes the links between public safety and greater investment in public sector housing estates. Crime rates are at their highest on inner city council estates. More resident caretakers, tower block receptionists and estate staff are important since would-be offenders are deterred by the presence of people. Increased staffing levels are vital in other areas too such as public transport. The facilities in an area will also affect crime rates, and in particular, the provision of constructive leisure pursuits for young people who commit a large percentage of crimes. One-half of all recorded offences and three-quarters of all recorded burglaries are committed by people under 21. Yet youth provision is often totally inadequate in the impoverished areas where it is most needed (Birley and Bright 1985).

Crime prevention is also crucially bound up with economic and social policies at national level. The present government has pursued policies which foster social division, which lead to poverty in the midst of affluence, which marginalize and alienate young people without jobs and without a stake in society. Crime will be tackled more effectively by reversing these policies than by inventing new sentencing options.

The government's proposals for the probation service flow against the current thinking on crime prevention. Born of political necessity they are doomed to fail in their main purpose, the reduction of the prison population, since the government has not been prepared to stand up to sentencers and reduce their power. The probation service is a softer target and a convenient scapegoat whose traditions and values risk being swept away. Perhaps one day with the benefit of hindsight we shall look back on punishment in the community as the high tide of the punishment philosophy. Sadly we may discover the remnant of a probation service committed to social work help amongst the discarded flotsam and jetsam washed up on the shore.

References

Allan, R. (1987) 'The dangers of an Orwellian future', *Social Work Today*, 26 October: 23.
—— (1988a) 'Punishment in the community', *Social Work Today*, 11 August: 25.
—— (1988b) 'Correct me if I'm wrong', *Social Work Today*, 16 June: 20.
Audit Commission (1989) *Promoting Value for Money in the Probation Service*, London: HMSO.
Ball, R., Huff, C. and Lilly, J. (1987) *House Arrest and Correctional Policy: Doing Time at Home*, Beverly Hills, Calif: Sage.
Birley, D. and Bright, J. (1985) *Crime in the Community*, London: Labour Campaign for Criminal Justice.

Fitzmaurice, C. and Pease, K. (1986) *The Psychology of Judicial Sentencing*, Manchester University Press.

Fowler, Q. and Voakes, R. (1989) *Sentencing, Race and Social Enquiry Reports*, Wakefield: West Yorkshire Probation Service.

Garland, D. (1989) 'Critical reflections on *Punishment, Custody and the Community*', unpublished paper prepared for the Second LSE International Criminal Justice Seminar.

Home Office (1974) *Home Office Circular 197/74*, Community Service by Offenders, London: HMSO.

—— (1986) *The Ethnic Origin of Prisoners*, Statistical Bulletin 17/86, London: HMSO.

—— (1988a) *National Standards for Community Service Orders: First Draft*, London: Home Office.

—— (1988b) *Punishment, Custody and the Community*, Cm 424, London: HMSO.

—— (1988c) *Private Sector Involvement in the Remand System*, Cm 434, London: HMSO.

—— (1988d) *Tackling Offending: An Action Plan*, London: HMSO.

—— (1989a) *Community Service Orders Rules 1989*, Statutory Instrument no. 191, London: HMSO.

—— (1989b) *National Standards for Community Service Orders*, London: HMSO.

—— (1989c) *National Standards for Community Service Orders*, Home Office Circular 18/1989, London: HMSO.

—— (1989d) *Intensive Probation Programmes*, letter to chief probation officers, London: Home Office.

ILPS (Inner London Probation Service) (1988) *Demonstration Unit Phase Two 1985–1988*, London: ILPS.

Jackson, H. and Smith, L. (1987) *Female Offenders: An Analysis of Social Inquiry Reports*, Research Bulletin no. 23, London: Home Office Research and Planning Unit.

Jones, D. (1989) 'The successful revolution', *Community Care*, 30 March 1988: i–ii.

LCCJ (Labour Campaign for Criminal Justice) (1988) *Punishment, Custody and the Community*, London: LCCJ.

Morris, T. (1988) 'Punishment, Custody and the Community', *Criminal Justice*, the magazine of the Howard League, 6, 4, November: 5–6.

NACRO (National Association for the Care and Resettlement of Offenders) (1989) *Imprisonment in Western Europe: Some Facts and Figures*, London: NACRO.

NAPO (National Association of Probation Officers) (1988a) *Magistrates Courts and Custody*, London: NAPO.

—— (1988b) *Response to the Home Office Draft National Standards for Community Service*, London: NAPO.

—— (1988c) *Punishment, Custody and the Community*, London: NAPO.

—— (1988d) *The Use of Schedule II Conditions*, London: NAPO.

—— (1989) 'What do Action Plans add up to?', *NAPO News* 11, London: NAPO.

Petersilia, J. (1986) 'Exploring the option of house arrest', *Federal Probation*, June: 50–5.

Schmidt, A. (1986) 'Electronic monitors', *Federal Probation*, June: 58–9.

Tuck, M. (1987) *Crime Prevention: A Shift in Concept*, Research Bulletin no. 24, London: Home Office Research and Planning Unit.

Ward, T. (1988) 'Privatisation and punishment', *Criminal Justice*, the magazine of the Howard League, 6, 4, November: 10.

4
Guardians of autonomy: work orientations in a social work office

Andy Pithouse

The impact of large organizational structures on the delivery of welfare services has traditionally been cast as a source of intrusion or diversion from the ideals of social work practice. The notion that social workers have been deskilled and have lost autonomy through working in large social services departments is a familiar theme (Clarke 1979). Yet polemics apart, there is comparatively little evidence of how social workers actually cope with today's work world, particularly in the way they handle their organization, manage their colleagues and deal with their clients.

This chapter seeks to address some of these areas in regard to the question of autonomy. By autonomy I mean the degree to which social workers can control the pace and content of their work given the boundaries of their role. In this chapter I will examine the experiences of a team of child care workers operating in a decentralized setting. It will be shown that there are considerable areas of practitioner autonomy which are the outcome of both covert and explicit negotiations within the organization. It will also be shown that the self-regulation enjoyed by workers contains certain disadvantages in that scrutiny and assessment of practice suffers in the contest over the control of work.

A year of participant observation together with a series of structured interviews with social workers and their immediate managers form the basis of the following commentary. The methods and theory employed stem from a symbolic interactionist tradition and the background to the study is set out in detail elsewhere (Pithouse 1987). The setting in question is a local authority social services area office and is the only detached fieldwork section of the social services department. The focus here is upon the child care workers in the office, who are organized into two teams, both with a complement of seven practitioners and a team leader. They share an open-plan office with other teams, who provide services for elderly people and people with learning difficulties.

All but two of the child care social workers are women. All are qualified. Most of the practitioners have been in post for more than two years; there are five veterans with more than five years in post. The two teams hold some six hundred cases between them. The social services department serves one of the many shire counties in England and Wales. The area office workers routinely visit homes in a coastal conurbation; these localities have suffered the long-run decline of local industry (steel, coal and dockland) and endure higher levels of unemployment than the national average.

The area office: insulation and control

The work orientations of the child care practitioners are best defined by a notion of conflict and control. Here the workers create a group response to their environment that seeks to reject or manipulate external influences in such a way as to protect their accustomed forms of practice. It is argued here that their organizational conduct is best viewed from the standpoint of groups in competition over the control of work. In this example, power is not simply drained off by higher management but is contested and negotiated by those lower down who share similar views about their occupational task and identity.

Here the social workers, female and male, enjoy and protect a considerable degree of self-regulation. This is particularly noteworthy since women as welfare professionals have in the past been cast as more amenable to administrative regulation (see Toren 1969: 156; Etzioni 1969: xv). It is of course the case that women have been marginalized in male-dominated professions (Spencer and Podmore 1987) but there remains substantial doubt as to whether male and female orientations about work are fundamentally dissimilar. This is not least because past research on work settings has either accepted stereotypical assumptions about women or has treated the question of gender superficially (see Dex 1985: 41). Indeed, it has been observed in some work-places that men, rather than women, are more responsive to hierarchy and authority (see Davies 1983: 50). The notion that women in social work may be more submissive to bureaucratic rules than men will not be discussed here, not least because there was no evidence that such a contention applied to the child care workers that were observed. If anything, the female workers were more assertive when claiming their right to self-regulating practice.

The area office is a segment of the social services department. The term 'segment' is located in a symbolic interactionist perspective that emphasizes conflict and competition over differing interests among professionals in organizations (see Bucher and Strauss 1961; Bucher and Stelling 1977; Heraud 1971). Segment implies a notion of groups in continual and spontaneous process and actively asserting or protecting their local interests. Here elements within the organization engage in claims for recognition and frequently negotiate the formal rules and objectives of the organization in favour of specific groups. The following account of the area office and its relationships with the city department draws on this notion of groups involved in processes of negotiation and competition. It will be shown that members have mapped out the boundaries around their segment and continually attempt to repair these in order to fend off intrusions from the departmental hierarchy.

In the course of the research, monthly meetings of the entire area office establishment were attended. These take place in the open-plan office and the area manager or his deputy usually chair the proceedings. Typically there is reference by the manager to some new administrative procedure but there are also frequent comments made on more local matters. For example, meetings often commence with news about important events in the lives of staff members present and past. This local and more 'domestic' account of 'births, deaths and marriages' among the staff and those who have left but are remembered, implicitly affirms an 'office' identity. New recruits are 'officially' welcomed by the managers at these meetings. Similarly, those who may soon be leaving are gently eased towards a new shift in their personal or occupational career. Here a warm farewell and commemorative card or gift marks the event.

These routine ovations of collegial concern help stake out the boundaries of the occupational group. Such warm affect is rarely reserved for higher management. For example, at one meeting new instructions were issued in respect of especially long journeys made to visit clients (such as children placed in care outside the county). New forms now had to be completed before the visit and permission sought from management. The news, delivered by the office manager, was received with snorts of derision by the social workers who were affronted by the implication that they were not the best judge of how to plan their visits and movements. These points were expressed at the meeting and one worker loudly stated that such long-distance visits were sometimes urgent and anticipatory form-filling was not always possible.

> *Social Worker:* These mileage forms are stupid! You don't always know when you'll visit, er you know – it could be a crisis and you have to go!
> *Manager:* [nods] I agree. Look, if we scrap this one [form] they'll [higher management] only invent another one. In fact they want to scrap all out-of-county visiting and have social workers in those areas doing the visiting, so we don't want to give them the opportunity of changing our ways of working.
> *Child care team leader:* But visiting the client wherever they are is a principle of the way we work, why don't they [higher management] understand this?
> *Manager:* I appreciate your point completely. But I don't think we ought to rock the boat on this one. We'll go along with it and you tell me when you come to do a visit or if it's immediate we can work something out. I don't think we need to worry about this one.

There followed several comments pointing to a shared concern that the 'department' was always trying to restrict the use of resources and complicate matters through administrative routines. Changes in procedure such as the one above are frequently submitted and commented on at the monthly area office meetings. This provides the participants with an opportunity to affirm their distinctive local identity through an almost ritual criticism of higher management. This is not unique to the office in question. Observation of other social work offices suggests that practitioners are interested in the organization to the extent that it affects them negatively (Satyamurti 1981: 188). Also, that a veritable 'Berlin Wall' exists between managers and practitioners in some social work departments has been noted by Parsloe (1981: 92). Similarly, workers have complained in many welfare settings about the layers of decision-making, particularly in relation to major child care problems (NISW 1982: 127–8).

Yet, it is equally evident that social work organizations do not always impinge upon workers as much as their complaints would indicate. Indeed, it has been suggested that some practitioners have too much freedom and discretion (NISW 1982: 131). In the office setting the social workers do not complain of ponderous chains of command, indeed they attempt to keep their contacts with the department to a minimum. Among the child care workers there is an embracing perception that all administrative regulation detracts from the 'real' work of visiting consumers. There is a marked similarity between their work orientations and those of other lower participants who work in organizations that process people's problems. For example, Manning notes that beat policemen invoke an 'individualistic' and 'entrepreneurial' work ethic unhindered by administrative routine as the ideal activity:

> Only the everyday activities of the constable even approach the form and function of 'real police work'. Paper work, court appearances, administrative tasks or report writing . . . are considered ex post-facto glosses upon real work on the ground.

> (Manning 1977: 269)

In the area office, administrative work is perceived as an intrusion and higher management the culprits of this diversion from 'real' work. Yet throughout the research there were no administrative directives or schemes advanced that sought to control closely the daily movements and practices that the workers individually produced. Daily work is very much a matter of workers' responding to demands rather than initiating services in relation to their cases. Nevertheless they visit consumers according to priorities they set themselves. They apply their own preferred modes of intervention, that is, the skills and relationships they feel most comfortable with. They ration their time and pace their energies in light of their own experience of case requirements. While they respond to the erratic demands made upon them, they do so with scant interference from supervisors, managers and team colleagues.

It is important to point out briefly that issues of practitioner control of work apply to clients as well as management. Those receiving the service are, in most cases, tutored by the workers in the part they will play in the welfare relationship. While practitioners cannot control the unexpected nature of emergencies nor the level of demand made by their clients they do, out of necessity, redefine the claims made upon them as legitimate or not, in order to manage their personal resources of time and effort. Furthermore, while clients have their own strategies for handling the welfare relationship they nevertheless have little control over the timetabling of encounters with the workers or with the content of the service they receive.

Ethical considerations apart, client regulation is for these workers a practical necessity as much as a form of control by professionals over the work they carry out. In this respect the practitioners often express their discomfort at fending off both organizational and client demands. None of the workers views client and organizational needs as mutual; rather they are seen as different but competing sources of influence that have to be managed or negotiated. Thus workers do not seek to lobby the agency as a means of improving services for clients. Instead the organization, already cast as intrusive rather than supportive, is kept at a wary distance. Similarly the clients are largely managed within a relationship established by the worker. While the practitioners do connect service-users to existing resources (residential, day care, nursery and so forth) they see no rewards in trying to assert some professional authority within the agency to enhance these or other means of satisfying demand. In this respect their autonomy stems from a subtle insulation of their practices from what is seen as a demanding and unfriendly environment beyond the office.

The above points are developed in detail elsewhere (Pithouse 1987). At this juncture it is simply asserted that work itself does not occur in some standardized and easily monitored sequence of time and event. Furthermore, in the office there are no formal attempts to check or scrutinize daily practice apart from supervision meetings with the team leader and these occur fortnightly or monthly in some instances. In general the qualified child care worker is left to get on with her cases free of any direct intrusion by her immediate colleagues and superiors. It is this basic element of day-to-day autonomy that workers take for granted. It is the basis upon which the job is routinely done. It is from this position they view all changes in the organization. Hence administrative intrusion in any shape or form is viewed as an unwarranted distraction or managerial threat to their accustomed self-regulation.

While social workers may have little or no control over the range of material services and resources that can be provided to consumers (residential, day care, nursery provision, finance) they nevertheless enjoy considerable self-regulation of their own activities. In the office the child care workers have learned they can create, expect and enjoy a certain day-to-day control of their own work. Their self-directed activities become a common-sense fact of organizational life, taken for granted. In turn this becomes a tacit rarely stated assumption and part of their cognitive map. Such a map is a way of seeing which, as Manning (1979: 209) suggests, 'provides the matrix for all deliberate considerations without itself being deliberately considered'. Hence, practitioner self-regulation remains largely unanalysed in the social workers' rhetoric and criticism of the organization. Yet is it because workers enjoy substantial space to manage their own practices that administrative directions are promptly cast as intrusive and restraining. Thus, simply noting the negative commentary about the department would lead the researcher (and reader) to a skewed understanding of the occupational experience of the area office.

In the course of gathering interviews it became apparent that members of the area office hold no positive attachment for the main organization in the city. Most responses indicated the beneficial effects of their geographic and social distance from the city department. Thus, the department as a whole, cannot be described in terms of some 'professional community' (Goode 1957) of consensual service ideals. Instead the area office represents a segment that carefully manages its local affairs in such a way as to prevent close scrutiny by the departmental hierarchy. For example, the city department depends upon reports and day-to-day telephone communication to monitor events in the detached area office. This gives the local management an opportunity to manage skilfully the exchange of information between themselves and the city department:

> Yes we are some distance from the department but I enjoy it. But it's good and bad. You see we can control the information that goes to them as we represent the office. They never come here to see what we do, but on the other hand, we are removed from contact and we can't influence things so much.
>
> (manager)

While the local managers are somewhat removed from the spheres of influence in the city department they can at least 'control the information'. This ability to be the 'gatekeeper' of delicate and potentially damaging information is described below by the manager. He reveals how, in the past, he has actively sought a degree of local autonomy and protection of his staff from scrutiny by higher management:

> I fight tooth and nail to keep the identity of the office. I might criticize people in the office, I would never criticize them outside or allow their files [case records] to go to [higher] management without me. These privileges I've had to win. In [city department] a social worker can be sent for without their manager or team leader knowing . . . and he's up there with the director explaining his actions – I won't have that and they know that. We're really a true detached office and our staff want to keep it that way.
>
> (manager)

The local managers and staff at the area office are keen guardians of their hard-won local autonomy. In this sense the office is part of a complex organization that contains negotiable working arrangements that have emerged from the initiatives of participants and not through formal rules or objectives. The setting in many respects reflects the view of Strauss *et al.* (1964: 165). They observe that complex organizations obtain order through the continual reconstruction of relationships stemming from processes of compromise, informal agreements and local discretion that is often hidden from higher administrators.

Interviews with the child care workers reveal similar perspectives. They too asserted the need for a well-managed distance from the city department and all commented on the belief that higher management are 'out of touch', unappreciative of 'real social work' and concerned only with undue restriction of their local activities. In their view their own day-to-day endeavours with consumers are the authentic realm of work and not their membership of a distanced department and the completion of their administrative requirements. 'Real' work is their face-to-face contact with service users and the deployment of their preferred skills and methods of intervention.

Workers' accounts of managerial dereliction have been cast by some occupational observers as unconscious displacement of the inherent anxieties of the job (Parsloe 1981: 92) or evidence of practitioner immaturity (see Scott 1969: 101–10). However, if we view organizational disaffection only as intrapersonal defences or deficiencies we lose sight of more compelling arguments, such as understanding organizations as made up of segments in competition. Thus if social work settings are frequently contested environments then we would do better to search for the cause of this in the structuring properties of organizational division and differentiation and not in some collective psychological impairment among the practitioners. In the area office for example, the social workers see themselves as separate from and 'superior' to the city department. This came across in most interviews:

> We're very much superior. I think we all feel superior, more organized and efficient than the people at [city department]. They don't seem to find any advantage in being that much closer to management. We can get on with things down here without too much trouble. It's rather nice that we're removed.
>
> (child care worker)

In the area office the workers see themselves as the definers of good practice and their comments about higher management are a means of asserting this shared perception of their occupational location. Gossip and criticism are a means of informal social control (Coser 1961) and it would be possible to submit at this point many accounts by practitioners about the shortcomings of higher management. However, the concern here is not to document the innumerable stories offered by social workers that serve to cast them as 'heroes' and the management as 'villains'. Rather, it is suggested here that such accounts (accurate or otherwise) are not psychological defence mechanisms but more plausibly a means of asserting a right to a cherished autonomy. This autonomy is rarely specified but remains a tacit base upon which stories are formulated by members of a close colleague group. Observations of other occupations engaged in welfare (Blau and Scott 1963: 73) and health care (Bennis *et al.* 1958) indicate how social workers and nurses look to their immediate colleague group as a resource for offsetting the impact of administrative intrusions. In the area office the workers look to their team colleagues as a source of reference for 'good work'. The higher management are seen as practically and morally estranged from everyday practice and hence unqualified to impose legitimate criteria for processing work.

The practitioners' social distance from the main department is recognized by all and carefully maintained by local management. As 'gatekeepers' the local managers are keen to stress that overt and hostile criticism of the city department might invoke a more interested gaze by higher administrators towards their local activities. Thus criticism of the department would never arrive there in its original abrasive form if in fact it arrived there at all. The department hierarchy, like other 'high ups', receive distilled information that barely reveals the feelings or climate of opinion lower down the organisation (see Merton 1968: 401). Thus the local managers take practitioners' complaints and refine them into constructive suggestions; there is an adept mediation of information described as follows:

> I respect and protect the staff . . . you see I don't stop complaints going through to [city department] as long as they're thought out – nothing hysterical. I don't allow that. Now, if management send memos that would really upset the social workers I would take it back and say is this really necessary? We try to recognize problems before they occur. I don't spend a lot of time at [city department] but I spend long enough to pick up what's going on – you know – someone's on to something – and I've then got our answers ready for them when they start asking questions! That often keeps the pressure off social workers.
>
> (office manager)

This extract again indicates the guarded and segmented character of the area office. The careful handling of information and communication helps create an insulated office with a colleague group who look to themselves and not the wider department for their reference to satisfactory practice. The child care workers have learned that it is the office and not the city department that is the source of their satisfactions. A negative view of the hierarchy prevails and a shared emphasis upon quiet insulation and skilled control of communication characterizes their contact with the department. Within the area office collegial solidarity and harmony typify the overt relationships between practitioners.

The implications of these consensual forms for the way work is shared and assessed is significant. To begin with, the impact of what is seen as an unfriendly work environment leads to the creation of a supportive ethos among colleagues. This defensive response also endorses the cherished forms of practice, that is, self-regulating practitioners who define their own preferred methods of work within a case-based mode of practice. This notion of autonomy or practitioners' control of work is assumed by all workers who know little about the sorts of cases their colleagues have or the way they work with them. Nor do they engage in uninvited scrutiny of another's work unless invited by that colleague:

> *Child care worker:* It's something we don't talk about. The names [clients] come out that trouble everyone, but as far as a [team mate's] caseload goes and what they do I wouldn't know . . .
> *Child care worker:* . . . we get on with out own cases, you wouldn't be very popular if you kept making suggestions even if you thought someone was going wrong.

Criticism of another's practice would not only corrode the supportive ethos but also assault the accustomed understanding about individual control of work. Criticism of colleagues is typically voiced quietly between parties that do not include the person concerned. Where criticism is brought to the notice of the practitioner is in the unobserved encounter between worker and team leader when supervision takes place. Here, the social worker has to indicate progress made in respect of her cases. Criticism by the supervisor typically takes the form of a corrective and informal 'talking to' that remains confidential and does not injure individual or team conceptions of practitioners as competent. This approach to problems of performance is a feature of other professional settings, particularly medicine (see Freidson 1975).

The claim made by practitioners to self-regulation requires that questions of competence are rarely examined openly. The notion that all workers are competent, albeit with different strengths and weaknesses, is a commonplace assertion among the members of the team. While it is clear to all that some colleagues are less able than others or that some forms of practice might call forth differences of opinion such events do not occur:

> There's a strong tendency that any critical analysis of what you're doing, er, would mean criticism of a colleague and we don't do it. We sort of play the happy family.
>
> (child care worker)

The child care workers do not practise in silence: they do of course talk about their cases to one another and conversation about work problems surrounds daily life in the office. But such talk carries no risk of censure or unwarranted enquiry. There are, however, particular collegial relationships whereby workers will select certain colleagues in order to seek advice or share uncertainties over some issue. These informal 'consultancy partnerships' exist in most organizations (Blau 1964) and are typically confined to colleagues who do not feel they are exposing some area of incompetence by declaring a lack of knowledge or doubts about some aspect of their work. Colleagues who consult in this fashion usually do so on the basis of friendship and commonality of role or experience. Thus in the child care teams it is likely, for example, that a more recent recruit will consult with someone of equal standing rather than go to a team 'veteran' for regular advice. Thus practitioners will avoid the 'over-use' of a colleague when looking for consultancy and they will avoid one whose experience or attitude might reflect the dependency of some 'expert and neophyte' relationship.

> Anita [veteran] is a bit, er, how can I put it, she's really nice but she'll take over if you let her. She's a good friend of mine, she's a good worker but her ways aren't my ways. I don't talk about my cases to her . . . I generally talk to Suzanne, she tells you what she thinks and leaves it there.
>
> (child care worker)

Not all members of the teams seek such partnerships. Some of the longer-serving staff feel themselves to be independent of such needs and some of the new members seek advice from any who will help. Generally, however, selective relationships for advice and an ethos of mutual support reduce the visibility of variable or questionable competence. Autonomy as the self-regulation of practice is a shared interest of all and demands that conflict between colleagues or differences of opinion be managed subtly. This is achieved typically by a cordial distancing from team mates thought likely to be a source of unwanted intrusion or comment.

Conclusion: The office as a social world

The colleague group of child care team mates and other office members acts as a reference group, not simply by dint of physical location, but, as Shibutani (1955: 587) states, as a locus of 'effective communication'.

Shibutani's use of reference group describes a communication system which has developed a special world-view that accentuates the difference between those in and out of the collectivity. This aptly applies to the area office whereby those 'outside' (city department, client, other agencies) are viewed as ineligible to assess the service or the worthy efforts of the membership. The workers are 'locals' (Gouldner 1954) in the sense that they look to the office rather than outside associations (BASW, trade unions, professional bodies) for a sense of purpose and esteem. They transform the office into a 'social world': that is, a structure of meanings and relationships that provide secure boundaries and a creditable identity.

The area office is a social world that provides both spatial and perceptual reference for the meaning of work. This concept of 'world' is one that offers a view of creative members who are not over-constrained by the limits of their organizational setting (see Strauss 1978: 120). Thus, the members of the office should be understood in the context of 'world-building' and purposive practitioners. This notion of 'world' emphasizes aspects of negotiation, process, identity and communication and these aptly reflect some of the themes discussed so far. For example, the office membership carefully negotiates its relations with the parent department. Their negative but careful orientation towards the city department, rather than depicting strict regulation of practice and procedures, stands as implicit praise of local arrangements.

The practitioners have to negotiate occasional forays from the city department as well as the burgeoning demands of their clientele. Those receiving the service have to be taught that it is the worker who determines the pace and content of the service. A similar lesson is learned by colleagues who readily appreciate that day-to-day practice is determined by the individual worker. The comfort of a caring and unintrusive colleague group helps manage the competing pressures of client and administrative requirements. Autonomy is cherished and keenly guarded and the solo case-based activity of self-directing workers is the largely realized practice of the office.

The advantages of autonomy are won through careful strategies and accommodations that insulate work and performance. The disadvantages of autonomy, such as invisibility of practice, limited accountability, concealed interests and variable performance also exist within these practical manoeuvres and professional claims to the control of work in large welfare organizations.

References

Bennis, W., Berkowitz, N., Affinito, M. and Malone, M. (1958) 'Reference groups and loyalties in the out-patient department', *Administrative Science Quarterly* 2, 4: 481–500.
Blau, P. (1964) 'The research process in the study of the dynamics of bureaucracy', in P. Hammond (ed.) *Sociologists at Work*, New York: Basic Books.
Blau, P. and Scott, W. (1963) *Formal Organisations: A Comparative Approach*, London: Routledge & Kegan Paul.
Bucher, R. and Stelling, J. (1977) 'Four characteristics of professional organisations', in R. L. Blankenship (ed.) *Colleagues in Organisations: The Social Construction of Professional Work*, New York: Wiley.
Bucher, R. and Strauss, A. (1961) 'Professions in process', *American Journal of Sociology*, 66, 4: 325–34.
Clarke, J. (1979) 'Critical sociology and radical social work problems of theory and practice', in N. Parry, M. Rushin and C. Satyamurti (eds) *Social Work, Welfare and The State*, London: Edward Arnold.
Coser, R. L. (1961) 'Insulation from observability and types of social conformity', *American Sociological Review* 26, 1: 28–39.
Davies, L. (1983) 'Gender resistance and power', in S. Walker and L. Barton (eds) *Gender Class and Education*, Brighton: Falmer.
Dex, S. (1985) *The Sexual Division of Work: Conceptual Revolutions in the Social Sciences*, Brighton: Harvester.
Etzioni, A. (ed.) (1969) *The Semi-Professions and Their Organisation*, New York: Free Press.
Freidson, E. (1975) *Doctoring Together: A Study of Professional Social Control*, New York: Elsevier.
Goode, W. (1957) 'Community within a community: the professions', *American Sociological Review* 22, 2: 194–200.
Gouldner, A. (1954) *Patterns of Industrial Democracy*, New York: Free Press.
Heraud, B. (1971) 'British social work: a profession in process', *Social Casework* 52: 347–55.
Manning, P. (1977) 'Rules, colleagues and situationally justified actions', in R. L. Blankenship (ed.) *Colleagues in Organisations: The Social Construction of Professional Work*, New York: Wiley.
—— (1979) *Police Work: The Social Organisation of Policing*, London: MIT Press.
Merton, R. (1968) *Social Theory and Social Structure*, New York: Free Press.
NISW (1982) *Social Workers: Their Roles and Tasks*, Barclay Report, London: Bedford Square Press.
Parsloe, P. (1981) *Social Services and Area Teams*, London: Allen & Unwin.
Pithouse, A. (1987) *Social Work: The Social Organisation of an Invisible Trade*, Aldershot: Gower.
Satyamurti, C. (1981) *Occupational Survival: The Case of the Local Authority Social Worker*, Oxford: Blackwell.
Scott, W. R. (1969) 'Professional employees in bureaucratic structures: social work', in A. Etzioni (ed.) *The Semi-Professions and Their Organisation*, New York: Free Press.
Shibutani, T. (1955) 'Reference groups as perspectives', *American Journal of Sociology* 60, 6: 562–9.
Spencer, A. and Podmore, D. (eds) (1987) *In a Man's World: Essays on Women in Male-Dominated Professions*, London: Tavistock.
Strauss, A. (1978) 'A social world perspective', in N. K. Denzin (ed.) *Studies in Symbolic Interactionism: An Annual Compilation of Research* vol. 1, Connecticut: JAI Press.

Strauss, A., Schatzman, L., Bucher, R., Erhlich, C. and Sabshin, M. (1964) *Psychiatric Ideologies and Institutions*, New York: Free Press.

Toren, N. (1969) 'Semi-professionalism and social work: a theoretical perspective', in A. Etzioni (ed.) *The Semi-Professions and Their Organisation*, New York: Free Press.

5
Planning for a
new generation of
older people

Anthea Tinker

Much of the discussion about ageing and provision for older people takes place against the background of the current group. Most have memories, if not experiences, of hardship and of the steady growth of state provision. The future generation are likely to be different in many ways. Many, particularly women, are more likely to be aware of their rights; some will not share the same culture and history; and the gap between those with considerable wealth, often home owners with occupational pensions, and those in poverty is likely to widen.

In the context of this changing group of people this chapter will address two main issues. The fist is what kinds of services should be provided. The discussion here will revolve around the kinds of innovation that are likely to take place including new models of home care and residential provision. The second is who should provide. Here the changing role of the state, including views about statutory agencies becoming enablers rather than providers, will be discussed. So will the likely development and role of the private sector. Finally the future role of informal carers will be examined together with factors likely to change the current position.

Older people: who will they be?

When thinking about the next generation of older people perhaps the most helpful approach is to think of the present generation of middle-aged people a few years on. It then becomes easier to see how much older people differ from one another and why it is so foolish to make generalizations such as 'older people will want'. If it is difficult to generalize about a group of middle-aged people why should it become so easy for others, especially professionals to lump together all older people as 'the elderly'? But it is also pertinent to raise a number of broad questions which may alter our perception of the composition and needs of the next generation of pensioners (see also Tinker 1984a).

The first important factor to consider is that of *gender*. Looking first at demographic trends the assumption is always made, and rightly to date, that the majority of older people will be women. Women live longer and more survive into old·age at present. For some cohorts of older people now there is also the effect of war to take into account. The dearth of men is partly due to deaths earlier in life. But what of the future? Will there always automatically be such a surplus of women? There is evidence that some women are now adopting some of the features of men's life-styles which are likely to lead to an earlier death. For example, many more women are smoking, drinking and driving. It can also be. argued that women are subjected to more stressful lives as a larger proportion enter paid employment. If employment is full time and family responsibilities have to be undertaken too, this can be doubly stressful.

It is also always assumed that women will be more disabled in old age than men. They are more likely to suffer mobility problems and to suffer from arthritis. They are also more likely to fall and be subject to fractures. All these medical factors have meant that health and social services are more likely to be in demand from elderly women than men. However, women are now paying far more attention to their own health in their younger lives and new initiatives like hormone replacement therapy (HRT) may further modify the position. If women do continue to survive for longer than men, it is at least possible that they may be healthier. From the point of view of services and costs, HRT or hip replacements may be less expensive than providing years of care to a very disabled elderly woman.

But it is not just over numbers and demands for services that the influence of women may become much more important. At the moment all the evidence points to society ignoring and undervaluing the lives of older women (e.g. Evers 1983; Peace 1986). A generation of women who have been part of women's formal or informal networks are more likely to demand a say in how services are provided. The influence of women in the provision of health care is a startling example of a group of consumers who are becoming increasingly articulate and assertive about their needs. If this is continued in old age, as is now beginning in groups like the Older Women's Project and Pensioners' Link, professionals may find that they have to change the way services are planned and delivered. It is also possible that the role of women as informal carers may be affected too. This is discussed at the end of the chapter.

When thinking about the next generation of elderly people cultural differences must not be ignored. In particular the number of *black and Asian elderly people* is likely to increase dramatically. In 1984–6 only 4 per cent of ethnic minority groups were aged 60 or over but large numbers in younger age groups will cause an increase in the future (CSO 1989). Questions have been asked about whether elderly people who came from abroad will wish to return to their original home in old age. What makes this a particularly difficult question is the very different backgrounds from which they come. An examination of the origins of this diverse group shows the different circumstances, ages and reasons for coming to the United Kingdom. For example the Jewish contingent who came to the UK in the 1930s driven from their homes by persecution will be different from those who came here willingly, perhaps hoping to return home after a period (Norman 1985; Barker 1984). Not only are cohorts varied but also they settled in different areas so that demands on, and contributions to, services will not be the same. Women who joined spouses in later life may present particular problems. Very little research has been undertaken in this area. One study found that of 619 Black and Asian old people interviewed in 1982 97 per cent of men and 84 per cent of women originally expected to return 'home' but at the time of the interview only 49 per cent of men and 26 per cent of women still expected to do so (Barker 1984). Only 5 per cent of men and 11 per cent of women had made specific plans to return. This position is likely to alter further as a growing proportion of black and Asian old people are born in the UK.

Not only must generalizations not be made about who black and Asian old people are, but also care must be taken not to make assumptions about future demands for services. For example, a higher proportion of heads of households from India, Pakistan and Bangladesh are owner-occupiers (75 per cent) than White (62 per cent) or West Indian and Guyanese (35 per cent) (CSO 1987). If this tenure pattern continues in old age it is likely that an area with a large number of owner-occupiers on low incomes will need agency services to help with repairs and improvements to property. An area with a large number of elderly council tenants may need a different solution.

What is clear from research evidence about services for these groups is the insensitivity of many of the services (Norman 1985). Lack of knowledge of existing services is also evident (e.g. Donaldson 1986). Apart from the obvious problems of language; religious, cultural and dietary differences also need to be taken into account. There is growing evidence that much can be learned from the response that different communities make to the needs of their older members. Some of the more imaginative schemes, especially those involving mutual aid or self-help, could serve as models for other groups.

A third factor to take into account when considering who the next generation of elderly people will be is *family relationships*. Much is written about the effect on children of the growing number of divorces, increase in cohabitation and remarriages. Less attention is paid to the effect that this will have on elderly people. Inter-generational patterns are likely to change and this may affect the physical and mental well-being of older people. This point is taken up when discussing carers. Another aspect is the number of elderly people who will have children from different partnerships.

Household composition must also play an influential role in plans for the future. In 1987 3.3 million people of retirement age lived alone in Great Britain. This number is forecast to rise to 3.9 million in 2001 (CSO 1989). The number of one-person households of all kinds is predicted to increase and this will include older people. What are the implications of this growing group of older people living alone? While this may mean the possibility of living an independent life is enhanced, those who plan services have to be alert to the help that may be needed for people who are frail. Of particular importance is the need to be able to contact someone in an emergency (Tinker 1984b; Research Institute for Consumer Affairs 1986). Equally significant is the need to keep in touch with relatives and friends. Recent research on the use of telephones has shown the key role of this form of communication in sustaining social networks (Tinker 1989).

Finally the *overall demographic picture* must be taken into account. Most commentators have rightly focused on the projected increase in the numbers of very elderly people but paid less attention to other age groups. The growing number of very elderly people must, however, be a starting point. The over-75s are forecast to grow from 3.8 million in 1987 to 4.4 million in 2011 (CSO 1989). The main reason for this is the high number of births during the early years of the century and a very large increase in 1919–21. Even more startling is the projection that the number of people aged 80 years and over will increase from 1.8 million in 1985 to 2.4 million in 2001, and 2.6 million ten years later. One reason for concern about increases in the numbers of very elderly people is the rise in disability with age (Martin *et al.* 1988). Besides questions of individual discomfort and restriction, there are significant resource implications. The estimated average cost for an elderly person aged over 75 in 1984 was £1,087 compared with £473 for a 65–74-year-old and an average for all ages of £254 (CSO 1987). However, the next generation of very elderly people may have very much better health profiles than their predecessors. As one writer has observed:

> The measurement of how the needs of people for care and support grow with increasing age presents great difficulties, even more so if needs at any age are changing over time. For instance is it the case that the 80 year olds of today are in aggregate fitter physically and mentally, and thus better equipped to lead independent lives, than were 80 year olds twenty years ago?
>
> (Thompson 1987)

Looking at 'young elderly' people there will be only a small increase in numbers. From 6.6 million in 1985 the number of people from retirement age to 75 will grow to 7 million in 2011. Overall between 1985 and 2011 the number of people of retirement age will increase by 1.3 million. However, as a percentage of the total population the rise of pensioners is very small. It will go up from 18.2 per cent of the population in 1985 to 18.5 per cent in 2016.

Apart from the growth in numbers of very elderly people the most significant demographic change will be one which has only recently been a matter of much public discussion. That is the effect of the falling birth-rate in recent years. Thompson has commented:

> The steep decline which has already been seen in the size of the child population is now feeding through to a reducing number of young people entering the labour market. Over the next two decades the population of conventional working ages will show an older age profile.
>
> (Thompson 1987)

She then concludes that the likely shrinking of the labour-force will have important implications for the economy. Those responsible for planning services for a greater number of very elderly people need to make a radical reappraisal of services.

Changes in resources and life-styles

Another major factor in planning for older people must be their own resources and life-styles. Many older people are likely to have access to more financial *resources* because more will own their homes and have occupational pensions. The growth in owner-occupation among middle-aged people has been substantial. In 1986 70 per cent of heads of households aged 45–59 were owner-occupiers compared with 56 per cent of 60–69-year-olds, 51 per cent of 70–79-year-olds and 45 per cent of those aged over 80 (CSO 1989). Not only does owner occupation mean fewer demands on state services such as housing from local councils or housing associations, but also it gives people an asset to sell or to borrow against. While schemes to enable elderly people to raise an income from their homes are in their infancy in this country (Fleiss 1985), they are more widespread in the USA. They are usually run by building societies or insurance companies and enable the elderly person to raise an income or lump sum while continuing to remain in their home. These home income or home reversion plans are obviously of less use to people in homes that are not worth a great deal. There will, therefore, be many older people for whom this kind of scheme is irrelevant. Nor should it be assumed that owner occupation necessarily goes hand in hand with a high income. Rather the reverse may occur. Many low-income pensioners already have a struggle to meet bills for the maintenance of their home. So while owner occupation may bring greater assets it may bring problems too. Less attention has been paid to another aspect of home ownership: this is the likelihood that the next generation of pensioners are more likely to inherit homes from their parents and therefore have access to an amount of capital of which previous generations would not have dreamed.

The spread of occupational pensions will bring greater financial security to many more people, especially women. In 1984–5 22 per cent of pensioners' incomes came from occupational pensions compared with 15 per cent in 1951. Similarly the spread of ownership of shares will mean that more financial resources are available. What is much less certain is how many elderly people will be in poverty. Endless debates take place both in political and academic circles about the meaning of poverty. Numbers are difficult to estimate and depend on the definition. If the figure for income support from the state is taken then in Great Britain in 1987–8 9.7 million received a retirement pension and 1.9 million a supplementary pension. In the absence of any large-scale survey, and there has not been a national one since the 1970s, it is difficult to quantify the scale of the likely problem. Further, the impact of the new system of income maintenance has not yet been adequately evaluated. It is not possible to tell, for example, what the abolition of single payments has meant.

Beyond questions concerning overall resource levels, the effect of *changing life-styles* on families and service providers has to be considered. What, for example, of the growing number of elderly people who choose to move abroad on retirement? The rich have long retired to the South of France and other warmer places but a growing number of older people are now choosing to move to places like Spain and the Canaries. No reliable statistics regarding the scale of the change exist and it is not known what will happen when they become very old and perhaps in need of a great deal of medical attention and personal care. Will they receive this in their retirement communities or will they return home to end their days? Some may not make the break completely but go abroad for the winter. There are signs that this is beginning to happen, encouraged by the holiday companies and tour operators who wish to increase trade out of season. Those who move to a better climate may enjoy better health and, hence, are unlikely to consume so many health services. But all this is uncharted ground and very little is known about the situation. While retirement migration has been studied over the years little work has been done on moves to new areas like the Canaries or on short spells abroad.

Also worthy of much more research and discussion is the effect of new technologies on the lives of older people. Obvious examples are aids to help very disabled people to communicate and to live more independent lives. But what of things like the growth in ownership of microwave ovens? They may make the provision of meals much easier, and combined with a freezer, make the distribution of meals much easier. Shopping via the television and the growth of sophisticated telephone and alarm systems are all likely to transform people's ability to remain in their homes. The next generation of elderly people are also more likely to be used to modern technology than the present one. They may also live different lives in other ways. More will own cars, dishwashers and washer dryers. They may be more used to sending out for food and not cooking. The ability to pay other people or to provide the service via a machine may bring greater independence than in previous years.

Medical technology comes in here too. If advances in medicine, such as hip operations, increase then the quality of life will improve dramatically. If, for example, more could be done to prevent the high number of falls by very elderly people, then there would be a decrease in numbers in hospital occupying beds for longer periods. Falls are the main cause of deaths of people over 75 and are the commonest accident to occur to elderly people. More research on causes, generally agreed to be complex, would enable better preventive strategies to be adopted with savings to the health service as well as human misery. Research already shows the general lack of attention paid to environmental factors (Gibson 1987).

What kind of services will be wanted?

Policy-makers and professionals are naturally concerned about what services should be provided. Those who are involved in gerontology are more inclined to take a broader view. Their immediate concern is not only with the minority who will need services but also with all elderly people. Many older people will live out their lives with little recourse to services of a statutory or voluntary nature. Apart from the pension which is almost universally claimed, the majority of older people do not have services like meals on wheels, are not in residential care or long-stay hospital beds, and do not attend day centres. It is always worth reminding professionals that they deal with a minority of older people.

For this minority it is likely that a different pattern of services will be wanted than those provided today. The first section has indicated that those who are likely to need help will be older and frailer than in the past. Because so many more will be very old, for example, it is likely that the prevalence of dementia will increase. This alone will pose great problems for residential and domiciliary services. The growing number of black and Asian older people too will mean that a different kind of service may be needed. Judging from the experiments in services for these groups, new kinds of provision may evolve, perhaps based on self-help (Standing Conference on Ethnic Minority Senior Citizens 1986).

Services are likely to be different for other reasons. Higher standards will almost certainly be sought for the new generation of older people who are likely to be more articulate. But here imponderable factors enter. If, for example, state services become more of a residual service, will the articulate members be removed from the state arena? Or will the growing movement of Advocacy mean that older people will be in a stronger position because they have someone to speak on their behalf (Greengross 1986)?

Research shows that the kinds of services which will be wanted are those which are individually tailored to needs. Surveys of nearly every service show that there are people receiving it who neither need nor want it. Either they have been assessed incorrectly, the appropriate service is not available or the service has been continued without any reassessment. Rather than fitting people into services perhaps it will be individuals and their needs which are thought about first. For example, rather than assuming that someone requires meals on wheels it is worth the time and trouble finding out whether the person needs food that is brought in by someone else. Or would they prefer someone to do the shopping so that they can cook, or would they prefer to have the money to go to a local café or a neighbour paid to bring in a meal they have cooked? Studies concerning meals (Dunn 1987) and day care (Tester 1989) show how services need to escape the strait-jacket of existing provision. Both new and lateral thinking are required if services are to be more relevant and varied. For example, in a number of significant respects, older people have few rights when compared with children. Greengross (1986) is among those who suggest that changes are needed here to give greater rights to older people.

But new services are not the only answer. Innovation, as has been shown in numerous studies, is often successful but there are two major problems which emerge. One is how to incorporate the innovation into mainstream services and the other is what to do about existing mainstream services. These kind of problems are currently well illustrated by home care services. These new services provide a different kind of provision from home helps with the emphasis on personal and home care rather than cleaning. The incorporation of this form of provision into a mainstream service has not always proved easy.

Who should provide?

Before asking who should provide services for elderly people it is salutary to see who the current providers are. The evidence from research is clear. All recent surveys show that by far the largest amount of personal and domestic care is given by families. The obvious exceptions concern the provision of specialized help such as medical care. Despite allegations that the welfare state has caused a diminution in family care there is no evidence to support this. Rather the reverse. Johnson maintains that families have never cared more (Johnson and Cooper 1983).

The state continues to play the major role in income support services. Nearly all people of pensionable age receive the state pension and the majority of people use the National Health Service. For other state services, whether national or local, elderly people feature strongly as consumers, for example in home-help services, meals on wheels and day care. But although they may be the main consumers only a small proportion use these services. For example, only 9 per cent of people over the age of 65 received a home help, 2 per cent meals on wheels and 5 per cent had seen the district nurse in the previous month (OPCS 1989). Housing is another service where older people are currently well represented in state provision with 36 per cent of people over the age of 60 being council tenants in 1986 (CSO 1989).

The private sector is increasingly featuring as a provider. Private sheltered housing, for example, is one of the fastest growing sectors of the housebuilding industry. It is significant that interest among developers and builders is now turning to ordinary small accommodation for those elderly people who do not want the sheltered element (warden and communal facilities). There is a growing market in private pensions and insurance for health care too. Perhaps the most dramatic increase in private provision has been seen in the rise of private residential homes. Numbers of residents in private and voluntary homes claiming supplementary board and lodging payments went up from 7,000 in 1978 to 42,000 in 1984 and the cost from £6 million in 1978 to £200 million in 1984 (Audit Commission 1986). The Griffiths Report commented,

> The separate funding of residential and nursing home care through social security, with no assessment of need, is a particularly pernicious split in responsibilities and a fundamental obstacle to the creation of a comprehensive local approach to community care.

> (Griffiths Report 1988).

The voluntary sector has always played an important role from the early days of old people's homes to the current large-scale involvement of bodies like the Women's Royal Voluntary Service. The major change that is happening in the late 1980s is the taking over of state, in the main local, services by voluntary bodies such as Age Concern England. Day care is a good example of this. What is likely to change this pattern of provision? It is suggested that there are seven main factors: these are politics, philosophical considerations, demographic and other changes, research and reports, attitudes, international events and internal and external events which could be labelled 'the unexpected'.

The *political dimension* is harder to assess than would appear. The last ten years of Conservative government have shown quite clearly that the role of the state is seen as moving away from what was claimed to be 'a huge, benevolent, all-embracing, all-providing state' and 'away from dependence toward independence' (John Moore, Secretary of State for Social Services on the future of the Welfare State 26.9.87). That the role of the state will not necessarily expand is shown from a passage later in the speech referring to changes in Social Security. 'Implicit in the new Social Security Act is, I think, to inject some long overdue modesty into the government's attitude towards its own role in welfare'. The concept of the state as an enabler, particularly in respect of local social services and housing departments, is another indication of Conservative thinking. Reluctance to give local authorities more responsibilities has undoubtedly been a major reason why the government did not implement the recommendations of the Griffiths Report immediately. The encouragement of the private sector to take on contracted out services and to establish provision alongside state services is a further element; as is the giving of tax relief to older people and their relatives to take up private health insurance in the 1989 budget.

Looking specifically at provision for older people there is remarkably little in the Conservative or other manifestos about this group. It does appear, however; from the statements and speeches of all the political parties that some growth of private provision is envisaged by each of them. The widespread support for the sale of council houses is one example. Some critics of policies to place less emphasis on state provision talk of 'cuts' without producing a great deal of evidence that these have occurred. Crude calculations of expenditure and staff numbers within, for example, social services departments, show increases in the last ten years. A much more sophisticated analysis needs to take place relating these figures to demographic changes and increases in legislative demands. It is also important to take into account public expenditure in related fields. For instance, while there has been a decline in public spending on housing by local authorities there has been an increase in public expenditure on housing associations.

The second factor which is likely to influence future provision is a change of *philosophy*. Although the major element here has come via political change, for example the increased emphasis on the individual and what they can achieve (the 'enterprise culture'), it is not possible to say that this is the sole source. Whatever the source this philosophy is bound to have an impact on older people in the future. It may mean an attitude of expecting less from the state, and being more self-sufficient, but it could also lead more dangerously to a disregard for those who are not able to help themselves.

The third factor is the practical implications of *demographic and other changes*. A growing number of very elderly people, combined with a smaller number of young elderly and a declining number of people of working age will almost inevitably pose problems. Not only will a smaller work-force mean likely difficulties in recruiting members of caring professions like nurses but numbers able to offer informal care may decline. The relative decline in the numbers of younger people, the greater numbers of women in paid employment and the break-up of a growing number of marriages may mean that there is not a ready source of informal care available. All these factors should lead to a radical reappraisal of sources of care. Strategies which may be needed include making part-time work more readily available and better paid, creating better working conditions for both men and women with time off for family responsibilities and more support and training for relatives and friends who are prepared to care. If very elderly people are to remain at home then those with physical and mental problems are likely to need imaginative schemes in the evenings and at night to supplement what other help is available in the day.

The influence of *research and official and unofficial reports* is difficult to assess. There is little doubt, however, that the combination of research (e.g. Challis and Davies 1987; Tinker 1984b; Wheeler 1985) and official reports (e.g. Audit Commission 1986; Griffiths 1988) which have shown the advantages of schemes to enable elderly people to stay in their own homes have played an important part in policy decisions. There is less evidence of a similar picture on residential care. The research summarized for the Wagner Report on residential care pointed to the reluctance of elderly people to opt for residential care, the need for alternatives for frail elderly people and problems within existing homes (Wagner Report 1988b). The report recommended that those who move into residential care should do so only as a result of 'positive choice' and that conditions must be improved (Wagner Report 1988a). If this report is implemented and a financial regime is devised which enables resources to be diverted to staying at home options, then social workers and other professionals will find that they may need different skills. In particular it will become even more urgent to liaise with other agencies like those involved with housing.

Changes in *attitudes* may have an impact too. For example a growing number of men seem to be involved in the care of their children (Jowell *et al.* 1988). Will they be both willing and able to give the kind of care which has traditionally been given by women to elderly people? There are signs that this may be beginning to happen. The recent study of informal carers showed that 2.5 million men were carers compared with 3.5 million women (Green 1988).

The effect of *changes in other countries* on plans has scarcely been discussed by policy-makers. The effect of 1992 on countries in the European Community is seldom mentioned. Social measures to accompany the completion of the Internal Market in 1992 have been given a high profile by the European Commission (Eurolink Age 1989). One proposal in the 1992 programme will directly affect older people. That is their automatic right to live in any member state. Not only will legislation have an effect but also so may the growing amount of research.

Finally there may be *unexpected factors* which cause changes in policy or practice. A scandal, sudden publicity in the media and the growth in influence of a pressure group are all examples of events which have changed social policy in other areas and could do so for older people.

Conclusions

This chapter has suggested that the new generation of older people may be very different from previous ones. They are likely to be older on average, more will be black and Asian, they are likely to have higher expectations and to be more articulate. Services will need to respond, often locally, to different groups and to find ways of providing services in a sensitive way. Not only must services change but also the providers are likely to increase in diversity. With more older people likely to look to the private sector because of increased wealth, those who continue to turn to the public sector may be stigmatized unless great care is taken (see Malpass in this volume, Chapter 7).

Perhaps the most important new dimension is that of the involvement of older people themselves in decisions. Any planning must take into account that the majority of older people are not physically or mentally disabled and need to be consulted about plans for their future just as much as other groups. Those less able to speak for themselves may need an advocate to speak on their behalf.

Finally it will be interesting to see if elderly people will be considered of greater importance because of their growing influence as consumers, voters and their value in the labour market. Whatever the reasons, the next few years represent a golden opportunity to put ageing on the agenda. Hopefully this will lead to more positive attitudes towards a group of people whom most of us wish to join.

References

Audit Commission (1986) *Making a Reality of Community Care*, London: HMSO.
Barker, J. (1984) *Black and Asian Old People in Britain*, Mitcham, Surrey: Age Concern England.
CSO (Central Statistical Office) (1987) *Social Trends, 17*, London: HMSO.
—— (1989) *Social Trends, 19*, London: HMSO.
Challis, D. and Davies, B. (1986) *Case Management in Community Care*, Aldershot: Gower.
Donaldson, L. (1986) 'Health and social status of elderly Asians: a community survey', *British Medical Journal*, 293, 25 October: 1,079–82.
Dunn, D. (1987) *Food Glorious Food: A Review of Meals Services for Older People*, London: Centre for Policy on Ageing.
Eurolink Age (1989) *The Grey Agenda*, Mitcham, Surrey: Eurolink Age.
Evers, H. (1983) 'Elderly women and disadvantage: perceptions of daily life and support relationships', in D. Jerrome (ed.) *Ageing in Modern Society*, Beckenham: Croom Helm.
Fleiss, A. (1985) *Home Ownership Alternatives for the Elderly*, London: HMSO.
Gibson, M. (1987) 'The prevention of falls in later life', *Danish Medical Bulletin* 34, April, supplement no. 4, Danish Medical Association: 1–25.
Green, H. (1988) *Informal Carers* London: HMSO.
Greengross, S. (1986) *The Law and Vulnerable Elderly People*, Mitcham, Surrey: Age Concern England.
Griffiths Report (1988) *Community Care: Agenda for Action*, London: HMSO.
Johnson, M. and Cooper, S. (1983) *Informal Care and the Personal Social Services: A Report to DHSS*, London: Policy Studies Institute.
Jowell, R., Witherspoon, S. and Brook, L. (1988) *British Social Attitudes – The 5th Report*, Aldershot: Gower.
Martin, J., Meltzer, H. and Elliot, D. (1988) *The Prevalence of Disability among Adults. OPCS Surveys of Disability in Great Britain, Report 1*, London: HMSO.
Norman, A. (1985) *Triple Jeopardy*, London: Centre for Policy on Ageing.
OPCS (1989) *General Household Survey, 1986*, London: HMSO.

Peace, S. (1986) 'The forgotten female: social policy and older women', in C. Phillipson and A. Walker (eds) *Ageing and Social Policy*, London: Gower.

Research Institute for Consumer Affairs (1986) *Dispersed Alarms*, London: RICA.

Standing Conference on Ethnic Minority Senior Citizens (1986) *Ethnic Minority Senior Citizens – The Question of Policy*, London: SCEMSC.

Tester, S. (1989) *Caring By Day: A Study of Day Care Services for Older People*, London: Centre for Policy on Ageing.

♦ Thompson, J. (1987) 'Ageing of the population: contemporary trends and issues', *Population Trends*, 50, winter: 18–22.

Tinker, A. (1984a) *The Elderly in Modern Society*, Harlow: Longman.

—— (1984b) *Staying at Home: Helping Elderly People*, London: HMSO.

—— (1989) *The Telecommunications Needs of Disabled and Elderly People*, London: OFTEL.

Wagner Report (1988a) *Residential Care: A Positive Choice*, London: HMSO.

—— (1988b) *Residential Care: The Research Reviewed*, London: HMSO.

Wheeler, R. (1985) *Don't Move: We've Got You Covered*, London: Institute of Housing.

6
The client's view in context

David Howe

It has always seemed a reasonable, indeed wholesome thing to ask the clients of social workers what they think of the help received. A satisfied customer appears a self-evident good for which any self-respecting chief officer or social worker should be striving. Hence the interest in seeking the client's view. Sainsbury (1975: 1) believes that 'an effective service requires us to know something about the responses and reactions of those we seek to help'. Clients have a right to be heard and they have interesting things to say (Fisher 1983: i). I want to give qualified support to this line of enquiry but not before casting a more stringent eye on the cosy idea that when the client speaks all the practitioner (and her boss) wish to do is listen. Much of what is heard depends on what the audience believes is being said and the reasons why it thinks it is being said. Between what some people say and what others hear is a vast gulf, filled with intention and interpretation, self-interest and explanation. The client speaks, but in a context bounded by expectations and criss-crossed with assumptions.

In general, I shall argue that how the client is seen determines what is heard and, to some extent, what is said. For example, managers are people who marshall resources and deploy them on 'target populations', or if consumers make the first move, welfare organizations experience them as 'bombardment rates'. Professional workers speak of 'dysfunctional families', 'abusing parents' and the 'at risk' elderly. The words chosen to describe clients are fascinatingly enough, often amusing, sometimes worrying, yet the language used does more than simply designate; it provides clues about how the client is seen, experienced and treated. Language is the medium in which the client is understood, approached and explained. When the client speaks, therefore, he or she is heard in the language of the listener and, as we shall see, many tongues are spoken in the world of social work. We shall consider three in particular;

those spoken by the scientist or professional expert, by the humanist or subjectivist, and by the social agent or welfare manager. Each one assembles what the client says in a different way.

The professional expert

Here, the argument is that the client's experience is best explained by experts: traditional professional social workers. These are the menders of broken performances, whether personal or social. Approaching the client as a phenomenon to be explained, the professional examines what is said and done in order to diagnose what is the matter. Diagnoses lead to treatment in which the expert directs, administers and controls the help offered, hoping to bring about a return to normal functioning. The framework in which the client is explained is held by the professional. Viewed objectively, whatever the other says and does makes sense only when examined within the logic of the framework. The client's utterances and actions are taken as evidence of that person's way of functioning. They become coherent and meaningful in the context of the theories held by the expert. Thus, when the client speaks, we may hear something of her personality or learn aspects of her sociobiology, but the client's opinion itself has no greater status than that of a piece of objective evidence. For example, in a study of family therapy, families who were critical of the technique and opted out of treatment, were said by some therapists to be showing further evidence of their pathological condition (Howe 1989). The argument was that change was painful and was to be avoided. Resistance is simply an unwillingness to change. It was the belief of the therapists that 'flight from the cause of such threatened pain is the instinctive course of action. It is not surprising that some families leave therapy' (Howe 1989: 86). So, said the therapists, families who fail to take advantage of treatment are bound to say rude things about it. The practitioner does not hear a criticism of family therapy, only utterances which confirm the family's pathological state.

Professional groups possess esoteric bodies of knowledge that allegedly explain what is going on and allow the practitioner to work out what to do when a problem needs resolving. The interpretation and application of this knowledge requires specialist training in the theories and methods of the discipline. Thus, knowledge gives the professional power to define problems and the manner of their resolution which is not available to either the lay person or the client. And just to complete the monopoly, once a group is in a position of power, it can then control what a situation means and therefore what kind of knowledge is to count as relevant in understanding that situation. Professionals actively create cognitive frameworks in which the client is to be explained. Having defined the situation in terms of the profession's knowledge base, the practitioner prescribes what courses of action are to take place if sound health, good conduct or emotional well-being are to be restored.

The rise of the professions coincided with the growing rationalization and systematization of knowledge in which nature was controlled and uncertainty reduced. From the seventeenth century onwards, men and women began to detach themselves from nature and the total order of things. No longer were they an integral, undissociated part of the world, but rather, as individual subjects, they stood outside the objects of nature and human affairs. The whole was split into a world of objects to be inspected by individual subjects. We now recognize that scientific knowledge seeks unchanging universal properties whose truth can be formally demonstrated. Objects are taken to have fixed meanings and it is the task of the scientists to identify them in the phenomena under scrutiny. Knowledge of objects is gained by an appreciation of the laws that govern their appearance. Nor was the scientific gaze limited to the world of things; people, individually and collectively, could be measured with an objective eye, with the subject on the outside looking in. If the observer, as subject, believes that objects are internally consistent and possess a fixed logic which can be discerned by examination, an interest in methodology must follow. A set of rules is required which must be applied when interpreting things, people and situations. The investigator is seeking to establish the mechanisms that determine the character and behaviour of the object. There is no notion that the object itself has any views on these matters.

The scientific method acted as a powerful exemplar for many occupational groups, including those whose concern was with the human condition, whether physical, behavioural or psychological. In this approach, the client exists as an object of study, available for clinical examination. If, by objective analysis, the expert could determine the cause of a problem, they could also work out what had to be done to fix it. Experts asks clients to speak only in order that they display their habits and operating characteristics. This is the way we learn about objects and other living creatures. They are prodded and provoked, and their reactions show how they work and reveal the things of which they are made. Plants grow towards strong sources of light; crystals reveal their molecular structure when they diffract a blaze of X-rays. If we ask clients to speak, we treat what they say as evidence emitted which is characteristic of their psychological and social make-up, a natural product of their essential character. On the basis of this spoken evidence, we can formulate theories to account for their nature and behaviour. In this way the structure of the individual is glimpsed. This gives the observer clues to decipher what the individual as object, is about.

The subjectivist

In this approach, the client's experience is believed to be of fundamental importance. It must be sought and understood, raised and explored if help is to be accurate and effective. Workers who adopt this view are the liberators of the other's experience. Whereas the professional, as expert, regards the client as someone possessed of certain essential properties there are others, with humanist sympathies, who believe that human nature has no essential fixed qualities; that we have free will and we are the agents of our own destiny. We impose meaning on the world. In our negotiations with everyday life, we define people, we interpret situations so that we know who we are, where we might go and how we might get there. No outsider, viewing the other as an object, can ever understand the other's experience. It is this subjective experience, though, that we must understand if the other's actions are to make sense.

There is an urgent need to learn what experiences mean to the other person, what the world looks like from his or her point of view, what reasons they have for doing what they do. This requires a very different approach. No longer is the client assessed, measured and explained. The other is asked to give voice to experience, to communicate the meaning of his or her thoughts, feelings and actions. All this, of course, is the attitude adopted by the researcher who seeks the consumer's view. Clients are encouraged to speak so that others may learn what the world looks like from their perspective. If the client's experience can be understood, the social worker may develop practices which are more sensitive to the needs of the consumer. Not only is the client's experience valued, but also it becomes *the* thing to understand. The social worker can be helpful only if she is able to appreciate the other's experience and understand the meaning given to that experience. It is not the task of the social worker to *explain* the client, it is her moral obligation to *understand* him or her, and this is possible only by trying to appreciate how the other constructs the world and gives meaning to experience.

The manager

In the position adopted here, the client's experience, although not necessarily denied, is ignored. An appreciation of the client's view is not relevant to the activities of welfare managers. Whereas experts want to explain and humanists want to understand, there are others who adopt an altogether more vigorous approach to clients and the users of the social services. Both experts and humanists seek to capture what they believe to be the inherent condition of the client in order for their help to be effective. However, if the client is defined, not in terms of some scientific theory or inter-subjective encounter, but by someone *deciding* what the other person shall mean, prediction and control is achieved not by explanation or understanding, but by decree. For example, many clients of social workers are defined by law, that is by *how* they behave rather than *why* they behave.

Most occupational groups seek to reduce the amount of uncertainty in their 'work environment'. Knowledge and skills are developed so that the 'raw materials' addressed can be controlled and manipulated to whatever ends the occupation has in mind. However, not all the raw material's characteristics need to be understood or acknowledged. A heating engineer may need to know that hot water rises but he or she may safely ignore the fact that water is at its most dense at 4°C. The extent to which an occupation or an organization has to attend to the inherent complexity and variability of the raw materials depends entirely on what is said to matter. Organizations, for example, whenever possible define their raw materials to suit their purposes. Thus, it may not matter what parents think about the quality of their relationship with a social worker if the social services department is involved with the family because of suspected child abuse. The child and the parents are defined primarily by statute and procedure and not by the state of their personality. Safety and protection inform the agency's style of involvement and not the wishes of the client. In this way, welfare administrators are able to determine and simplify what the client means to the organization. Social services managers do not passively respond to clients – the organization's 'task environment' – they actively define and shape them whenever possible to suit their obligations, skills and interests (Howe 1986). To this extent, the client's meaning is constructed, not out of his or her psychological state or existential condition, but by welfare laws, agency practices and organizational resources. In other words, how a client is understood is externally imposed and not objectively discovered.

Clients are asked to speak simply in order to announce what kind of social and welfare entity they represent and hence what sort of demand they are likely to make on the agency and its agents. Having announced their presence, the client is judged, categorized and evaluated by the procedural machinery of the welfare organization.

Interpreting what the client says

Therefore clients may speak, but different audiences, hearing the same words, make a different sense out of them. This hermeneutical explanation of the consumer's experience concedes that there is no bedrock of truth that can be discovered when welfare workers relate to clients. Like the social scientist, the social worker is engaged in the interpretation of social meaning and not in the search for an objective truth. However, each of the three positions – expert, humanist and administrator – seeks to place itself on one side of the subject–object divide. To this extent the positions are static; only one side of the relationship is allowed to announce or reveal meaning. Experts establish meaning by investigating the other while remaining on the outside, subjectivists ask the other to disclose his or her subjective meaning, and managers define what the other shall mean according to how they interpret their welfare responsibilities. But there are those who would like to see conversations with clients take a more dynamic turn. Dialogue, rather than one-sided conversation, produces the richest understandings, the profoundest meanings. Dialogue, in this sense, is more than an exchange of words. It is the activity in which meaning is generated; it is the route along which we understand the nature of our being. Understanding occurs in dialogue with the other.

We find out more about the world, of people and things, not by developing more penetrating methods of enquiry and examination, but, in the words of Rorty, by finding 'new, better, more interesting ways of speaking' (1979: 360). It is not simply a case of asking the client to speak. The intention is to learn how to explore meaning and experience as one relates and seeks to understand the other within the structures of the situation that brings them together.

Understanding as dialogue

Understanding is developed in conversation when two people consider a matter of mutual interest. In the case of the social worker and the client, the matter of mutual interest is the nature and purpose of the occasion that requires them to speak to one another. However, each conversationalist brings his or her own history and experience, presuppositions and anticipations to the dialogue. These direct the 'reading' of the other, just as the other's assumptions and intentions affect what he or she is trying to say. There is a mutual requirement to recognize that what is said and what is heard is bounded and saturated by the outlooks that are part of being that person at that time in that place. This leads us into some important ideas about what we say, how we think and who we are. As individuals, we have a location in time and place, there is a context in which our thoughts, ideas and understandings take their shape. What is said bears all the traces of the context in which it is uttered, though the speaker or author may remain unaware of much of the 'situated-ness' of the speech. This is true for both partners in the dialogue. The depth of understanding remains limited if only the theoretical or experiential perspective of one partner in the conversation is allowed to fathom meaning.

> Understanding begins with a response to something that appears as a sign of something else. Someone addresses me; a text interests me; an event happens to me. In responding to the meaning of what appears, I understand what the person, text, or event says to me. . . . In the nature of the case, understanding is a dialogue with the other. My response to any such meaning-bearing sign initiates a dialogue of questions and answer, or give and take. An interaction unfolds between myself and the other person, text, or event that claims my attention. . . . Like any other good conversation, good will must be present between speakers in order for the dialogue to take place.
>
> (Klemm 1986: 30)

The focus of attention is the subject matter about which those in dialogue are speaking and not the person, text or event as such. Understanding comes only if both parties are able to submit themselves to the meaning of the text or the nature of the occasion that brings them together. We all bring perspectives and prejudices to any situation. But whereas the objective observer believes that proper understanding can come only when one is free of all such prejudices, those who recognize that understanding emerges in dialogue also know that prejudice is inevitably a part of who we are and where we are. We are obliged to bring our histories and outlooks with us into the activity of understanding. In conversation, we are required to open ourselves to the other, to recognize what fundamental issues and concerns animate our talk (Klemm 1986: 32).

Escaping the subject–object divide

Social workers, clients and managers meet in contexts created by laws and resources, expectations and needs, upbringings and experience. Those who investigate are just as saturated with ideas, experiences and intentions as those who are investigated. The reasons which bring social agent and client together preform much of what is asked, what is said and what is heard in the encounter. A detached objectivity is not available either to the worker or the client for no meaning can emerge that is independent of the situation and the reasons that brings them together. It is not sufficient to seek understanding by standing on one side of the subject—object divide; understanding emerges as one addresses the question of how that meaning arises in that context for those participants. It is the task of the researcher, the practitioner and the client to pursue understanding through dialogue. Understanding is the outcome of an interaction between the interpreter and the text, the social worker and client; it is a 'constructive performance' (Klemm 1986: 37). Human beings constantly reinterpret the situations in which they find themselves even though there are others who attempt to pre-define those situations through rules, histories, habits, conventions and assumptions. It is to the interpretations and reinterpretations themselves that those who seek understanding must go.

Meaning can never be a constant thing. Texts and people are created in one time and one place and read and listened to in others. The reader and the read, the speaker and the spoken to create meanings peculiar to their context. Practical philosophy recognizes that the meaning of the other is always brought into the interpreter's system of values and meanings; there is no objective point of view to fix the account to some foundation of truth.

This last point requires amplification. Just as there is no fixed truth in viewing the other as object, there is no bedrock of truth in learning of the other's private world of subjectivity. No primacy can be given to the client's views and experiences. Meaning is not generated in the individual but in the collective context and the structures in which they find themselves. Interpretative social scientists who interpret subjective meaning appear to give the actor's meaning primacy in the constitution of meaning. This would mean that there is something more truthful and superior in the client's view than those of others in the situation.

Hekman (1986) describes the debate between positivists and humanists as ultimately sterile. Although at first sight it may appear that the humanists are offering an alternative view of the world, upon closer examination both 'share a fundamental epistemological assumption; the opposition of subject and object . . . positivism and humanism are, in essence, two sides of the same coin' (Heckman 1986: 168). One finds meaning exclusively located in the objective examination of phenomena, the other finds meaning present only in the subjective experiences of individuals. Either way, 'man', the knowing subject, is placed at the centre of understanding, the individual person who determines what people and situations mean. But for some time there has been a powerful movement to locate meaning not just in the objective eye or the subjective mind, but in the contexts and structures in which those eyes and minds find themselves. It is within structures that we generate our ideas and understandings of situations. We are not on the outside of structures and understandings, we are fully immersed in them, though as Bhasker (1979: 47) notes, natural structures are like the rules of grammar which impose limits on the speech acts we perform, but they do not entirely determine what we say.

What the client says and understands is said and understood in relation to the presence, views and purposes of the social worker. What is said cannot be understood without reference to the situation that allowed them to come together. Human thought and action emerges partly in response to existing structures and in part is formed by those structures. Those who seek help or become of social concern know something of what it is to become a client (an object of social definition) – a failing parent or a wayward youth. Similarly, the social worker is situated within a history, or horizon of her own – welfare laws and social agencies that say what a client shall mean; professional theories that explain what is happening; community expectations that say what should be done. She has her training; she knows her role and duties; she has her skills and experience. The social worker acts, interacts and has a view of herself within this context. Meanings cannot be wrenched from the contexts for that is the medium in which they take on their form. The client becomes an object of enquiry that does not exist in itself but is constituted by the motivation of the enquirer (Hekman 1986: 106). Only in the discourse of welfare encounters is the client formed. Therefore what the client says can be understood only in the context of this discourse. Meaning is the relationship of the text, speech or event, to the pre-existing structures in which texts are written, words are spoken and events take place.

Participation in the dialogue

This way of understanding represents a shift from seeing the other as object to understanding the participants in context. Establishing what actions mean to the participants has to be followed by understanding the contexts in which these meanings arise. Understanding, for both the actor and the interpreter, always takes place within a context. Moreover, meanings are mediated by language. It is important to recognize that language can stand outside the subject of the dialogue and hold some objective reality independent of the individual subject who understands. It is within the structure and stricture of language that texts are created and read. But herein lies the potential for new understandings to arise. Within the dialogue, new words are spoken, new contexts forged. This new speech and fresh arrangement of language composed of the open interplay of both perspectives, offers the possibility of new thoughts being thought and new meanings being appreciated. In this way individuals, as subjects, can develop different understandings within the new linguistic context. 'In this view, texts are no longer repositories of objective meaning so much as they are potentialities for recontextualising meaning. Understanding is no longer a mode of knowing, but a dialogical activity' (Klemm 1986: 38).

When we ask clients to speak, it is not simply to report the world as they experience it. Their experience and the meaning which they give it is expressed into the world of the other and the history and values which the other brings. The context which this creates is the one in which the dialogue takes place.

An example of research and practice that picks up many elements of the dialogue is that of Fisher *et al.* (1986). In their study of the experiences of parents, social workers and children who had been 'in and out of care', they conclude that a partnership is required between all participants, particularly the family and the state.

> Partnership is more akin to a philosophy of practice which could inform all the actions undertaken by social workers, so that clients could reasonably ask for an account to be given, and expect their views to carry weight in connection with the child care processes they are experiencing.
>
> (Fisher *et al*. 1986: 140)

The authors employ a research style and advocate a social work practice that are 'based upon explicit and jointly shared information about problems, aims, and desired outcome (1986: 140).

In an earlier paper, Marsh (1983) acknowledged that client studies could profitably explore the contrast between participants' views and understandings. He recommended that the ideas and activities of the social worker be counterposed with those of other participants. 'Practice was seen as an 'interactive process' in which all those involved had views about what was happening and what they wanted to happen. This model overcomes the simple notion of asking whether the client is satisfied or not with the service, a notion peculiarly inappropriate in the case of those clients who become involved with social workers on an involuntary basis.

Adding the structural context to participation studies

Although participatory studies have opened up the dialogue in a most refreshing way, it is possible to take one more step in theorizing about the client's view. Adding the cultural and historical horizons to the analysis of the users' experiences gives further support to the argument that the client's view does not have a privileged epistemological status. It also requires that all views are located within and related to the contexts in which and about which they are offered. The upshot is a more dynamic, subtle understanding in which what clients say is explored in relation to the situation in which they say it. Participatory research is democratic research. It seeks the views of all those involved in constructing the social action under consideration. The research style demands everybody's involvement; ideas are fed back, reworked and wherever possible agreed. But the insistence that meaning is not simply sited in the heads of individual subjects but arises as actors find themselves embedded in established structures, facing particular situations, and possessed of their own histories, means that understanding the experiences of others is more than just adding the various views together and seeing where they blend and where they clash. In the strategy advocated, the accounts of the participants have to be seen as situated within the deeper structures of the occasion.

For example, in child abuse work both social workers and parents meet in the context of a vast discourse concerning the relationship of the state to family life, the proper development of children, and the rights of parents. That workers and parents should be meeting at all, never mind the views they have about their encounter, is something which cannot be accepted as obvious and so taken for granted. In the field of voluntary counselling, where statutory duties do not stalk the relationship, fascinating questions arise over the 'medicalization' of seeking and giving personal help. Morgan (1985), in his sociological analysis of the family, notes the growing emphasis placed on the quality of interpersonal relationships as the measure by which to assess marriages and family life. Personally driven interaction and not custom, duty or a working economic union is the demand made of the modern marital partnership. In the face of marital difficulty, problems are explained in terms of the couple's faulty relationship and help is required of the doctor, therapist or counsellor and not the priest. Treatment is sought and not guidance. A medical model of marriage is offered, implying that there is a class of problems called 'marital problems' which manifest themselves when relationships are 'dysfunctional'. Thinking about a marriage in this way is part of a larger universe of meaning that helps shape ideas and understandings about the 'nature' of social phenomena that we all take for granted and yet which are clearly the products of the ideas, knowledge and needs of particular times and particular places. The views of couples and counsellors about their encounter are formed and expressed within the logic of the situation that guided their interaction. There is still a client's view, though the perspective is no longer especially privileged. The researcher 'de-centres' the locus of understanding so that rather than see the world exclusively from the subject's perspective, there is a greater appreciation of how action and experience form in a cultural context.

The place of the client's view in social work has mirrored developments in the social sciences. In an attempt to understand the client, the words he or she speaks have been placed, using a range of theoretical orientations, in four different sites. Each site generates a particular kind of sociological question:

1 What does the expert say of the client?
2 What does the client say of the expert?
3 What does everyone in the action say about themselves and everyone else?
4 Why is everyone saying the things they say?

Initially, the client was simply the object whose behaviour was under scrutiny. Research into the effectiveness of the professional worker measured what the client was doing before and after treatment. In the second sociological site, we meet the early client studies. These were an influential reaction to the positivism that characterized the effectiveness studies. In seeking the views of the subject, the client was given a voice, a voice which resounded with a welcome clarity throughout social work, disturbing many of the profession's therapeutic pretensions. But ironically, during this long period of measuring effectiveness and seeking subjectivity, the voice of the social worker herself was missing. In the third site of enquiry, a bout of democratization burst on to the scene. Attempts were made to obtain and incorporate the views of all the participants in the action – clients, social workers and other interested parties. No one perspective assumed primacy or was accorded moral superiority. However, it is the contention of this chapter that there is one more site in which to locate the client's view and one more question to ask.

Participatory, multi-perspective research still retains a whiff of subjectivism. The individual subject – whether social worker, client or manager – remains at the centre of understanding, though there is an insistence that these individual understandings are shared in what amounts to the beginnings of a useful dialogue. The extra dimension that has to be added is that of structure and context, the relationship of thoughts, actions and utterances to the ideological, material and intellectual practice in which all meetings between social worker and client are constituted. In this relationship, the perspective of the client as either object or subject is lost. The words of the participants both form the occasion and are informed by it. Listening to the voice of the client demands a sophisticated sociological ear. The meaning of social actions – the views of clients and others – can be understood only in context; separating those views, giving them a discrete and independent status cuts off social action from the situation which provoked it. The participants' views make some sense, but out of context their meaning is diminished. A word wrenched out of a line of poetry can be recognized, valued, defined but outside of its context it is not fully understood or appreciated. The context (the poem) creates the word and the word helps form the context. It is the relationship between context and event, situation and person, that has to be understood by those who wish to make sense of the views of others.

Client study researchers have tended to be stronger on moral prescription than on sociological theorizing. Their wish to give the client a good hearing has had a healthy and welcome impact on social work research and practice. But without an equal measure of social theory there is always the danger that understanding is sacrificed to reforming zeal. Asking clients to speak remains a fundamentally important research task. Adding theory to the client's view not only tells us how practice is experienced but also helps us to understand something of the nature of social work itself and the times in which it is formed.

References

Bhasker, R. (1979) *The Possibility of Naturalism: A Philosophical Critique of the Human Sciences*, Brighton: Harvester.

Fisher, M. (1983) 'Preface', in M. Fisher (ed.) *Speaking of Clients*, Joint Unit for Social Services Research, University of Sheffield.

Fisher, M., Marsh, P. and Phillips, D. (1986) *In and Out of Care: The Experiences of Children, Parents and Social Workers*, London: Batsford.

Hekman, S. J. (1986) *Hermeneutics and the Sociology of Knowledge*, Oxford: Polity Press.

Howe, D. (1986) *Social Workers and their Practice in Welfare Bureaucracies*, Aldershot: Gower.

—— (1989) *The Consumers' View of Family Therapy*, Aldershot: Gower.

Klemm, D. E. (1986) *Hermeneutical Inquiry Volume I: The Interpretation of Texts*, Atlanta, Ga: Scholars Press.

Marsh, P. (1983) 'Researching practice and practising research in child care social work', in M. Fisher (ed.) *Speaking of Clients*, Joint Unit for Social Services Research, University of Sheffield.

Morgan, D. H. J. (1985) *The Family, Politics and Social Theory*, London: Routledge & Kegan Paul.

Rorty, R. (1979) *Philosophy and the Mirror of Nature*, Princeton, NJ: Princeton University Press.

Sainsbury, E. (1975) *Social Work with Families*, London: Routledge & Kegan Paul.

7
Housing policy and the Thatcher revolution

Peter Malpass

The pace of change in housing provision and housing policy in Britain was unusually rapid during the 1980s, and the pattern seems set to continue in the 1990s. The housing market was characterized by expansion of home ownership at a rate markedly faster than in previous decades, although there was also considerable instability in prices, with a low rate of increase in the early 1980s giving way to an overall increase of 32 per cent in 1988 (Nationwide Anglia Building Society 1989). Private housing production reached a twenty-five-year low point in 1981, although activity later recovered, in contrast to the experience of the local authority sector where output fell year by year, to the lowest levels since the very early 1920s. The housing market was shaken up by changes affecting the construction industry (Ball 1988) and a major restructuring of mortgage lending and estate agency services. The building societies faced a strong challenge from the banks and sought new powers to operate more competitively (Boddy 1989). The new climate was reflected in the widespread acquisition of estate agency businesses by building societies, banks and insurance companies.

For the local authorities, falling output was accompanied by the sale of council houses on an unprecedented scale. Well over 1 million dwellings were sold, with the result that the total number of council houses fell each year after 1980, something which had never happened before. At the same time the private rented sector continued its long-term decline, losing some 600,000 dwellings between 1981 and 1988 (DoE 1988a). Overall, therefore, there was a significant decline in the supply of rented housing, despite the modest growth achieved by the housing associations, which survived a period of uncertainty and ended the decade as the officially favoured providers of social rented housing.

From the point of view of housing consumers the 1980s was a decade of stark contrasts. While some home owners, especially in London and the south east, accumulated wealth at a rapid pace, there was a growing problem of homelessness and increasing use of expensive temporary accommodation (Bramley *et al.*, 1988). Demographic trends and economic recession made conditions difficult for young people seeking to establish independent homes of their own, and the growing numbers of elderly people, combined with the closure of long-stay mental illness and mental handicap hospitals, put further pressure on the housing and community services.

Not surprisingly, then, evidence such as this, together with other indicators showing a rising tide of disrepair in both public and private sectors (Cantle 1986; Gibson 1986; Audit Commission 1986a) led to talk of a new housing crisis (Fleming and Nellis 1982; Lansley 1984; Malpass 1986a). However, this contrasted with the government's view that its policies were highly successful. It was impatient with critics who emphasized problems of shortage and homelessness, preferring instead to trumpet the success of its measures to increase home ownership. There was an apparently widening gulf between the concerns of the housing lobby and the perceptions and preoccupations of the government.

After major legislation in the early 1980s the government returned with further far-reaching proposals in the wake of its third election victory in 1987. In this it displayed an eagerness for change going far beyond anything envisaged by previous Conservative governments in the period following the Second World War. What emerged in the 1980s was, on the one hand, a determination to explore the limits to growth in owner-occupation, and, on the other, a challenge to local authority housing *in principle*, as distinct from the changes of policy emphasis which have occurred from time to time in the past. What also emerged was a departure from the concerns of previous decades, such as shortage, unfitness and inadequate standards; instead there was a gathering preoccupation with questions of housing tenure, and in particular issues of prices and wealth accumulation.

For the radical right housing provided an obvious and easy target for privatization, given that most households were already accommodated in the private sector. In a number of ways the first Thatcher government targeted housing as a key policy area in its longer-term project of social and economic restructuring. Housing was identified as the programme area in which spending cuts could be most readily achieved (House of Commons 1980). The introduction of the right to buy for council tenants proved to be electorally successful, with the added bonus that substantial capital receipts were generated, exceeding the receipts from all other privatization exercises put together in the period 1980–2 to 1985–6 (Forrest and Murie 1988: 10). The right to buy also bolstered the growth of home ownership in the early 1980s when private sector building was in recession; in the period 1980–4 sales of council houses in England and Wales exceeded private sector new building by some 45,000 dwellings (DoE 1988a).

It is against this background of change and right-wing radicalism that this chapter seeks to focus in on the latest phase of policy-making and implementation, and to consider the implications for the 1990s. The next section outlines the various provisions of the Housing Act 1988, and includes reference to the restructuring of local authority capital and revenue finance arrangements from April 1990. This is followed by a discussion of the ways in which housing policy in the 1980s reinforced the link between poverty and poor housing, with council housing becoming more clearly reduced to the narrow role of providing welfare housing for elderly people and 'special needs groups'. The last main section then goes on to look at some of the contradictions of contemporary housing policy, arguing that the outcomes are often at variance with government objectives and rhetoric.

The gathering obsession with housing tenure

A striking feature of British housing policy in the 1980s was the emphasis on tenure – the number of council houses sold came to be a more potent indicator of policy implementation than the figures for new building. Table 7.1 shows the rapid growth of owner-occupation since 1979, in contrast to the declining fortunes of council housing and private renting.

The government's overall approach has been described as being more a tenure policy than a housing policy (Donnison and Maclennan 1985), the basis for this view being that there seemed to be greater interest in redistributing the ownership of existing dwellings than in addressing the conventional housing policy issues of quantity, quality and price. This interpretation was strengthened by the government's statement of its housing policy objectives in the White Paper of September 1987:

First, the Government will continue to spread home ownership as widely as possible, through encouraging suitable market conditions, continuing tax relief on mortgage interest, and pressing ahead with the right to buy . . .

Second, the Government will put new life into the independent rented sector. The letting of private property will again become an economic proposition . . .

Third, the Government will encourage local authorities to change and develop their housing role. Provision of housing by local authorities as

Table 7.1 Housing tenure in Great Britain (%)

	Owner-occupied	Rented from local authorities and new towns	Rented from		
			housing associations	and	private landlords
1977	54.1	31.7		14.2	
1979	55.3	31.5		13.1	
1987	64.1	25.9	2.5		7.5
1988	65.1	25.2	2.5		7.2

Source: *Annual Abstract of Statistics*, 1989 edn, p. 48

landlords should gradually be diminished, and alternative forms of tenure and tenant choice should increase . . .

Fourth, the Government will focus the use of scarce public money more effectively so that tenants are given a better deal.

The tenure-specific nature of the first three objectives is apparent, as is the positive endorsement of home ownership and private renting, in contrast to the negative attitude to council housing. Support for home ownership has been forthcoming from successive governments, Labour as well as Conservative, since the early 1950s, and Conservative governments have always expressed their commitment to private renting. What was different about the attitudes of the Thatcher governments in the 1980s was, first, the faith placed in home ownership as a form of housing consumption that was suitable for up to three-quarters of the population; second, the belief that private renting could actually be made to work in the late twentieth century, and third, the hostility of their stance in relation to council housing. Twenty years ago the development of new council estates was seen as an essential component of the policy response by any government to the twin problems of shortage and unfitness. By the late 1980s a continuing and largely successful campaign had shifted the terms of public debate against council housing. In short, council housing had been transformed from a solution into a problem.

The legislative assault on council housing in the Housing Act 1988 was prefaced by a series of ministerial pronouncements highlighting its deficiencies. For instance, John Patten (then Minister of Housing) wrote a piece for the *Guardian* in 1987 in which he dwelt at length on the failings of local authorities as providers and managers of housing. The initial assumption underlying the article was that council housing was a failed solution, characterized by a whole litany of deficiencies: poor design and layout, serious disrepair, rising rent arrears, increasing numbers of void properties and unmanageably large housing departments. He described council housing as an 'extreme' solution to the problem of providing social rented housing, and argued that, 'Above all there is the growing dissatisfaction among many tenants of many estates about the conditions in which they live, and about their lack of control over their own environment and housing' (Patten 1987a).

Patten's successor, William Waldegrave, also compared council housing unfavourably with the market:

> What we now have to do is to change the ethos of the rented sector, to get some of the same sense of commitment on the part of tenants to their property that owner occupation achieves, or to get people off that most deadly of all social drugs, the drug of dependence on the state, or bureaucracy, or whoever.
>
> (Waldegrave 1987)

Ministers received a certain amount of support from some academic commentators, such as Coleman (1985) who attributed design faults to bureaucratic interference with the market mechanism, Power (1987) who was critical of local authority housing management practices, and Minford *et al.* (1987) who called for a return to a free market in housing. The latter authors argued that subsidized council rents and restrictions on access to council housing had been key causes of distortions in the housing and labour markets. Amongst their policy proposals for reducing the scale of public housing was the idea that authorities should have the statutory power to evict tenants who were deemed to have the capacity to find alternative accommodation in the private sector.

That particular suggestion has not yet been taken up by the government, but the Housing Act 1988 did contain measures designed to implement the next great step forward in the break-up of the public sector. Hitherto the right to buy had been the main policy instrument for reducing the council stock, although the Housing and Planning Act 1986 had launched, in a rather tentative fashion, estate sales and further diversification of control (Usher 1988). By 1987 over 150,000 dwellings had been sold in block schemes. The majority of these were in two areas, Thamesmead in south-east London and Cantril Farm (renamed Stockbridge Village) in Knowsley. However, some authorities, notably the London Borough of Wandsworth, had sold estates with vacant possession, allowing developers a free hand to refurbish and to dispose of individual units on the open market.

The provisions of the 1986 Act were essentially concerned with local-authority-initiated disposals, but the White Paper of 1987 tried to link disposal of estates to the idea of tenant power and choice. Ministerial statements referred to a 'right' for tenants to transfer to a new landlord, but the publication of the Housing Bill made it clear that in fact what was being proposed was a right for landlords to acquire selected parts of the public sector. Part IV of the Housing Act established powers by which approved landlords can exercise the right to acquire parts of the municipal housing stock, unless a majority of tenants vote against the sale. The novel voting procedure, in which abstentions count as votes in favour of transfer to a new landlord, attracted considerable criticism but the government refused to revert to a more conventional system. However, the first time the system was used, in the proposed voluntary transfer of the entire stock of council houses in Torbay to two housing associations, its unfairness was clearly demonstrated. Of those entitled to vote only 15 per cent voted in favour of the transfer and 42.5 per cent voted against, but because the turnout was only 59 per cent all the abstentions were added to the yes vote, producing an apparent majority in favour of the transfer (*Inside Housing* 18.11.88). The subsequent public outcry led the secretary of state to request a re-run of the ballot, but in the event the council withdrew their proposal.

The voluntary disposal of the whole of an authority's stock was not a key element of government policy and was not covered by the Housing Act 1988. Nevertheless the government welcomed transfers and issued a consultation paper setting out its position (DoE 1988b). However, given that authorities proposing such transfers often justified their decision on grounds of protecting social rented housing from break-up and predation by private landlords, it remains unclear just how far large-scale transfers are intended to accord with government policy. It is also interesting to observe that of the first eight authorities to ballot their tenants five found their plans rejected in quite decisive fashion.

Further erosion of the public sector stock is envisaged in Part III of the 1988 Act which established powers for the Secretary of State to set up Housing Action Trusts (HATs). These bodies, similar in conception to urban development corporations, are intended to take over those parts of the local authority stock which are deemed to be so problematic as to be beyond the abilities of local authorities to deal with them. The HATs are independent bodies, run by people appointed by the Secretary of State, and funded directly by central government. The first six HATs to be set up were announced in July 1988, after a considerable delay. This was widely understood to be the result of a vigorous anti-HAT campaign by tenants in the Hulme area of Manchester which was seen by the government as a prime candidate for HAT treatment. The plan was that the first round of HATs would remove 24,500 dwellings from local authority control in Sunderland, Leeds, Sandwell, Lambeth, Tower Hamlets and Southwark. Equipped with a budget of £125 million for the first three years, the HATs were charged with the task of improving the environment and housing conditions so that the estates can be sold, to individual home owners, new landlords, or just conceivably, back to the local authority. The original proposals for the six HATs were subsequently modified in the light of tenant reaction and consultants' reports, but the Secretary of State made it clear that in order to secure an injection of financial resources to improve their estates tenants would have to accept the HAT as well (*Inside Housing* 31.3.89). This reveals that the real motive behind HATs is privatization rather than improvement for the benefit of tenants.

Taken together the right to buy, the change of landlord scheme and HATs constitute a comprehensive package of measures designed to carry forward the break-up of council housing. Two of the three schemes also have the effect of adding to the supply of dwellings in owner-occupation, while transfers to new landlords add to what the government began to call the independent rented sector. This term was coined to embrace both conventional profit-motivated private renting and the housing association sector. The government's commitment to market forces led it to return to the deregulation of private renting, a policy which had been tried by a previous Tory administration in 1957, with almost complete lack of success (Banting 1979). What was different in the late 1980s was that in addition to deregulating the private rented sector the government simultaneously embarked on a process of privatizing the housing associations, using them as key instruments for the development of independent renting. The success of the policy, therefore, did not rely on a revival of private renting in its traditional form; if this were to happen then the government would welcome it, but it had put in place measures designed to develop a new form of independent renting.

Part I of the Housing Act 1988 introduced deregulation of the existing private rented sector. This meant that new lettings were to be assured tenancies (or assured short-hold – for details see Burrows 1989), giving landlords both a market rent and the prospect of more easily obtaining vacant possession. From the tenants' point of view, therefore, there was the certainty of higher rents and the uncertainty of reduced security of tenure. Previously, assured tenancies could be established only by approved institutional landlords, but the 1988 Act abandoned these restrictions, and the protection for tenants which they implied. In order to stimulate investment in new privately rented housing the Chancellor's 1988 budget extended the Business Expansion Scheme (BES) to cover investment in housing (Coleman 1989; Boleat 1989). Nevertheless, there remained considerable doubt as to the scale of the revival of private renting which these measures would generate.

The basic problem, as always, was the gap between the level of rent that a landlord needed to charge to secure a competitive rate of return and the amount that could be afforded by people in need of rented housing. There remained a need for some element of subsidy, and this is where the housing associations had a role to play. From the government's point of view, housing associations had a number of advantages as contributors to the new model private landlordism. Specifically they already had a form of subsidy, the housing association grant (HAG), which could be modified to fit the new privatized approach. Hitherto HAG had been paid at a level which typically covered 80 per cent or more of the capital cost of new schemes, but the new financial system for associations was designed to provide a lower level of HAG, balanced by a higher level of private sector investment. The higher rents that would result from this change were to be set at 'affordable' levels, supported by housing benefit in the case of low income tenants. This was essentially a proposal for shifting from a system based on high levels of general subsidy (HAG) and fair rents (set by independent rent officers) to a system based on lower levels of general subsidy and unregulated rents with means-tested assistance. In this respect the policy mirrored the experience of local authorities which had experienced a major restructuring of subsidy from general to means tested assistance in the early 1980s (Cooper 1985; Malpass and Murie 1987).

Among the housing associations' other advantages perceived by the government were the fact that they had an established expertise and managerial capacity in relation to rented housing. They were free of the negative imagery associated with the ruthless Rachman-type private landlord. And, equally important for the deeply ideological Thatcher government, they were not local authorities. One interpretation of policy formulation in the late 1980s is that the government had to accept that owner-occupation had its limits, that commercial private renting would not be able to provide for lower-income households and that, therefore, there was a continuing need for new investment in social rented housing. However, the government was so entrenched in its opposition to local authority provision that it had to rely on the housing associations as the only politically acceptable agencies capable of delivering the necessary dwellings.

So far this section has concentrated on the measures in the Housing Act 1988 but in addition it is necessary to consider the contents of a Bill published in February 1989 in which the government outlined yet more radical proposals for the advancement of its programme to revolutionise housing provision in Britain. The Local Government and Housing Bill 1989 combined a number of different proposals, including measures affecting the conduct of local government business as well as housing matters. It is appropriate here to refer to the proposals affecting local authority capital expenditure, housing revenue accounting and subsidy, and home improvement grants.

By the late 1980s it was clear that the system of central government controls on local authority capital spending in general were not satisfactory from either the central or local point of view. Authorities were subject to severe restrictions and continual changes in the rules governing their activities, while central government found it difficult both to plan the overall level of spending and to target resources to areas of greatest need. Key factors in this were the slack drafting of earlier legislation and local authority agility in exploiting opportunities to avoid constraints on spending. In addition, the very success of council house sales had generated capital receipts worth an estimated £12.5 billion by 1987–8 (DoE 1988c). Some local authorities, therefore, had large amounts of accumulated capital receipts, although others had effectively disposed of their receipts, and there was a marked mismatch between the accumulation of receipts and the need to invest in new provision.

The government proposed that from April 1990 a new system would take effect in which the loopholes of the old system would be closed and three-quarters of all capital receipts would be applied to the redemption of existing debt. In future authorities will receive an annual 'credit approval' which will determine how much capital can be raised by borrowing (or its equivalent), giving central government much tighter control over local spending, and allowing it, for the first time, to take into account capital receipts when deciding each authority's credit approval limit. Hitherto, central government has been required to determine Housing Investment Programme (HIP) allocations (i.e. annual borrowing limits) according to local need, and each local authority has been free to augment its allocation by a fixed proportion of receipts from asset sales. The scale of aggregate accumulated receipts had a distorting effect on the HIP system and the government has belatedly moved to bring receipts within the scope of its powers to control spending by each local authority.

On the revenue side the government proposed what it called a 'new regime' for local authority housing finance (Grant 1988; Ward 1988). This again was motivated by the government's frustration at its inability to control local authority decisions. By the mid-1980s the housing subsidy system, through which the centre sought to control local rent increases, was breaking down (Malpass 1986b; 1987; 1988). That system was based on central government leverage on rents by means of subsidy withdrawal. However, as increasing numbers of local authorities lost all their general subsidy, so they were freed from that source of pressure to raise rents. The new regime represents an attempt by the centre to regain control of rent increases. It does so by, first, prohibiting the rate fund contributions (or poll tax fund after 1990) by which some local authorities have subsidized housing rents. Second, it prohibits transfers from the housing revenue account into the general fund. These two measures together constitute the so-called 'ring-fence' around the housing revenue account. However, the really important part of the new system will be the running together of existing housing subsidy, which is paid to a small proportion of authorities under the Housing Act 1980, and housing benefit subsidy, which is paid to all authorities under the Social Security Act 1986. The latter is the aggregate amount of the Housing Benefit entitlement of local authority tenants, and is clearly an income maintenance payment, not a housing subsidy as such. However, by rolling these two payments together the government is moving to a new definition of the deficit on the Housing Revenue Account, based on net rents (i.e. what tenants actually pay from their own pockets). The new combined subsidy, to be known as housing revenue account subsidy, will be paid only where net rent income is less than approved expenditure. Where the housing revenue account can balance without subsidy then none will be paid, which has led to the accusation that this system will require tenants as a whole to pay for their own rent rebates. From the point of view of central government, however, the main feature of the new regime is that it provides very powerful leverage on rents across the country, a fact which could prove to be highly significant in influencing tenants' decisions about whether to opt for a new landlord. In the early 1980s very large rent increases were used to provide an incentive to tenants to buy their homes, and the same sort of strategy seems to be in preparation for the 1990s.

The final radical new measure to be mentioned is the means testing of home improvement grants (Leather and Mackintosh 1989). Financial assistance for improvement work has been available in various forms since 1949, but it has never been means tested. The important criteria were always taken to be the condition of the property and the nature of the works required, although rateable value limits tended to operate as a means of excluding high income earners. Space does not permit a full discussion of the new system, but it is sufficient to note that it will be based on the type of assessment used for housing benefit, taking into account regular income and assumed income from savings, but making allowance for household composition and certain disregards. This will produce a 'surplus income' figure, 20 per cent of which will be assumed to be available to service a loan to finance the necessary work. Thus the grant will be the difference between the cost of the necessary work and the notional borrowing power of the applicant.

This section has reviewed the latest phase of housing policy formation and has shown how the rented sectors have continued to be the focus of reform. It is important to note that nothing has been done, or proposed, by the government to confront the issue of the subsidies and tax incentives poured into the owner-occupied sector. Mortgage interest tax relief, to take just one indicator, was estimated to reach £5.5 billion in 1988–9. Despite the rhetoric of targeting resources and assistance on those in greatest need, nothing has been done to redistribute the assistance given to home owners in a more equitable way. Meanwhile, building societies repossessed nine times as many houses from defaulting mortgagors in 1987 compared with 1979, and serious mortgage arrears increased by a factor of nearly six in the same period (Building Societies Association 1989).

Reinforcing the link between poverty and poor housing

It is quite clear from the above discussion that privatization is the main theme of policy in relation to housing, as it is in so many areas of life in contemporary Britain. Privatization can bring real benefits to certain sections of the population, and there can be no doubt that many people have benefited from buying their council houses. However, as the reference to mortgage default and arrears indicates, private provision does not guarantee satisfaction and affordability. In the private market there is inevitably a close link between income and wealth on the one hand and quality of housing on the other. It has always been so.

The purpose of this section is to make two points concerning the housing conditions of households on low incomes and the way in which housing policy under Thatcher has made their position worse. First, the growth of owner-occupation towards two-thirds of the population has depended upon a continuing broadening of the social composition of the tenure. It is no longer (if, indeed, it ever was) safe to regard owner-occupation as a relatively uniform category comprised of affluent households in modern high-amenity dwellings in leafy suburbs. As owner-occupation has grown it has spread into more and more of the pre-1919 stock of urban housing, most of which was formerly owned by, and often neglected by, private landlords. Inner city residential neighbourhoods of small terraced housing have been taken over by young first-time buyers, and in particular by those forced by income constraints to operate at the bottom of the market. The people with the least purchasing power and with least choice are driven into the smallest, meanest and least desirable dwellings (Karn *et al.* 1985).

The spread of home ownership into such areas has taken place during a period when state intervention in the form of first slum clearance and more recently area improvement has been in decline. This means increasingly that young, low-income, first-time buyers have taken on responsibility for maintaining and improving the physical fabric of dwellings which would probably have been subject to planned and well-resourced area-based intervention by the local authority if previous policies had continued. It is arguable that these purchasers are least well placed to discharge this important responsibility, and that in this sense privatization entails an unreasonable redistribution of the burden of urban renewal. It is also a reminder of the point that privatization individualizes the costs as well as the benefits of ownership.

To add to the burden of home ownership for marginal purchasers in the 1980s interest rates were at record levels in both nominal terms (15 per cent in 1980 and 1981, and hardly below 10 per cent throughout the decade) and real terms (i.e. taking account of inflation). At the same time the ratio of house prices to earnings rose to record levels, reaching 4.61 in 1989. These two factors together mean that recent purchasers had to commit very large proportions of income to mortgage repayments.

The demand for home ownership remains buoyant, however, partly because of the prospect of long-term advantage and wealth accumulation, and partly because of the diminished supply of public sector housing. This brings us to the second main point, and it concerns the way in which council housing has been transformed into a tenure for the least well off, providing less choice of accommodation and the threat of declining standards. In principle council housing historically offered a real chance to break the link between poverty and poor housing. The provision of subsidy and the opportunity to allocate according to need, rather than ability to pay, meant that the market link between income and standard of accommodation could be broken. However, in practice the periods of highest quality housing production (in the 1920s and 1940s) were associated with wider policies which tended to result in the better-off working class being the main beneficiaries. When housing policy tilted towards a clearer focus on the less well off then the quality of new building tended to fall (as in the 1930s and 1950s). Despite these fluctuations, council housing remained a relatively modern high amenity stock compared with the private rented sector, in which the least well off continued to be concentrated until the last twenty years or so.

In recent years council housing has changed its character, partly because it now contains a growing proportion of dwellings which are more than sixty years old, partly because its image was tarnished by the construction of a lot of high-rise and high-density housing in the 1960s and 1970s, and partly because the differential impact of sales has reduced the proportion of attractive three-bedroomed houses with gardens. At the same time the continued decline of private renting has left the poorest with little real alternative to council housing, and government policy has emphasized the residual role of the public sector as the tenure specializing in providing for special needs and those on the lowest incomes (Forrest and Murie 1988: ch. 4; Malpass 1990: ch. 1).

A range of evidence emerged during the 1980s confirming social polarization in the housing system and showing the growing concentration of the least well off within the public sector. By 1986 58.9 per cent of council tenants were in the lowest three-income deciles, compared with just 14 per cent of home owners (Department of Employment 1987: Tables 4 and 22). Hamnett's study of tenure differences showed that 'Skilled manual workers have moved increasingly into the owner occupied sector, leaving behind them a council sector increasingly dominated by the semi-skilled, the unskilled and the economically inactive' (Hamnett 1984). Forrest and Murie state that by 1984 more than half (53 per cent) of households in council housing were headed by an economically inactive person, and that overall nearly two-thirds of council-housing heads of household were not working (Forrest and Murie 1988: 69). Table 7.2 shows how elderly people became heavily over-represented in local authority housing by the early 1980s. These figures also indicate important changes in younger age groups, with the under-25s becoming over-represented while there were reductions in the proportions of people aged 30 to 59 who were council tenants.

It may be argued that the proper role of local-authority housing is indeed to provide for the poorest and those who the market cannot satisfactorily accommodate. The point being made here, however, is that whatever position one takes on what local authorities should be doing, the fact remains that as council housing increasingly accommodates the least well off it does so in a situation where some authorities (especially the large urban authorities) face mounting criticism of their management and maintenance performance (Audit

Table 7.2   Proportions of households of different ages in local authority housing

Age of head of household	1971 (%)	1985 (%)
24 and under	21	32
25–29	24	24
30–44	29	19
45–59	35	27
60–69	32	36
70–79	31	39
80 and over	31	39
All households	31	28

Source: *Social Trends 1988*, London: HMSO, Table 8.20

Commission 1986a; 1986b), and where they can offer only a restricted choice of dwellings.

The backlog of repairs in the council sector is huge. In the mid-1980s the Association of Metropolitan Authorities estimated the cost of these repairs to be £19 billion (Cantle 1986), and in 1985 a Department of the Environment survey indicated that 85 per cent of the stock was in need of repairs averaging some £4,500 per dwelling (DoE 1985). In addition the Audit Commission calculated in 1986 that new repair problems could add £900 million each year to the total council house maintenance bill (Audit Commission 1986b). However, it should be understood that responsibility for this situation lies partly with the government, for in the early 1980s it forced authorities to raise rents substantially but did not allow the whole of the increased rental income to be spent on improved services to tenants. Instead a large part of the additional income was creamed off by central government in the form of reduced subsidy, meaning that authorities wishing to improve services had to make even bigger rent increases than the government required.

In both the owner-occupied and local-authority sectors, then, housing policy in the 1980s tended to reinforce the link between poverty and poor housing, implying a restructuring of the housing problem rather than a solution to it.

Conclusion

In conclusion it can be argued that the long-term changes in housing tenure, to which the Thatcher revolution has contributed with such enthusiasm, are producing outcomes which are at variance with government policy and posing new problems for policy in the 1990s. On the one hand council housing is proving to be remarkably resilient in the face of the attacks launched against it in the 1980s. Although the government boasts of the success of the right to buy around 85 per cent of the stock remained unsold, which was one of the main reasons for the development of new policies to sell off whole estates via tenants' choice and HATs. But as the evidence presented here has shown, the government mis-read the attitude of tenants, who emerged as strong defenders of council housing in their opposition to HATs and in several ballots on transfers to new landlords.

On the other hand, mass home ownership has so far failed to provide the panacea to all housing problems. On the contrary, reference has been made here to growing problems of mortgage arrears and disrepair. Access to home ownership became very difficult and expensive for young people in the 1980s, and in addition wider regional variations in house prices generated distortions in the labour market.

The evidence points to the conclusion that the policies of the Thatcher decade were directed towards tenure restructuring rather than housing problems as such, and that in future the requirement is for policies which can deal with problems within each tenure. Specifically it is increasingly necessary to move on from a policy focus designed to draw yet more people into owner-occupation and to confront the problems generated within this sector. This means reorganizing the grossly inequitable systems of financial assistance and providing new services to help home owners with the continuing problems of repair and maintenance work. In the case of the council sector the requirement is for a more balanced approach, capable of acknowledging the virtues of collective ownership by local authorities, and going beyond the narrowly based and ill-conceived obsession with privatization.

References

Audit Commission (1986a) *Managing the Crisis in Council Housing*, London: HMSO.
—— (1986b) *Improving Council House Maintenance*, London: HMSO.
Ball, M. (1988) *Rebuilding Construction*, London: Routledge.
Banting, K. (1979) *Poverty, Policy and Politics*, London: Macmillan.
Boddy, M. (1989) 'Financial deregulation and UK housing finance', *Housing Studies* 4, 1: 92–104.
Boleat, M. (1989) 'The transformation of rented housing', *Housing Finance* 1, January: 8–15.
Bramley, G., Doogan, K., Leather, P., Murie, A. and Watson, E. (1988) *Homelessness and the London Housing Market*, SAUS, Occasional Paper 32, University of Bristol.
Building Societies Association (1989) *Housing Finance* 1, January.
Burrows, L. (1989) *The Housing Act 1988*, London: Shelter.
Cantle, T. (1986) 'The deterioration of public sector housing', in P. Malpass (ed.) *The Housing Crisis*, Beckenham: Croom Helm.
Coleman, A. (1985) *Utopia on Trial*, London: Hilary Shipman.
Coleman, D. (1989) 'The new housing policy – a critique', *Housing Studies* 4, 1: 44–57.
Cooper, S. (1985) *Public Housing and Private Property*, Aldershot: Gower.
Department of Employment (1987) *Family Expenditure Survey 1986*, London: HMSO.
DoE (Department of the Environment) (1985) *An Inquiry Into the Condition of the Local Authority Housing Stock in England*, London: DoE.
—— (1988a) *Housing and Construction Statistics*, London: HMSO.
—— (1988b) *Large Scale Voluntary Transfers of Local Authority Housing to Private Bodies*, mimeo, London: DoE.
—— (1988c) *Capital Expenditure and Finance: A Consultation Paper*, London: DoE.
Donnison, D. and Maclennan, D. (1985) 'What should we do about housing?', *New Society* 11 April: 43–6.

Duncan, S. and Goodwin, M. (1988) *The Local State and Uneven Development: Behind the Local Government Crisis*, Cambridge: Polity Press.

Fleming, M. and Nellis, J. (1982) 'A new housing crisis?', *Lloyds Bank Review*, April: 38–53.

Forrest, R. and Murie, A. (1988) *Selling the Welfare State: the Privatisation of Public Housing*, London: Routledge.

Gibson, M. (1986) 'Housing renewal: privatisation and beyond', in P. Malpass (ed.) *The Housing Crisis*, Beckenham: Croom Helm.

Grant, C. (1988) 'Making tenants foot the bill', *Roof* September–October: 15–17.

Hamnett, C. (1984) 'Housing the two nations: socio-tenurial polarisation in England and Wales, 1961–1981', *Urban Studies* 21, 4: 389–405.

House of Commons (1980) *Enquiry into the Implications of Government's Expenditure Plans 1980–81 to 1983–84 for the Housing Policies of the Department of the Environment*, First Report of the Environment Committee, Session 1979–80, HC714, London: HMSO.

Karn, V., Kemeny, J. and Williams, P. (1985) *Home Ownership in the Inner City*, Aldershot: Gower.

Lansley, S. (1984) 'The growing housing crisis', in Labour Housing Group (eds) *Right to a Home*, Nottingham: Spokesman.

Leather, P. and Mackintosh, S. (1989) 'The means testing of home improvement grants', *Housing Review* May–June: 77–80.

Malpass, P. (ed.) (1986a) *The Housing Crisis*, Beckenham: Croom Helm.

—— (1986b) 'Councils that cheat their tenants', *Roof* May–June: 12–20.

—— (1987) 'Ridley's one way ring fence', *Roof* September–October: 23–4.

—— (1988) 'Council tenants overcharged by half a billion pounds', *Roof* September–October: 12.

—— (1990) *Reshaping Housing Policy*, London: Routledge.

Malpass, P. and Murie, A. (1987) *Housing Policy and Practice*, 2nd edn, Basingstoke: Macmillan.

Minford, P., Peel, M. and Ashton, P. (1987) *The Housing Morass: Regulation, Immobility and Unemployment*, London: Institute of Economic Affairs.

Nationwide Anglia Building Society (1989) *House Prices in the First Quarter of 1989*, London: Nationwide Anglia Building Society.

Patten, J. (1987a) 'Housing – room for a new view', *Guardian*, 30 January.

—— (1987b) 'Yes minister, but . . .' *Roof* January–February: 23–5.

Power, A. (1987) *Property Before People*, London: Allen & Unwin.

Usher, D. (1988) *Council Estate Sales*, SAUS, Working Paper 74, University of Bristol.

Waldegrave, W. (1987) Address to the Institute of Housing Annual Conference, Brighton.

Ward, M. (1988) 'Priced out', *Housing* October: 9–11.

8
Doubts, dilemmas and duties: ethics and the social worker

Sarah Banks

The 1980s have been a period of uncertainty for social workers: one when the public, and the profession itself, has frequently asked what the role of the social worker is and what it ought to be. Many of the questions raised are essentially ethical – about how far the rights and freedoms of individuals, families or communities ought to be limited by the state; and about whether certain goods and services ought even to be provided by the state and how they should be distributed. Yet while there has been a recent growth in publications relating specifically to ethical issues in social work (Leighton *et al.* 1982; Timms 1983; Clark with Asquith 1985; Watson 1985; Rhodes 1986; Horne 1987), it is doubtful whether practising social workers are able to make sense or use of the literature and relate it to the acknowledged ethical dilemmas experienced in their practice. It seems particularly timely, therefore, to take stock of the kinds of ethical issues involved in social work, to review the literature in this field and to evaluate its usefulness for practitioners.

Definitions

Before discussing some of the ethical issues in social work, it may be helpful to clarify briefly my use of the terms 'social work' and 'ethics'. Social work is taken to be the work done by people called 'social workers' in their job descriptions, whose main task is counselling and social care planning as defined in the Barclay Report (NISW 1982), and who work for/or are monitored by a local authority within the terms of reference of the Local Authority Social Services Act 1970. Strictly speaking, ethics, or moral philosophy, is the study of morals: morals are the norms of behaviour which people follow concerning what is right or wrong, good or bad (Raphael 1981: 1–10; Frankena 1973: 1–11). Despite this distinction between morals and ethics, the two words are often used interchangeably – for example, the code of ethics for social work is in fact a code of norms of behaviour and therefore strictly speaking a code of morals (BASW: 1988). Similarly the adjectives 'moral' and 'ethical' are both used to mean pertaining to what people ought to do, what is regarded as good or bad, right or wrong. It is in this sense that I will use the terms 'ethical' and 'moral' interchangeably.

Moral judgements

Much of social work is concerned with making decisions about how to act in particular cases; for example, whether to commit an elderly woman to hospital against her will. This involves making moral judgements. One such judgement might be 'it is morally wrong to commit this woman to hospital against her will'. Philosophers have spent many years disputing the demarcation of the sphere of the moral. I do not intend to enter into that debate here, but simply to make four statements which summarize the position adopted in this chapter and which is implicit in much of the social work literature on ethics:

1 Moral judgements are about human welfare – for example, the promotion of human happiness or the satisfaction of needs (Norman 1983: 225–52; Warnock 1967: 48–72). What counts as a 'human need' will be relative to a particular society, or ideological belief system and will change over time.
2 Moral judgements are prescriptive, that is, they prescribe action. If a social worker makes the moral judgement that an elderly woman suffering from confusion ought not to be committed to hospital against her will, then the worker should be prepared to act on this prescription; this might include making plans for her to stay at home and being prepared to argue the case to her family and to professional colleagues.
3 A moral judgement should be universalizable, in that it should apply to all people in similar circumstances. The social worker should make the same moral judgement about another elderly person, unless it could be demonstrated that the situation was significantly different.
4 Moral decision-making is an essentially rational process. It makes sense to ask social workers to justify particular moral judgements and they may do so with reference to some more general moral judgements or principles. In this case, one such principle might be 'all individuals have a right to decide for themselves what they want to do' (self-determination). This in turn might be justified with reference to the principle that 'all persons should be respected as rational and self-determining beings'. Ultimately a stage is reached where no further justification can be given and certain beliefs about the nature of human welfare and needs have to be taken as given.

This view does not entail that people always make moral decisions through a process of neat deductive reasoning from general principles. Very often the principles may only be implicit and not fully worked out; or, we may be so practised in an area of decision-making that we do not need to refer to fundamental principles on each occasion. The claim being made is that moral judgements should be capable of rational justification (Hare 1963: Warnock 1967). Not all philosophers would accept this view.

Ethics and social work

Practitioners and theorists seem generally agreed that social work is intimately connected with ethics. For example, the British Association of Social Workers describes social work as 'the purposeful and ethical application of personal skills' (BASW 1977: 19); Butrym's introductory textbook proclaims 'the inherently moral nature of social work' (Butrym 1976: 40). In talking to social work students about ethics, there is never any shortage of examples of ethical dilemmas in practice (Banks 1985).

There are two ways in which social work can be viewed as an inherently moral activity. First, considering the context of social work, it is part of a system (the welfare state) for the distribution of material and emotional goods. This is based on moral judgements (by the state, administrative officials and social workers themselves) that certain goods ought to be provided (for example, home helps or bereavement counselling) and about how they ought to be distributed. It can also be regarded as a form of socially mandated control (for example, in the case of mental illness and child abuse), which may entail limiting certain individual rights and freedoms. From this perspective, the kinds of ethical issues faced by social workers may include balancing the interests of different clients and questioning their role as part of the welfare state – whether the services provided are fair, whether the law within which social work operates is just and whether social workers act primarily as agents of social control.

The second sense in which social work can be regarded as an ethical activity relates to the content of social work. Social work is about relating to people, and this is what morality is all about. Further social workers tend to have more power than clients – especially in relation to access to resources or the application of legal sanctions. Clients tend to be more than averagely deprived and the social worker holds an official position. As a profession social work has a code of ethics, one of the purposes of which is to protect clients against exploitation and mistreatment. The kinds of dilemmas that arise in this area might include consideration of how much freedom to allow the client, whether it is possible to be non-judgemental and non-discriminatory, and what are the limits to confidentiality.

A theoretical framework for social work ethics

We shall now briefly consider whether the theoretical literature on social work ethics might help to clarify and resolve some of the ethical dilemmas in social work practice. Until recently, much of this literature has focused on lists of principles about how the social worker ought to treat the individual client (that is, the content of the relationship). This approach owes a lot to the work of Biestek, an American Catholic priest, whose book, *The Casework Relationship* (first published in 1957), has been very influential. Biestek's list of seven principles has been adopted and modified by a number of British writers, as Table 8.1 demonstrates. In addition to Biestek's principles, some writers have stressed the importance of 'respect for persons' as the ultimate principle underpinning social work, and indeed, as a basic presupposition of any system of moral thinking (Plant 1970; Downie and Telfer 1969). The term 'person' refers to beings who are capable of rational thought and self-determined action. As such they are worthy of 'respect', which is a form of 'active sympathy' towards others. In a social work context, Downie and Telfer argue that clients who are not fully capable of rational thought and self-determined action (for example, children or mentally handicapped adults) should still be treated with some respect, which is due to them as potentially rational beings, or as members of a species of rational beings (Downie and Telfer 1980). Although Biestek did not explicitly state this principle (which derives from the nineteenth-century German philosopher, Kant) there is no doubt that it underpins his liberal, Christian thinking.

Some of the more recent literature has been critical of both the 'list' approach (Timms 1983: 45–65) and of the focus on the individual social-worker–client relationship (Clarke with Asquith 1985; Horne 1987). The lists are often a mixture of principles of different status. For example, surely 'purposeful expression of feelings' is a method of effective practice, whereas 'self-determination' is a general moral principle? Second, no indication is given of how to rank the principles, or what to do in cases of conflict. For example, how do we judge between promoting a client's self-determination at the expense of revealing a confidential secret? Finally, many of the principles are broad generalizations which are open to interpretation. For example 'self-determination' as described in Table 8.1 actually embodies two concepts of freedom: negative freedom – the right of the client to freedom from interference in making choices and decisions – and positive freedom – the right to be enabled to have more choices and to become self-realizing (Berlin 1975; McDermott 1975). The former might be interpreted to recommend that social work intervention should be minimized, whereas the latter might justify intervention from the social worker ranging from paternalism to social control.

Another set of problems with the 'Biestekian' approach is that it tends to focus on the one-to-one relationship between the social worker and an individual client, giving little guidance as to how to balance the conflicting rights of several clients (for example, mother and child) and paying less attention to the societal and agency context where this happens. In philosophical terms we might say that the Biestekian approach is based within the Kantian tradition (Kant 1964). One feature of this approach is a focus on the rights and duties of individuals. A second feature is that in making a judgement about whether an action is morally right or wrong, the moral agent would look to the nature of the act itself, regardless of what consequences it will have. For example, lying or manipulation would always be morally wrong because they violate the fundamental principle of respect for persons, regardless of whether, for example, by lying someone's life could be saved (for a detailed discussion of problems around truth telling in the public professions, see Bok 1980). Yet in

Table 8.1 Principles of the social-worker–client relationship

Biestek's principles	*Examples of their adoption/modification*					
	Biestek 1961	Moffet 1968	Plant 1970	CCETSW 1976	Butrym 1976	Ragg 1977
Individualization: recognition of each client's qualities	X	X	X	X	X	X
Purposeful expression of feelings: recognition of clients' needs to express their feelings freely	X	X			X	X
Controlled emotional involvement: social worker's sensitivity to clients' feelings and appropriate response to them	X				X	
Acceptance: social worker accepts clients as they are, maintaining a sense of their dignity and worth	X	X	X	X	X	
Non-judgemental attitudes: social worker should not judge the guilt or innocence of clients	X				X	
Client self-determination: recognition of clients' rights to freedom in making their own choices. Social worker also has a duty to help activate clients' potential for self-direction. This right can be limited by a client's capacity for decision-making, by the law and by the function of the agency	X	X	X	X	X	X
Confidentiality: preservation of secret information concerning clients disclosed in the professional relationship. This right may be limited by higher duty to self, by rights of other individuals, the social worker, agency or community.	X	X		X	X	
Basic or ultimate principle						
Respect for persons: active sympathy towards other people as beings who are self-determining and rational (i.e. who have choices, desires which should be respected).			X	X	X	X

reality, social work takes place within a framework which also takes into account notions such as 'public good' and involves weighing up the consequences of actions. Philosophically, the latter approach would be termed 'Utilitarianism', variations of which have been derived from the work of J. S. Mill (Mill 1972; Smart and Williams 1973). According to this theory actions are judged morally right according to whether they produce a greater balance of good over evil, distributed as widely as possible. Its ultimate principle (which is, in fact, two principles) can be stated as the promotion of the greatest good (utility) of the greatest number (justice).

More recent texts on social work ethics and values do take into account the Utilitarian dimension (Clark with Asquith 1985; Rhodes 1986; Horne 1987), but tend not to suggest how it relates to, or conflicts with, the Kantian perspective. There is only one detailed attempt to develop a unified Kantian – Utilitarian system of moral theory for social work: this is by Downie and Telfer (1980) in their book *Caring and Curing*. They argue that the principle of utility (taken as the promotion of happiness) presupposes the principle of respect for persons (because it entails that the beings whose happiness is to be promoted matter; and to matter in this way entails respect). However, regardless of whether or not this argument is valid (for a more detailed critique see Banks 1985: 29–30), they still do not claim that the principle of utility can be derived from respect for persons. Therefore the latter cannot serve as the one ultimate arbiter between conflicting principles.

We may conclude that in social work, as in other aspects of life, moral-decision-making appears to involve elements of both Kantian and Utilitarian thinking, working at balancing individual rights and freedoms against the public good. This reflects the tensions and contradictions inherent in a welfare-capitalist society, where the welfare state exists both to sustain capital accumulation (based on values of individualism and competition) and to ensure social harmony (based on values of collective responsibility and equal distribution) (O'Connor 1973: 6; George and Wilding 1985: 110–19). It is not surprising that social workers are caught in these contradictions, operating, as Statham comments, 'at a meeting place between the dominant economic values and welfare values as they are defined and accepted within capitalism' (Statham 1978: 94). What ultimately influences a social worker's decision on whether to stay in the job, or how to act in a particular case will often be based on non-moral assumptions about what is the nature and good of humankind and of society. These 'non-moral' assumptions about whether human beings are essentially free or determined, whether they are essentially individuals or social beings, have long taxed philosophers (see Lukes 1973) and I do not propose to enter into the various debates here. However, a brief mention of the underlying assumptions of moral theories may aid understanding. Both the Kantian and Utilitarian moral theories are premised on the assumption of the individual human being as a moral agent who is free to make moral choices and judgements and to act on these choices. For it makes sense to accord moral praise or blame to people only if they determine their own actions without external constraint.

There are alternative analyses of society which do not regard human beings as free in this sense. A Marxist view, for example, regards human thought and action as being predominantly influenced by the social and economic structures of society. Moral principles therefore, cannot be regarded as absolute, or universally valid, even within a particular society at a particular time. What is to count as right, wrong, good or bad will be relative to the interests of groups or classes in society. On this view, the Kantian–Utilitarian morality would be regarded as a set of norms working in the interests of the ruling class, while purporting to be absolute and universal to all classes (for a detailed articulation of a class-relativist view, see Fisk 1980). This is why Marx dismissed morality (at least, the prevailing morality) as a bourgeois illusion (Marx and Engels 1848: 494–5) and why he did not develop an ethical theory, comparable, say, to Kantianism or Utilitarianism. Yet Marx's writings are full of explicit and implicit moral judgements, demonstrating his belief in the dignity and potential of human beings and in a 'higher' form of collective society where this potential would be realized (Lukes 1985: 1–36). Lukes identifies the morality underlying Marx's views as consequentialist (actions are judged right or wrong according to their consequences) and perfectionist (the end we are heading towards is fully realized human beings in a communist society). There have been many different ethical theories developed by subsequent Marxists, including versions of Kantianism and Utilitarianism as well as ethical relativism (for an overview see Nielson 1986: 92–112; see also Kamenka 1969; Ollman 1976: 41–51).

Social work theorists in the Marxist tradition, in common with Marx himself, have generally tended not to articulate an ethical theory as such. However, within the literature of 'radical social work', particularly as represented by Corrigan and Leonard (1978) there is a tendency to emphasize the consequences of action, with the prescription for social workers being to try to change clients' views and involve them in collective action (see also Bailey and Brake 1980; Statham 1978; Simpkin 1983; Bolger *et al.* 1981). The problem, as with Marx's consequentialism, is that the end (a communist society) which justifies the means used, and against which actions are judged right or wrong, is a long-range end which focuses on the future benefits of future persons and ignores the interests of people here and now (Lukes 1985: 146). This presents a particular problem in social work, where the essence of the work is dealing with people's immediate situations, and has always been an uneasy position for radical social workers (Rhodes 1986: 38–9).

Figure 8.1 is an attempt to sketch possible frameworks of moral thinking, tracing the links between underlying non-moral assumptions through basic moral principles to some principles relevant to social work practice. The principles are some of those generally found in the literature. The sketch does not aim to be exhaustive, but simply to make a beginning in locating the different levels of moral thought and their relation to each other. It is a very schematic attempt to bridge the gaps in the literature between the ideological or political and the ethical; and between moral theory and social work practice.

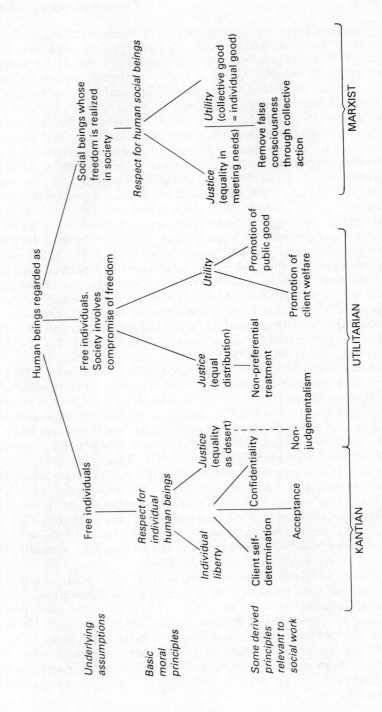

Figure 8.1 Kantian–Utilitarian and Marxist frameworks of moral thinking

Theory to practice

How does this help social workers in their day-to-day practice? The response of many workers might be that it does not. And this is not because they think ethical dilemmas do not arise in social work, but because very little guidance has been given in the literature about how to put these 'moral principles' into practice. With a few recent exceptions (Horne 1987; Rhodes 1986) there is a dearth of texts which actually combine detailed theoretical discussion of ethical issues with detailed application to case studies. This reflects a problem in social work generally of the gap between the theories and the practice (Howe 1987: 8–17). A second feature of the literature on social work ethics is that it seems to have had little impact on social work thought generally, remaining curiously separate from the wider literature on social work's aims and methods. For example, Howe's recent book, which provides an excellent analysis of the major theories in social work (e.g. psychoanalytic, behaviourist and Marxist), does not explicitly examine the ethical positions entailed by each theory. A much earlier, but still influential, text (Butrym 1976) similarly does not even relate her summary of the different models adopted in social work to her lengthy discussion of 'values' in the same book. Indeed, in the majority of current literature on social work in general, or particular methods and approaches, ethical or value issues, if covered, occupy only a few pages and are not related to further discussion (e.g. Barclay Report – NISW 1982: 145–50; Pincus and Minahan 1973; 37–52; Breakwell and Rowett 1982: 122–5; Davies 1981: 22–32; Jones *et al.* 1987: 317–18). This type of coverage encourages social workers in the already prevalent idea that ethics is an academic area, which is mandatorily, but briefly, covered in social work courses, and which is to be regarded not only as separate from any other academic study of theories of practice, but also as providing little help to workers experiencing ethical dilemmas in practice.

The code of ethics

The code of ethics for social workers (BASW 1988) might be thought to be an obvious avenue down which social workers could look for help regarding ethical dilemmas in practice. The code was adopted by BASW in 1975 and is based on the premise that social work, as a professional activity, entails certain obligations beyond those of the ordinary citizen. The stated objective of the code is to make explicit the implicit ethical principles, 'for the protection of clients'. The code contains both a statement of the broad principles upon which social work is based (for example, 'the value and dignity of every human being') and a list of 'principles of practice' which are supposedly more concrete and should guide practice. Within the statement of principles can be found versions of respect for persons, acceptance and self-determination, along with a commitment to use skills and knowledge with integrity and to contribute towards changing policy. However, this statement, and the list of principles of practice which follows, have all the shortcomings of 'the list approach' mentioned earlier. The principles of practice are a confusing mixture of statements of professional standards (e.g. 'professional education and training are basic to the practice of social work'), recommendations for effective practice (e.g. 'the need to collaborate with others') and moral principles (e.g. 'respect . . . clients as individuals and . . . seek to ensure that their dignity, individuality, rights and responsibility shall be safe guarded'). In short, the code lacks clarity and consistency.

Further, although the code clearly acknowledges in its foreword that social workers have an obligation not only to their clients, but also 'to their employers, to each other, to colleagues in other disciplines and to society', its principles of practice are largely concerned with how social workers should behave towards clients. Such an emphasis is to be expected in a professional code of ethics, and is found in the codes for counsellors (British Association for Counselling 1984), medicine, and nursing (both reprinted in Campbell 1984: 167–70). However, there is some debate as to whether social workers are autonomous professionals in the same sense as, say, doctors. For, as Payne points out, social work is generally practised within an organization, and social workers are usually more subject to the authority of their employers as opposed to being directly accountable to their clients (Payne 1985: 104). This is less so in medicine. For example, it is not the function of the National Health Service to treat patients, but to provide doctors who will do so. By contrast, it is the duty of the local authority to care for children; and for this purpose it employs social workers. So the relationship is always at least three-way including the local authority, the social worker and in many cases more than one client (e.g. child and parents). Since the social worker is in fact just the instrument used by the local authority, it follows, for example, that confidential information given to the social worker is, in fact, given to the local authority (Sutherland 1985: 162). Therefore social workers are not always autonomous professionals; their responsibilities to their agencies very often conflict with, and have to take precedence over, say, treating clients with dignity or respecting confidences. A code of ethics which assumes the centrality of clients' rights and takes little account of the agency and societal context of social work, seems at best inadequate and misleading, and at worst meaningless.

This may explain why many social workers (if they are even aware of the code's existence) claim to find it of little use. However, they may also have unrealistic expectations of what a code of ethics can or should be (Rice 1975; Watson 1985). A code cannot prescribe action to be followed by a social worker in all possible situations; its function is briefly to define the broad ethical framework within which a profession works. Precisely because the nature of the work makes it easy for clients' interests to be marginalized, there is some justification for retaining a code of ethics, or at least a statement of principles, including clients' rights. A code can encourage practitioners to reflect on their work, particularly if agency procedures or practice appear to be contravening principles embodied in the code. It can also be used as a baseline for more detailed codes of practice laid down by individual agencies, and as a defence of standards when the profession is under attack. Yet a more realistic code of ethics, or statement of principles for social work, would pay greater attention to the agency and societal context within which social work is practised. The broad areas that might be covered by such a statement of principles, might include the following:

1 Duties to clients: this would include many of the 'Biestekian'-type principles, and those listed in the existing code, such as respecting clients as people with rights to make their own decisions and choices; being honest with clients; not discriminating on grounds of race, age, sex, class, or ability; respecting confidentiality; and being non-judgemental. Clients have a right to such treatment, including the right to complain.

2 Duties to society: for example, executing the responsibilities of local authority social services departments as laid down by statute; maintaining social order; promoting the greatest good of the greatest number of people.

3 Duties to the agency/employer: for example, carrying out the duties as described in the job description; following prescribed rules and procedures; safeguarding the reputation of the agency; distributing service and goods fairly between clients.

4 Duties to the profession: for example, upholding the 'good name' or credibility of social work by maintaining effective and ethical standards of practice.

5 Rights of the social worker: social workers as people, have rights to be treated with respect; as employees they have contractual rights to certain working conditions; this should include protection from violence.

Obviously none of these areas is straightforward and non-controversial. Each statement needs clarifying and even then will be open to interpretation. For example, 'clients' rights to make their own decisions' needs clarification as to how far the social worker should go to provide information and resources to broaden the scope of a client's choice. The principle will also have to be qualified; for example, clients' rights to have their own choices respected may be limited if the interests of other people, or of themselves, are threatened, or if they are judged incapable of making rational decisions. There may be conflict between two sets of duties. For example the duty to promote client self-determination may conflict with the duty to society to maintain the existing social order in the case of deciding whether compulsorily to admit someone to psychiatric hospital. Duties to the agency may conflict with duties to clients. For example, safeguarding the reputation of the agency might entail allowing a client less freedom in order to minimize the risks of a scandal (for example, acting cautiously in cases of suspected child abuse). Another area of conflict may occur when an agency requires a social worker to act contrary to the principles of the profession – for example, in allowing very easy and wide access to confidential information in clients' files to any social worker, doctor or health visitor.

There will also be cases when a social worker's personal moral principles (e.g. anti-abortion) may conflict with principles of the profession (e.g. self-determination of a pregnant client), or when a worker seriously contravenes the code, perhaps by revealing confidential information to the press or exhibiting racial discrimination in allocating resources. Such conflicts are usually resolved through conscientious reflection by social workers (who come to the work with their own sets of values reflecting both societal values and their political or religious beliefs), through discussion with colleagues, departmental disciplinary proceedings, or, in extreme cases, through legal action. The existing code of ethics appears to play very little part in these deliberations; indeed, it applies only to BASW members and has never been used as a basis for disciplinary action.

Perhaps one should ask if there is a case for a universal, nationally agreed and enforceable code of ethics for social work? In medicine, there is a General Council, established by Act of Parliament, which holds a register of qualified practitioners and has the power to strike them off for professional misconduct (British Medical Association 1980: 10). It could be claimed that this would be in the interests of clients (who could lodge complaints) and of the profession (to maintain standards and strength in an increasingly hostile climate). On the other hand, many social workers would reject such a proposal as a step more towards professional elitism than a genuine empowering of clients. Whether or not such a system is desirable, its implementation would require restructuring the training, employment and status of social workers, as well as giving them more professional autonomy; this seems highly unlikely given the current governmental ethos of de-professionalization and a particular distrust of welfare professionals. Consequently a more effective starting-point would be an integration of ethics into social work theory and practice, especially on professional training courses, and a clearer, more realistic statement of ethical principles by BASW to be used as a basis for all agencies to establish codes of practice.

Codes of practice

Once the ethical framework for social work is made clearer, it then becomes easier to operationalize some of the principles and to begin to put some practical flesh on the ethical bones. One way of moving from general ethical principles to practice is through the drawing up of codes of practice. It is interesting to note that the code of ethics for counselling is published alongside a brief code of practice which states, for example, that the counsellor should request permission to confer with other professionals, clarify the number and duration of sessions, and make explicit the nature of any conflict between obligations to an employing agency and to the client. Obviously there are many differences between the role and duties of a statutory social worker and those of a counsellor who may be independent or working for a voluntary agency, whose involvement with a client may frequently be at the client's request and where it is easier to determine who the client is. Nevertheless, a similar code of practice for social workers might be helpful both to social workers and clients.

There is, in fact, a growing trend in social work towards establishing codes and procedures for practice. This reflects both an increasing concern with protecting and operationalizing clients' rights and also a desire to protect the reputation and interests of agencies. There has been a movement in recent years towards what BASW has termed 'the new professionalism', based on the idea of clients as consumers of a service, who have the right to be treated as equal citizens (BASW 1989: 1; Leslie 1989). Examples include allowing clients access to their files, establishing complaints procedures and the use of contracts in social work. In each case, the rights of the clients are operationalized through a set of procedures laid down by an agency. The extent to which clients' rights are actually respected or protected depends upon how the procedures are designed and publicized, and how committed the agency is to putting them into practice. For example, many of the procedures for clients to gain access to files (now a legal right) are ill-publicized, cumbersome and off-putting, and seem to take more account of agency interests (such as convenience, use of staff time, fear of redress by clients) than client rights. There is similar controversy over the use of contracts in social work – as to whether they are, or indeed can be, in the interests of clients, given the unequal power structure of the social worker–client relationship (Corden and Preston-Shoot 1987; 1988; Rojeck and Collins 1987; 1988). It has also been argued that contracts tend to focus on individual and personal problems and rarely bring in the societal context of class inequality, patriarchy or racism (Rojeck and Collins 1987). Whatever view one holds on how these procedures work in practice, there is no doubt that respecting clients as people must involve giving them as much information as possible about what the purpose of social work involvement is, whether it is voluntary or involuntary, to what extent confidential information will in fact be kept secret and what they can do if they have a complaint about a worker or the service.

It is important to link such procedures and codes to the stated ethical principles underlying social work. Otherwise we will see a continued piecemeal growth of rule books, which may be contradictory and which reduce the scope of social workers' professional judgement. In some areas of the work, particularly child abuse, there has been a massive growth in sets of rules, procedures, guidelines and handbooks, the aim of which is much more about the protection of agencies and workers than clients (Harris 1987). This is not surprising, nor is it unjustified, given the unrealistic expectations that seem to be placed on social workers. However, it is unrealistic to think that the implementation of the recommendations of each new child abuse inquiry will actually solve the problems for social workers. Despite recommendations for improved guidelines, more inter-agency collaboration, better training or changes in the law, the role of the social worker remains fundamentally the same – to balance the contradictions and tensions within society itself between promoting individual welfare and maintaining the existing social and economic order. No matter how many new procedures or rules are introduced, the ethical questions are still there: for example, just how much interference by the state in family life is justified; what are the rights of children and how are they to be balanced against the rights of parents? The judgements involved, I would argue as a consequence, are essentially ethical rather than practical.

Conclusion

It is important for individual social workers to have thought about these issues and to know where they stand on them. It is also important for the profession to make some clear and accessible statements on ethics. The time seems particularly ripe at present, with a number of developments in practice, in public opinion, and in theory which have ethical implications. There is an increasing concern with non-discriminatory practice – anti-racist work in particular. There is a growing emphasis on clients' (or consumers') rights and with client participation and empowerment. Changes are proposed in children's legal rights, with a shifting emphasis towards parental responsibilities (as opposed to rights) and there is a growing literature in the legal field on children's rights (for example, Franklin 1986; Bainham 1988; Children's Legal Centre 1988). The publicity attaching to recent child abuse cases has thrown up many questions regarding social workers' rights to intervene and to whom they owe duties (whether to society, parents or children). At the same time, as already noted, several texts focusing specifically on ethical and value issues in social work have been published. Yet there seems to have been little cross-fertilization between the discussion of ethical issues and issues in current policy and practice. If the 'new professionalism' in social work is to constitute a genuine empowering of clients, as opposed to a growing defensiveness by an arm of an increasingly repressive and minimalized state, then it would benefit from clear underpinnings in a set of well-articulated ethical principles.

References

Bailey, R. and Brake, M. (1980) *Radical Social Work and Practice*, London: Edward Arnold.

Bainham, A. (1988) *Children, Parents and the State*, London: Sweet & Maxwell.

Banks, S. J. (1985) *Ethics and the Social Worker*, unpublished MSW thesis, University of York.

BASW (British Association of Social Workers) (1977) *The Social Work Task*, Birmingham: BASW.

—— (1988) *A Code of Ethics for Social Work*, Birmingham: BASW.

—— (1989) *Rights, Responsibilities and Remedies*, Birmingham: BASW.

Berlin, I. (1975) 'Two concepts of liberty', in F. E. McDermott (ed.) *Self-Determination in Social Work*, London: Routledge & Kegan Paul.

Biestek, F. (1957) *The Casework Relationship*, Chicago, Ill: Loyola University Press.

Bok, S. (1980) *Lying: Moral Choice in Public and Private Life*, London: Quartet.

Bolger, S., Corrigan, P., Docking, J. and Frost, N. (1981) *Towards Socialist Welfare Work*, London: Macmillan.

Breakwell, G. M. and Rowett, C. (1982) *Social Work: The Social Psychological Approach*, Wokingham: Van Nostrand Reinhold.

British Association for Counselling (1984) *Code of Ethics and Practice for Counsellors*, Rugby: BAC.

British Medical Association (1980) *The Handbook of Medical Ethics*, London: BMA.

Butrym, Z. (1976) *The Nature of Social Work*, London: Macmillan.

Campbell, A. V. (1984) *Moral Dilemmas in Medicine: A Coursebook in Ethics for Doctors and Nurses*, Edinburgh: Churchill Livingstone.

CCETSW (Central Council for Education and Training in Social Work) (1976) *Values in Social Work*, London: CCETSW.

Children's Legal Centre (1988) 'Children's rights after Cleveland', *Childright* 50: 13–20.

Clark, C. with Asquith, S. (1985) *Social Work and Social Philosophy*, London: Routledge & Kegan Paul.

Corden, J. and Preston-Shoot, M. (1987) 'Contract or con trick? A reply to Rojeck and Collins', *British Journal of Social Work* 17: 535–43.
—— (1988) 'Contract or con trick? A postscript', *British Journal of Social Work* 18: 623–37.
Corrigan, P. and Leonard, P. (1978) *Social Work Practice Under Capitalism: A Marxist Approach*, London: Macmillan.
Davies, M. (1981) *The Essential Social Worker: A Guide to Positive Practice*, London: Heinemann.
Downie, R. S. and Telfer, E. (1969) *Respect for Persons*, London: Routledge & Kegan Paul.
—— (1980) *Caring and Curing*, London: Methuen.
Fisk, M. (1980) *Ethics and Society*, Brighton: Harvester.
Frankena, W. (1973) *Ethics*, Englewood Cliffs, NJ: Prentice-Hall.
Franklin, B. (ed.) (1986) *The Rights of Children*, Oxford: Blackwell.
George, V. and Wilding, P. (1985) *Ideology and Social Welfare*, London: Routledge & Kegan Paul.
Hare, R. M. (1963) *Freedom and Reason*, Oxford: Clarendon Press.
Harris, N. (1987) 'Defensive social work', *British Journal of Social Work* 17: 61–9.
Horne, M. (1987) *Values in Social Work*, Aldershot: Wildwood House.
Howe, D. (1987) *An Introduction to Social Work Theory*, Aldershot: Wildwood House.
Jones, D., Pickett, J., Oates, M. R. and Barbor, P. (1987) *Understanding Child Abuse*, London: Macmillan.
Kamenka, E. (1969) *Marxism and Ethics*, London: Macmillan.
Kant, I. (1964) *Groundwork of the Metaphysics of Morals*, New York: Harper & Row.
Leighton, N., Stalley, R. and Watson, D. (1982) *Rights and Responsibilities*, London: Heinemann.
Leslie, A. (1989) 'A challenge to the system', *Social Work Today* 9 February: 22–3.
Lukes, S. (1973) *Individualism*, Oxford: Blackwell.
—— (1985) *Marxism and Morality*, Oxford: University Press.
McDermott, F. E. (1975) 'Against the persuasive definition of self-determination', in F. E. McDermott (ed.) *Self-Determination in Social Work*, London: Routledge & Kegan Paul.
Marx, K. and Engels, F. (1848) *Manifesto of the Communist Party*, in K. Marx and F. Engels (1975–) *Collected Works, Vol. 6*, London: Lawrence & Wishart.
Mill, J. S. (1972) *Utilitarianism, on Liberty and Considerations on Representative Government*, London: Dent.
Moffett, J. (1968) *Concepts of Casework Treatment*, London: Routledge & Kegan Paul.
Nielson, K. (1986) 'Marxism, morality and moral philosophy', in J. Demarco and R. Fox (eds) *New Directions in Ethics*, London: Routledge & Kegan Paul.
NISW (National Institute of Social Work) (1982) *Social Workers: Their Roles and Tasks*, Barclay Report, London: Bedford Square Press.
Norman, R. (1983) *The Moral Philosophers*, Oxford: Clarendon Press.
O'Connor, J. (1973) *The Fiscal Crisis of the State*, New York: St Martin's Press.
Ollman, B. (1976) *Alienation: Marx's Conception of Man in Capitalist Society*, Cambridge University Press.
Payne, M. (1985) 'The code of ethics, the social work manager and the organisation', in D. Watson (ed.) *A Code of Ethics for Social Work: The Second Step*, London: Routledge & Kegan Paul.
Pincus, A. and Minahan, A. (1973) *Social Work Practice*, Itasca, Illinois: F.E. Peacock.
Plant, R. (1970) *Social and Moral Theory in Casework*, London: Routledge & Kegan Paul.
Ragg, N. (1977) *People not Cases*, London: Routledge & Kegan Paul.

Raphael, D. D. (1981) *Moral Philosophy*, Oxford University Press.

Rhodes, M. (1986) *Ethical Dilemmas in Social Work Practice*, Boston, Mass: Routledge & Kegan Paul.

Rice, D. (1975) 'The code: a voice for approval', *Social Work Today*, 18 October: 381–2.

Rojeck, C. and Collins, S. (1987) 'Contract or con trick', *British Journal of Social Work* 17: 199–211.

—— (1988) 'Contract or con trick revisited', *British Journal of Social Work* 18: 611–22.

Simpkin, M. (1983) *Trapped Within Welfare*, London: Macmillan.

Smart, J. J. C. and Williams, B. (1973) *Utilitarianism, For and Against*, Cambridge University Press.

Statham, D. (1978) *Radicals in Social Work*, London: Routledge & Kegan Paul.

Sutherland, J. K. (1985) 'A doctor looks at a code of ethics for social work', in D. Watson (ed.) *A Code of Ethics for Social Work: The Second Step*, London: Routledge & Kegan Paul.

Timms, N. (1983) *Social Work Values*, London: Routledge & Kegan Paul.

Warnock, G. J. (1967) *Contemporary Moral Philosophy*, London: Macmillan.

Watson, D. (1985) 'What's the point of a code of ethics for social work?' in D. Watson (ed.) *A Code of Ethics for Social Work: the Second Step*, London: Routledge & Kegan Paul.

9
Language for autonomy

Ahmed Gurnah

'Hapana marefu yasiyo na ncha'

(Kiswahili proverb)

Community language schools occupy a special place in the evolving politics of black people in Britain, and yet little is known about them. It is where many of the black young women and men first acquire social, political and cultural self-confidence; for some it is also where they learn to take up and participate in their parents' social and political struggles. The reports concerning the Schools Council Mother Tongue Project (Tansley and Craft 1984) appear to conflict with black people's experiences of local education authorities (LEAs). The one HMI report on this subject is somewhat dated and bears the imprint of the DES (HMI 1984). While both are sympathetic to the teaching of mother tongue, their orientation is not that of the communities, but, rather, one which sets out to praise LEA contribution to the schools and their commitment to black people. From what *is* known of them, some people find it hard to understand why so much is made of the mother-tongue schools by black communities. Many people have stereotypical and routinely racist views of them; they are often easily dismissed as backward and tyrannical. The community language schools are, in fact, badly resourced; their teaching methods, standards, curricula and the general learning milieu and experience of children and adults who attend them, all come woefully short of what educators would these days consider sound learning (Shaif 1989). But much of that is due to state neglect of the education they provide, rather than resulting from deliberate philosophical stances in the black communities.

The resourcing of these schools is pitiful. Most of them are run on a few hundred pounds per year grant aid given to them by reluctant local authorities, occasionally enhanced by small contributions from working-class or un-employed black men and women. The teachers in these schools are usually enthusiastic women volunteers, mullas, university students or community activists, all of whom have most likely had no formal training to teach children or adults (CRE 1983: 1, 5 and 12). Teaching methods and the curricula are therefore often traditional, disorganized or repetitive, as they are hardly ever backed up by effective teaching materials or aids. Meanwhile the learning environment too is generally uncomfortable and unattractive.

When black men and women in the communities are asked to justify retaining such schools, their replies contain deep conviction and determination to keep them open. What may seem more puzzling is that both young and old people continue to attend these schools after school or work, and sometimes on three or four occasions per week. Furthermore, despite all the listed disadvantages, large numbers of young men and women learn mother tongue and some older people pick up some English from these schools, which is often more than many state schools and adult education services have been able to achieve, and certainly not on such meagre resources.

What is the issue?

So what is so compelling about these schools? Why are they so successful despite being neglected by LEAs and the DES? What is it about them that commands strong loyalty and raises such passions? In an attempt to give answers to these questions, I shall argue that the survival and development of community language schools has significance far beyond their appearance and resourcing. Their particular appeal lies in offering the mother-tongue language learning which state schools fail to provide. Additionally, they make available a wide range of educational, political, religious and cultural services. These enhance the development of girls and boys in primary and secondary schools by fostering a more mature relationship with their parents. The community schools' curriculum provides for mother tongue and some English development and includes elements which constitute counterweight to state school, college and societal racism. The linguistic and cultural affirmation that is the trade-mark of these schools not only helps to maintain and develop a knowledge base, but also reasserts the implicit rationality that is appropriate to black communities in struggle. Subsequently, they foster internationalism that brings back a Third World perspective on to the agenda of British black people. Thus, the potential of influencing state schools and colleges to move in similar directions is greatly increased by the existence and flourishing of community language schools.

In short, while these communities preserve what is specific about them through their schools and maintain a sense of autonomy of their group, they are simultaneously also constructing the *other*, to relate to, to engage with and maybe struggle against, or even overcome. Ultimately, the emergence of this contrast between black groups and others is about the recognition of own rights before joining in and becoming part of the larger community (Cabral 1973; Levi-Strauss 1966). But it is an organized merger, a rational and controlled participation, a participation of people who have learnt in struggle, often collectively transgressing age and gender cleavages. It would not be an exaggeration to claim that for many black groups the attempts in setting up such schools is often the first and main context through which they collectively come in contact and learn to tangle with the LEA. The lessons that are learnt from this language struggle can usually be transferred into their other struggles and be generalized to benefit the British educational system as a whole. In sum, for many black communities, the experience of setting up these schools represents the symbolic instigation and reinforcement of the process of black community development: it is a cultural and social regeneration in a hostile foreign country. Subsequently, the success of these independent schools may well serve to make British society much less parochial; but that, to some extent, would depend on how LEAs and educational institutions respond to their challenge. In addition, many of these schools are co-educational and can therefore provide a context for examining gender equality from a very early age, but without having to cope with the racist stereotypes usually embedded in some of the discussions when conducted by the state sector.

I want to make this argument in stages. First, I shall briefly outline the ambiguous policy attitudes and assumptions towards mother-tongue teaching, support and backing for black cultural traditions held by the DES, LEAs and the Home Office. Second, I shall present some background facts and figures that are known about them. Third, I shall then examine why these schools become necessary for boys and girls, what is interesting in their curriculum, who attends the schools, and evaluate what they are offered when they get there. Fourth, in order to make this review come alive, I shall focus on the schools run by the Yemenis of Sheffield, both because they are some of the most interesting and best organized in Britain and in order to examine the phenomenon in detail. Finally, I shall outline the political, linguistic and cultural significance of the schools for black people in Britain and for state educational institutions in the long run, by generalizing from the specific observations above.

Policy background

The absence of DES and LEA policy and resourcing strategies for community language schools is very instructive. As the Commission for Racial Equality observes, however, 'the linguistic diversity of British society has so far been either ignored or viewed as a liability rather than as a national resource' (CRE 1983: 1). But articles of the European Commission Directive of July 1977 required member states to

> in accordance with national circumstances and legal system, and in cooperation with States of origin, take appropriate measures to promote, in accordance with normal education, teaching of the mother tongue and culture of the country of origin for the children.
>
> (quoted in DES 1981: 5)

The intentions of so directing member states is 'principally to facilitating their [children's] reintegration into the Member State of origin' (DES 1981: 4). But the DES in its 'School Curriculum' document insists that this diversity of languages 'constitutes a valuable resource' for the children and the nation and seeks their accommodation in modern language programmes so that 'this resource does not whither away' (quoted in CRE 1983: 15). In its Circular 5/81, however, the DES dilutes this firm stand and the EC Directive in the advice it gives LEAs whom they ask to 'promote mother tongue and culture teaching in co-ordination with normal education . . . during or outside schools hours'. Then the Circular reminds LEAs that 'they are not required to give such tuition to all individuals as of right' (DES 1981: 2). In addition, the DES has, so far, not identified much funding for the implementation of Article 3 of the Directive (CRE 1983) which, as subsequent events show, means that LEAs are extremely unlikely to take much notice of it. It did not help that the Home Affairs Select Committee Report of 1981 states 'we are not convinced either that a local education authority is under any obligation to provide mother tongue teaching or that it is necessarily in the general interest that they should do so' (quoted in CRE 1983: 17).

This ambiguity about mother-tongue teaching still continues at the DES and no clear policies have come from there. Its present views were admirably summarized by an HMI at a recent Secondary Examination Council conference. In answer to questions about the place of community languages in the secondary curriculum he confirmed that the government was convinced of the need to maintain black community languages, but that was the responsibility of the communities themselves. It has always been difficult to find the best 'slot' for them in the national curriculum. The problem is therefore left to LEAs and individual schools, and presumably outside the national curriculum (*Education* 21.10.88).

The prospect of achieving this in schools without including community languages in the national curriculum and identifying specific resources to support their syllabus is very slim indeed, which is probably why the HMI appears to be advising black parents to teach their children mother tongue at home, and expect nothing from state education. One never hears, for example, that the teaching of English should be left to parents. Indeed, a great deal of effort and thought is given and (quite rightly) matching resources are linked to the teaching of English in state schools. In that context, though LEAs have given qualified support to the teaching of community languages and 'work in education for a multi-racial society', mother-tongue teaching and bilingual education are usually excluded from this (CRE 1983: 17).

This is not a new problem; LEA policies for community languages, or the absence of them, has caused concern in the black communities for many years. The recent howls from various urban LEAs about the monstrosity of this government's refusal to support community languages under Section 11 of the Local Government Act 1966 thus sound very hollow. For even when it was possible to do something about community languages, it was impossible to find many LEAs that would support even modest developments. Possibilities included diversifying the profile of modern and foreign language teachers; introducing language assistants and probationers; setting up language awareness and tasters; affecting exchange of students with other countries and even simply developing a more realistic grant aid budget for communities themselves to subsidize the state by providing the service themselves. The plea has always been that no extra funding can be bound to cover this priority area. But funding always seems to appear for other priority areas. Given the relatively small amounts needed for this work to be done, that rather more correctly reflects a lack of conviction or absence of policy to support this teaching than absence of funding (see Brumfit *et al.* 1985).

Given the attitudes in the DES, and the LEAs referred to, it is therefore not surprising that the Home Office has also refused to fund this work any longer under Section 11, though this funding was set aside specifically to assist in the black community development in Britain. The refusal to fund the teaching of community languages by the Home Office thus completes the vicious circle started by the DES and LEAs. For faced with the prospect of providing language services to black people without receiving 75 per cent extra funding from the Home Office, very few LEAs are willing to meet their moral, educational and legal duty to give foundational education to black children. The fact is, even when the funding was available, it was quite hard to get LEAs to apply for it and to use it for black people and not on some multi-cultural or anti-racist education for white people. Nevertheless, the possibility of this funding did constitute a powerful argument for LEA compliance. Its withdrawal now, equally, poses a compelling disincentive to finance the development of community language teaching.

Resourcing background

The absence of comprehensive policy nationally or locally on voluntary schools or mother-tongue teaching has resourcing implications. Most urban authorities give direct grants or support in kind to black community groups. The support will take the form of free or cheap accommodation, materials, lighting and heating or money for a few part-time teaching hours per week. The average total support to voluntary community language schools per annum amounts from the equivalent of one to three full-time teaching salaries. This is the situation in Brent, Wolverhampton, Haringey, Bradford, Sandwell and Sheffield, where it can probably be said there is greater understanding of the issues. A recent survey of these schools by the Sheffield LEA and South Yorkshire Open College Federation (Shaif 1989) gives us some very detailed information.

In Sheffield sixty-two languages other than English are spoken by school children (City of Sheffield 1988). There are between thirty-one and forty functioning community language schools in the city. Of the 4,731 bilingual pupils in the city, 1,560 children (811 male and 749 female) attend the thirty-one surveyed schools. There are only ninety tutors for these schools, 95 per cent of whom are unpaid volunteers. The City Council gave a grant of £14,100 to twenty of these schools in 1988 as part of its Community Education allocation. There were two additional amounts of £3,500 from the Schools Budget, and £2,100 as a one-off amount from the Youth Service Budget, making a total of £19,700 per annum (Shaif 1989: para 2). Of the buildings used in 1988 by the community language schools, 60 per cent were poorly maintained and lack basic amenities. Until this year, there was no in-service training or advisory support for volunteer teachers and 50 per cent of the tutors are not even paid bus fares.

In over 90% of the schools there is a total absence of curriculum. The lack of resources and inadequate funding makes this problem even worse. The teaching approaches were found to be rigid and traditional in style. There is great emphasis on reading aloud in front of the class, copying from outdated books and memory work. Some of the children were unsure what it was they were memorising.

(Shaif 1989: para 4)

But for all this deprivation 'a striking feature found in this review is the readiness of children to respond to their teachers, and they evidently worked extremely hard with great enthusiasm' (Shaif 1989: para 4). Some groups complained that they had no desks, chairs or blackboards and children sit on the floor. 'Some schools have no books at all, in others one book could be used for the whole class as a point of reference'; despite all this hardship

30% of the community language schools operate 5 evenings a week, some open at weekends and others are open 3 evenings a week. Four of the classes visited are open 7 days a week during the holidays. Class sizes varied: where in some classes there are as many as 70 children, in others I found about 20 children. Most classes are overcrowded.

(Shaif 1989: para 4)

These Victorian conditions have not abated attendance, which is 'excellent' for all schools visited. Standards varied: older children were able to speak mother tongue and are 'used as interpreters and translators by their parents'. The extra work, furthermore, did not appear to affect their standard schooling adversely, though 'some consideration must be given to how state schools can reduce this burden on the children by providing standard provisions' (Shaif 1989: para 4).

Why are they necessary?

To put it simply, these schools are necessary not least because a lot of local authorities offer none or very little provision in community languages: they are a self-help response. Shaif observed that 90 per cent of the classes are organized and managed by 'elected management committees of their respective centres' and the classes themselves are run by parents and volunteers.

There is a great deal of effort by members of the community in continuing to develop their educational provision. Many of them have made donations to keep the school functioning, others have used their own transport and energies to ensure continuity. All those visited showed a great deal of commitment to maintain existing provision.

(Shaif 1989: para 5)

It is a commitment that is not lost on the young men and women. They observe their uneducated, often unemployed parents making sacrifices to ensure they learn their mother tongue: they remember this as adults and pick up the responsibility.

For most LEAs too, notions of culture, learning, personal and intellectual development and communal development for black people are already defined by their traditional service strategies and give no recognition to minorities' versions of these. Some progressive authorities may well insist on multi-cultural or anti-racist education in their schools or colleges, or give curricula space to world studies, and certainly not tolerate overt racism, but when it is all said and done, what this adds up to is educating *white* and not black people. Some black people may receive English as a second language support delivered, still, by mostly monolingual teachers. In short, the multi-cultural and anti-racist curriculum is defined by white teachers and educators for the benefit of white communities. In itself, there is nothing wrong with this as long as LEAs did not continue to ignore black needs. If we were seeking to be unkind, we can make a parallel to our colonial experience and find that even this was more enlightened in some ways than the present situation.

During the time of British foreign adventures abroad, the state, educational and publishing institutions provided plenty of multi-cultural education at home. Then, as now, this information and education about the Third World was not necessarily to benefit Third World people here or there, but to humanize attitudes at home. Past and present accounts of black people are exotic and a little voyeuristic. Given the levels of colonial consciousness, in fact, those accounts would appear more thorough and scholarly than a lot of the superficial material that presently passes for multi-cultural education or world studies today (see Frazer 1915; Malinowski 1954; Evans-Prichard 1941). There was no anti-racist education then, but equivalent rhetoric in the form of liberal values was abundant. The concern was expressed in terms of accepting the responsibility for the welfare of Blacks in their dominions, colonies or commonwealth, but made no more resources available to black people than those uttering anti-racist slogans today, but readily exploited their labour and resources instead. Then and now, cultural, personal and intellectual development, forms and content of learning, are all measured according to time-honoured and proven standards of European education and worth. Within their framework, community languages appear to have even lower status now to an average teacher, than they had to an army officer of the Raj.

What was required then in the colonies, and is desperately needed now in Britain, is a decent education for black people. Education which addresses their concerns and explores their cultures as they enjoy and understand them, from their own perspective and critically. This task was not accomplished by anthropology and much of contemporary British development studies in its various political shades still tell the story that will interest fellow white professionals at home than say much that is worthwhile to working-class black and white people about other societies (Gurnah 1985). What is still absent is the critical learning that celebrates their languages, poetry and drama, and promotes an honest comprehension of Third World people's social arrangements and world views. Indeed in the colonies, both because they posed a lesser linguistic threat and the threat was in any case a fair distance from Britons, the British state was more willing for local languages to be part of the curriculum. Interestingly, however, these languages were not represented as Urdu, or

Kiswahili or Arabic or Hausa, but as the so-called 'vernacular' which, according to the dictionary translates as 'native' or 'native dialect'. Indeed, the Cambridge Overseas Examination Board allowed O levels to be taken in these languages, but usually not A levels for many of them. But even then universities in Britain did not consider O or A levels in these languages to be in themselves admissible qualifications for pursuing further and higher studies in the same way as were English Language and Literature or Science and Mathematics. During the colonial era, the British educational establishment attached little status to these languages. Subsequently, when students study them and wish to use them as qualifications for access to further and higher education *in their own countries*, they were denied this right by the colonial authority. While the British colonial education authorities were, on the whole, prepared to concede to the teaching of vernacular or 'native dialects' and in primary schools through them, and allow students to take O and A level examinations in them, it was thought a little excessive to make passes in these languages legitimate qualifications for further studies.

If this behaviour was unacceptable in the colonies, it becomes scandalous that even in those areas of high black populations, very few schools or colleges in Britain today routinely offer students Urdu, Creole or Arabic on their GCSE syllabuses. It is partly this devaluation and neglect of Third World languages and the culture, knowledge and rationality that goes with them from the British curriculum, which has stimulated many black groups to set up community language schools and passionately defend their continued existence, regardless of quality.

> On the issue of community language schools the *relationships between the black community and the LEA* is quite tense. All those visited felt that the budget . . . is too small [and] unconnected to state schools.
>
> (Shaif 1989: para 5)

There is another reason why these schools are necessary. We saw from the Sheffield Survey of 31 schools that they are attended by 811 boys or young men and 749 girls or young women learners. Whether deliberately or not, these schools provide both young people and their parents the opportunity to re-examine traditional values on gender equality in a safe environment. The discussions of, and relationship accommodations towards, greater equality are evident and fruitful. Furthermore, they significantly do not in this case get mixed up with standard racist stereotype criticisms which sometimes accompany legitimate criticisms of male domination of all societies. In community language schools, black girls and young women collectively get the opportunity to begin to share their grievances, construct counter positions, demand equality of treatment and challenge male domination. It must not be imagined that these struggles are any less painful for those involved than any other context. The difference here is that young black women are beginning to unite against sexism without rupturing other solidarities they value in the black community. The experience, furthermore, forces the boys and young men to question given positions and reconstitute themselves.

These are yet more reasons why black communities are so determined to set up voluntary schools despite inadequacy of resources. What has to be understood clearly, however, is that this attitude towards community languages is merely symptomatic of a whole range of other views about black cultural traditions and reflects strongly on a lack of interest by British educators in the knowledge, science and rationality they contain.

Yemenis of Sheffield

Yemenis of Sheffield have run mother-tongue classes since the early 1970s. There are two groups; the one from the South Yemen is represented by the Yemeni Community Association and from the North by Yemeni IG Union. In the context of Sheffield, the two groups are becoming increasingly politically allied and seek closer operational links. For the moment, however, they run separate language classes for 80 children each (equally divided between male and females) from the ages of 7 to 17 years old. The City Council has been grant-aiding both groups these last few years and in 1988 each received £1,800. The Yemeni Community Association classes, on which I shall concentrate my comments, meet three nights per week, Monday to Wednesday, at Crookesmoor Middle School, from 6 pm to 8 pm. The community school employs five teachers and two minibus drivers who collect and return children and students to their homes for every session. The Yemeni IG Union holds classes five nights per week, from Monday to Friday, at Earl Marshal Education Centre, from 6 pm to 8 pm and employ four teachers.

Background to the Yemeni community in Sheffield

There are about 2,000 Yemenis presently living in Sheffield. In the 1970s, before the full devastation of the steel and engineering industries was experienced by the City, many more Yemeni families lived and worked there. According to estimates compiled from Association advice centres and membership registers, there must have been up to 5,000 Yemenis in Sheffield in 1979. Almost all of them were working class and the majority of the employable men did unskilled jobs in heavy industry. Though many returned to the Yemen after the closure of heavy industry, a recent City Council survey (Yemeni Community Profile) showed that over 70 per cent of those still here have remained unemployed. It confirmed that as many as 87 per cent of the Yemeni men and women in Sheffield needed literacy and oracy education in English at some level. Of those questioned, 95 per cent favoured and supported the proposed joint LEA/community Yemeni Literacy Campaign.

What this profile confirmed is that, despite the fact that Yemenis have lived in Sheffield since the 1950s and contributed to the local and national economy, the LEA (and its adult and college services) has largely failed to address their educational needs anywhere at the level and scale required by these statistics. Equally, it has still not appointed a single full-time teacher of Arabic in any school or college in the city, despite the fact that thousands of Yemeni children went through these schools and 250 are doing so presently, with a complementary number in colleges. It was these sorts of considerations that forced this and other black communities in the city to set up their own mother-tongue provision, without finance or educational expertise, back in the early 1970s.

I interviewed thirty past and present female and male users of community language schools from the Yemeni community aged between 12 and 17 years. I shall here concentrate on four of them represented by the names of Moh'd (14 years), Leila (16 years), Fatma (16 years) and Abdul Razak (30 years). I have selected these four both because they presented the collective view of the interviewees but also because I had conducted more detailed follow-up interviews with them. I have chosen these standard Arabic names to preserve their anonymity. All the reference to these four names are from the interviews.

Reflections of the community

The struggles around the establishment of these schools have made an important contribution to the development of the Yemeni community. Apparently the struggle to build the Yemeni school and community centre gave members of the Yemeni Community Association the experience on

> how to be accountable, how to elect, how to nominate, how to integrate teachers, run minibuses . . . little detailed things, very important technical things and knowledge, the know how and experience of setting up the school, interview teachers, recruit volunteers, relating to State school headteachers and LEA representatives, when to open and close schools.
>
> (Abdul Razak)

Many in the community learnt about their rights, officer and member racism in the Council, and increasingly what are the most effective ways of getting those rights and how to deal with institutional racism. It would appear that the community was in constant struggle with Sheffield City Council from 1972 to 1984 'to try and get the Council to recognize the Yemeni Community Association . . . its management committee and fund its advice centre' (Abdul Razak). It is a struggle that still continues and does not occupy only the older members of the community, but often serve as a bond with young people. It would be no exaggeration, then, to suggest that the establishment of these schools has significant community development implications.

The contact with the Council did not really start until the early 1980s. For the community, this turned out to be a mixed experience. In the first instance, it was an initiation into the complex world of bidding for grants and Council services. The community then realized that unless it organized itself and developed some expertise in acquiring legitimate rights and resources, as confirmed by past experience, nobody else was going to do it for them. Thus, in the last 5–7 years the development of structures, personnel and ideas in the community has led to an identification of what people's needs are and ways of fighting for services. Young men and women increasingly play an important role in these developments. The contact with the Council has also led to disenchantment, to a loss of innocence. As a community group, the Yemeni Community Association fully supports the Socialist Republic of South Yemen.

Its present management committee is made up entirely of working-class (mostly) unemployed, unskilled workers in need of literacy education. Their view of the City Council was positive because of its reputation as a left-wing authority. The community contact with some officials and members, however, has been unfortunate and has made many of them revise their views of some of the councillors and officers.

Thus loss of innocence too is positive. It has not only made the community more alert about their rights and less naive about the Council but also reaffirmed their commitment and determination to make their voluntary services, particularly the language schools, successful and lasting. Now disenchanted, men and women in the community are learning ways of putting the right political pressure in appropriate sections of the Council. More importantly, they realize that they neither have to go without, nor depend entirely on the local authority for all their needs. Thought is going into the development of self-help projects, women's independent organizations, young people's recreation, external funding and making alliances with other groups and sympathetic members and officers in the city.

The establishment of these schools, and the search for resources to run them, has additionally brought this issue of education for adults forward and has brought about the Yemeni Literacy Campaign. The Literacy Campaign has been kept alive by the work of eight heroic young women and four young men, who have transformed community expectation. Such projects, though modest still, are providing working-class Yemeni men and women with knowledge and expertise of officialdom that is later bound to be used to deal with the greater problems of unemployment, retraining and general disadvantage in the Yemeni community. Greater numbers of younger Yemenis are getting involved in taking on the struggle in the community. Many are learning the tactics of how to get heard by headteachers or housing officers. Some of these issues, furthermore, get back to the younger Yemenis through the language schools, when it concerns their resourcing. Women have set up their own management committee, which organizes their own education forums, campaigns for resources from the Council and increasingly challenge male power at the community centre. But can these broader community development issues justify the continuation of such schools deprived of teachers, pedagogy, resources and curriculum? The answer to this question may be connected with the other services the community language schools provide.

Educational, political, religious and cultural studies

The general impression I got of the Yemeni school from the students was complex and ambiguous. They were, in the first instance, very positive.

> I was very happy when I used to go to those schools. It was a way of finding out more about my community, more about my culture, more about my language.

> (Abdul Razak)

In addition, that experience stimulated Abdul Razak to find out more about Yemen and its revolution. He became obsessed about the fact that working-class Yemenis drove the British out of Aden in 1967.

> How did we do it? From what I learnt in the mainstream school, I thought that was impossible: that we could kick anybody out . . . so I started asking people in the community.

He also asked his state school teachers and found that the untutored members of the community were, in fact, more knowledgeable on these issues that obsessed him than his teachers. This too was a new experience for him. In this case, at least, the community language school not only reaffirmed Abdul Razak's cultural background, but also led to his politicization and increased his motivation to learn.

> That gave me a lot of enthusiasm to go and change and fight, you know . . . the achievements of those schools reflect the struggles of our community.
>
> (Abdul Razak)

Fatma was more ambiguous, but does recall at the age of 11 when

> we used to really like it . . . I remember when I used to get home from school and could not eat anything, because I was so excited about going to Arabic school.

She really wanted to learn Arabic; reading, speaking and writing it.

> I speak Arabic without thinking . . . with a Yorkshire accent.

At the school they produced plays on the revolution and the women's role in it. They heard it described how schools were like in the Yemen and met many of their friends and enjoyed reading the books which were different since they were in Arabic and from the Yemen, about Yemeni issues.

Between the ages of 12 and 15, almost all of them became disillusioned with the language classes. Quite predictably, as they discovered their teens, they sought other interests.

> When you get home, all you want to do is watch films, *Top of the Pops*, do other things, go to after-school things . . . boys.
>
> (Leila)

But apart from becoming teenagers, they all had serious criticisms of the teachers, the curriculum, materials and so on. By then, they found the teachers too strict, boring and had insufficient skills to retain their interest for two hours, three nights per week. They discovered that the curriculum was becoming repetitive both because the volunteer teacher changed and there was no laid-out curriculum to follow and therefore sometimes new teachers went over ground covered by others before them. The lack of materials was contributory to the dullness: 'went through the same books three times' (Leila) and 'like hearing, you copy down, that's it, nothing exciting' (Moh'd). The books are out of date and too few and some teachers then slip back to the old faithfuls: religion and nostalgia.

Despite all of this, all the interviewees said they liked their teachers. Fatma summed up the general view of the school: 'But I'll recommend it to kids between 7 and 12 years old.'

The advice they gave about how to improve the school was as perceptive as it indicated how much they implicitly learnt by attending it. They suggested that children of 3–4 should not be mixed with the older children and those between 13 and 15 years should be engaging in activities more appropriate for young people, rather than children. Moh'd wished to see 'football, quizzes, Arabic sports, revision and tests' replace some of the present learning. They thought in-service training which will improve the presentation skills of some of the teachers would be welcome; organized curriculum and more and newer books and materials would much improve their interest after the age of 12.

Implications

The inescapable conclusions one reaches from reviewing such schools are that they are making a major contribution in mother-tongue ·learning and maintenance and the realization of bilingualism in Britain. The importance of all three is justified in terms of cognitive development, access to learning, the opportunity to occupy different cultures and languages and the pure functional value of having more than one language (for detailed discussion see Gurnah 1989).

These schools additionally provide social and political education which not only introduces new materials, but also from perspectives which will stimulate the children, challenges the mono-rational ethnocentric views they meet in state schools. This political programme can be deliberate or implicit. Some of the groups see it as part of their responsibility to ensure that their young people have a good grasp of local social and political struggles which restrain their communities from developing. They explain to them about central and local state racism and initiatives which are being taken to counter it. The aim is to raise awareness and mobilize black young people not to accept poverty and isolation as given. The schools also provide the context for the development of greater quality between men and women. These initiatives also help the whole community shift its primary political orientation from the country of origin and to learn to demand services, employment and justice from Britain and from each other.

The process is enhanced by developing a good grasp of the politics and struggles of their 'countries of origin', to give them the motivation to find out more about them. Their involvement in British society therein becomes conscious and deliberate and is not forced upon them by purely negative pressures or ignorance or stereotypes. The young people then become familiar not only with the one-sided views they get from the state school, but also with their community's perspectives and rationale and the political stances it assumes locally. They learn the reasons why their communities are fighting for language provision for Creole, Urdu, or for example Halal meat in schools and colleges. They gain confidence about the distinctiveness of their culture and how to participate in the 'host' one. They come to understand why there are alignments or quarrels with the Council or other black groups. Though often tiresome too, an exposure to such gutsy intra- and inter-community differences ends innocence, initiates young black men and women in community struggles and induces a minority to seek a platform for black community solidarity.

But the very practice of gathering young people scattered all over the city in a class is a political act. A context is then created where common experiences are exchanged and upon which solidarities and change strategies can follow. It is also a context through which men and women, young people and older ones, meet in common struggles and come to respect each other and share experiences. The older people contribute through their greater knowledge of the past, their colonial and imperial experiences and their culture and young people by sharing their greater knowledge of different forms of learning and politics. It may be partly for such reasons that despite the absence of resources that community language schools are so well attended. The improved link with their community makes young black people confident learners with a clearer agenda and a symbolic image that better prepares them for the racism in state schools and college. They are then less likely to relate to racism existentially and be damaged by it and will instead relate to it politically and feel angered and more resolved to tackle it.

Lest I have created the impression that these developments are completely harmonious and without problems, I want to correct this here. What is impressive about the achievements of these black communities is that these changes take place despite all the professional negativity and lack of resources. Black groups, like any other groups, disagree, but their conflicts are exploited by officialdom to make their demands contradictory and incoherent. But it is perhaps the deep injustice of their position and their intense individual and group determination to revise this, which overcomes all the odds.

This much must persuade educators of the importance of properly resourcing such schools. They do, however, also raise different kinds of questions of great interest and ambiguity in pedagogy, content of the curriculum, formality and the message of the curriculum, and so on. For example, what are the implications of using traditional and uniform – but may be partially culturally appropriate – methods of teaching? If they are successful in making children learn, to what extent do we condemn them as being reactionary and at what point do we re-evaluate some of our approaches? How much will the structure and content of European education be enhanced or damaged by structures and contents of other traditions? How far do we take the notion of 'student centredness' with regard to black children? Do we, for example, use religion as a tool to teach, as do other traditions? Is there an argument to be made about an immanence between education and community organizations? Does the informality of the curriculum of community language school create certain spaces which the formal curriculum lacks?

Whatever the answers one wishes to give to the above questions, they clearly may at least lead to an honest re-examination of existing approaches, and may stimulate diversification or synthesis of approaches and philosophies. A new formula may emerge, which will not only benefit community language schools in raising their standards, but also state schools and colleges in diversifying their curriculum and thus make it more relevant.

Regardless of whether state schools and colleges do subsequently and routinely offer community languages in their programmes, I would conclude that these voluntary community language schools still have an important role to play in the education of our bilingual children. It ought to be the inclination of all educators not only to ensure their survival, but also to redirect resources and support towards them and secure their development.

Acknowledgements

I thank Abdul Galil Shaif, Jeremy Hamm, Clara Green, Munitta and Mohammed Kassim, and Diana Haimheed for all their assistance in preparing this article.

References

Brumfit, C., Ellis, R. and Levine, J. (eds) (1985) *English as a Second Language in the United Kingdom*, Oxford: Oxford University Press.

Cabral, A. (1973) *Return to Source*, New York: Monthly Review.

City of Sheffield (1988) *Language Survey 1988*, Sheffield: Education Department.

CRE (Commission for Racial Equality) (1983) *Ethnic Minority Community Languages: A Statement*, London: CRE.

DES (Department of Education and Science) (1981) Circular 5/81, London: DES.

Education (1988) 'Raising the status of community languages', *Education* 21 October: 390.

Evans-Prichard, E. E. (1941) *The Nuer*, Oxford: Clarendon Press.

Frazer, J. G. (1915) *The Golden Bough*, 3rd edn, London: Macmillan.

Gurnah, A. (1985) 'Whither Paradigon?' *Review of African Political Economy*, 32: 116–21.

—— (1989) 'After bilingual support?', in M. Cole (ed.) *Education for Equality*, London: Routledge.

HMI (1984) *Mother Tongue Teaching in School and Community*, London: HMSO.

Levi-Strauss, C. (1966) *The Savage Mind*, London: Weidenfeld & Nicolson.

—— (1973) *Structural Anthropology*, Harmondsworth: Penguin.

Malinowski, B. (1954) *Magic, Science and Religion and Other Essays*, London: Anchor.

Shaif, A. (1989) *Struggle for Language*, Sheffield Education Committee (SUMES) and South Yorkshire Open College Federation.

Tansley, R. and Craft, A. (1984) 'Mother tongue teaching and support: a school council enquiry', *Journal of Multilingual and Multicultural Development* 5, 5.

10
Empowerment of staff: a prerequisite for the empowerment of users?

Alan Stanton

Collective working is consistent with our way of working with people in the community. In all our work we encourage people to become independent, skilled, and responsible for their own actions. It is therefore important to have a management structure which reflects those beliefs.
(Newcastle-upon-Tyne Family Service Unit, quoted in Stanton 1989:24)

The rhetoric of participation and involvement is one of the last areas of social policy without cuts. On the contrary, we've seen a distinct expansion, with terms like 'active citizen', 'advocacy', and yes, 'empowerment' becoming widely used. For instance, in 1989, the British Association of Social Workers made 'the empowerment of both service users and workers' the theme of its annual conference. To the organizers' credit, they were dismayed at 'how easily the language of empowerment had been colonized by some very traditional proposals', and 'just how easily old practices could be tarted up with the new words' (Mitchell 1989: 14).

Perhaps some readers are already wondering if this chapter is a double dose of the same thing. If so, their scepticism is welcome. Must the empowerment of people who use services go together with the empowerment of service-providers? To reach a judgement, we need to dig beneath the rhetoric to the values being urged, and further still to the practical day-to-day implications.

To examine these values and this practice, I'll look in particular at teams which explicitly adopt an 'empowerment' model. The research I'll refer to – my own and other's – is with 'democratic' social services agencies trying to run collectively and collaboratively (Stanton 1989). They range from law and advice centres to Women's Aid refuges from social work offices to residential homes. Some are formally 'collectives' with equal pay and equal power, and perhaps rotation of work; others are collaborative teams trying to combat the dysfunctions of the hierarchies inside which they develop, including problems like fragmented parallel working, or a lack of trust and fear of sanctions.

But plainly, the argument here is not limited to self-managing teams. To say there is 'fit' – an internal logic and coherence – between how an agency operates with its users and the relations among staff, applies to any 'human services' agency. In fact, in a number of fields, professionals have reached similar conclusions (Menzies 1970). Here, for example, is Oliver Sacks, a neurologist, observing what we might call the growth of 'overpowerment' as the regime changed in a hospital, very far from a collective team.

> A strict administration has come into being, rigidly committed to 'efficiency' and rules; 'familiarity' with patients is strongly discouraged. Law and order have been ousting fellow-feeling and kinship; hierarchy separates the inmates from staff; and patients tend to feel they are 'inside', unreachably distant from the real world outside.
>
> (Sacks 1982: 24)

Maria Brenton has argued for worker and user participation on the basis of the 'core values inherent in social work' (Brenton 1978: 289). These included, she said, 'the dignity of the individual' and 'self-determination', as well as enabling clients to have 'the highest possible level of self-reliance and autonomy'. That being so, Brenton urged 'the need for continuity of principle. In other words, the social service organisation should embody the values it professes to promote'.

A moral criticism?

A key feature of self-managing teams is that their aim is not simply good care, better therapy, or even client and user participation in the affairs of the agency. They want greater democratic control – by workers of their work-place and by users of their own lives.

> Women's Aid refuges should be committed to the principles of self-help and self-determination, and will encourage women seeking advice or refuge to determine their own futures. . . . Refuges should be run on a democratic basis, with all women having a say in decision-making.
>
> (from *Policies of the Women's Aid Federation*, quoted in Thomas and Thomas 1989: 6)

Running on a democratic basis is not only an ambitious aim: presented as a principle in this way, it also raises a fundamental challenge for all 'helping' agencies. Because it implies that trying to empower people who use services *without*, at the same time, developing a collaborative and empowering culture among agency staff, is inconsistent – even bad faith.

> If we're talking about community action and community control, or giving people a say, and then we work where we have no say – when someone else is dictating to us – it's a complete contradiction.
>
> (Pensioners' Link worker, quoted by Stanton 1983b: 203)

Outsiders can feel such comments as a moral criticism. And on one level they are right. A statement of values is being made: that if working towards empowerment is *right* for an agency's users, then the same principle should apply to staff. How can it be fair or just to extend democracy and control over their lives to the first group and not the second?

Van der Linden, in research with Women's Aid refuges, found this consistency of values a strong central core. Ideals of empowerment, self-help and involvement in the running of the refuges linked the residents, staff and the women who acted as outside support group and management body. Van der Linden saw such values operating less through clear-cut rules or formal organizational structures, than as part of the 'style or a culture in the refuge, into which workers in particular put a lot of invisible efforts' (van der Linden 1989: 52).

How you do it is what you get

The argument for empowerment from a common value basis (value rationality) challenges agencies to achieve a consistency of *ends*. However, as I suggested before, the 'fit' rests on more than this. For example, as van der Linden makes plain, the involvement of women in running women's refuges is also viewed as an instrument – a *means* of empowerment in itself.

> Although we will see that value rationality remains a very useful concept in our understanding of Women's Aid refuges, the importance of 'instrumental rationality' should not be overlooked either. It makes once more clear that members of this organization are not solely against 'bureaucratic' or hierarchical ruling because they don't like its values. It is also rejected because it would be ineffective in the light of the aims of the organization.
>
> (van der Linden 1989: 45)

The idea, then, is that means and ends are complementary; we need both. Empowerment at work can be argued as a good thing in itself. But in addition, how a social service agency runs should be judged by its effectiveness in encouraging and strengthening democratic services, and control by users over their own lives. The implication is also that if we use the wrong means we won't achieve the desired ends. As the Green slogan says: *How You Do It Is What You Get*. The key proposition here is that social relations among workers colour and shape and change the relationships between an agency and people who use it.

'We are doing this already'

The argument that social services agencies should 'practise what they preach' seems a powerful one. Yet, as suggested above, it's open to the same sort of watering down and colonization which has dogged efforts at fostering participation by people using services. As many readers will recognize, there is often a wide gulf between an agency's policy statements and what actually happens 'on the ground'. For instance, Beresford and Croft (1990), surveying statutory and voluntary agencies, found that a high proportion reported written policies and practical initiatives to involve service users. But actual examples given ranged from self-advocacy projects aimed at giving users influence and power, to consumerist schemes which were no more than asking clients for information.

If 'empowerment' can be stretched to mean 'old practices tarted up with the new words', an appeal to moral consistency won't work. Whether it's in involvement of service users or of staff, an agency can fend off the challenge by stating that 'We are doing this already'. It therefore becomes crucial to examine the practical links between an empowerment approach in principle and in day to day practice. What are the processes at work here?

Possibilities for change?

Moving from general statements of principle to more specific practice will, I hope, serve a further purpose. When discussing these ideas with social services staff around the country, I've frequently met the response that: 'It's all very well for teams that self-manage or collaborate successfully. Where *we* work it's just not like that'. Many readers may share this view. After all, research into social services agencies has consistently painted a gloomy picture of fragmented uncooperative work groups and departments, adding up to far less than the sum of their parts. Staff tend to work mainly as individuals; often feeling unsupported and distrustful. They may be suspicious of what they label as 'the hierarchy' or 'management' (Stevenson and Parsloe 1978: 312; Pithouse in this volume, Chapter 4).

So a common response to the material here has been for people to say how much they agree with the idea of a 'fit' between an agency culture and structure. Because their own work-places amply demonstrate the fit working *in reverse*. In other words, closed, controlling, hierarchical staff relations undermine attempts to work openly, equally and in ways that respect the rights of people who use the agency. Individuals and small groups struggle to make improvements *despite* what goes on in an office or department. However, it is precisely these struggles that suggest the remainder of this chapter need not deepen the gloom. The features I'm describing are neither frozen nor determined. And it's likely that by looking at specific areas, rather than the broad picture, readers will see possibilities for change. Becoming aware of the processes operating, we're in a better position to find the small spaces and build the small alliances that offer the best chance of altering the culture and social relations of our work-places.

What people know

Let's begin with the point about teams failing to 'team up'. Argyris and Schön observe that: 'There are too many cases in which organisations know *less* than their members. There are even cases in which the organisation cannot seem to learn what every member knows' (Argyris and Schön 1978: 9). Why is this? One cause is a work culture which weighs and takes notice of who people are, rather than what they say or know.

There's an incident I like to tell about a London collective team – a community arts and resources centre (Stanton 1983). I was halfway through an interview with one member, when we were interrupted. A second worker was on duty downstairs, and something unusual had come up. 'What's our policy on this?' she asked the person I was speaking to. I listened closely, tuned to issues of 'heavy votes' and 'hidden hierarchies'. Then the duty worker ended by saying: 'Thanks, I'll go and get another opinion from someone else'. And I suddenly realized what I'd heard. Heads put together to seek a better answer, with no feathers of status ruffled or faces to save. It was an example of 'Who knows', with nothing of 'Who's who'. But the astonishing thing was, later, that these team members *did not understand* why I felt this important. They took it for granted. When I tried to explain, they found it hard to recall the sort of office I'd worked in – a social work agency where everyone had to tiptoe round the bosses' sensitivities if they wanted their views listened to and taken seriously.

But now think, more generally, about the people who use services and what they know. Are clients' views respected and valued? Are their experience and opinion seen as valid and legitimate? There are some staff and agencies committed to giving such respect and value. But I suggest that where the prevailing culture has its normal force lines of 'Who's who' this will work against the validation and verification of what users know.

Who learns?

Asking 'Who knows?' leads on to 'Who learns?' A central issue for empowerment is making opportunities for people who use services to build their own knowledge. And by 'knowledge' I don't mean giving out information leaflets. The aim is a critical understanding of their social world and how they might act to change it, 'not as a closed world from which there is no exit, but as a limiting situation which they can transform' (Freire 1972: 25).

Often, the successful examples here are independent groups, stressing their separation from or even opposition to established agencies. Groups like Sickle Cell Societies (Anionwu: 1990) and Parents Aid (for people whose children are in local authority care) have pooled their own experiences and understanding, providing mutual aid and often making demands on practitioners.

But a more likely situation is when agencies realize it makes sense to give 'consumers' a say. They begin to listen – not just informally in the way that every sensitive social service worker has always listened to and learned from clients – but explicitly as agency policy, perhaps with consultation procedures.

Unfortunately, in a top-down and overpowering staff culture, there is a real danger that what users know is seen as something from which mainly the *professionals* learn. Even supposedly radical agencies campaigning, for example, on behalf of people who are poor or unemployed, may conduct their lobbying 'over the heads' of these groups, effectively excluding them from substantive decision-making and public debates. And we have the relatively new field of 'client studies' with its in-built risk that users' data, channelled as practitioners' information, may be appropriated as academics' knowledge.

Each of these examples can be partly explained by the features of a hierarchical, individualistic non-collaborating culture. This has its own 'fit' with traditions stressing professional status, the privatization of knowledge, and individual ownership of 'intellectual property'.

The difficult (but not impossible) alternative is to try opening a dialogue, among and between people who work in and who use services. Such a process of jointly gaining and creating knowledge, can be 'simultaneously education and development of consciousness, and of mobilization for action' (Gaventa 1988: 19). In concrete terms, this can even mean a collaborative staff team working with local residents to decide the entire future and form of an agency's services (Dobson 1987).

Healthy communication

Let me pause here and make something clear. I'm well aware that using words like 'dialogue' and 'mobilization for action' can readily evoke those misty-eyed visions of 1960s radical social work: with workers and clients, arms linked and fists raised. But my purpose is neither to idealize collective teams – who have their own generous share of internal conflict – nor to paint a picture of consensus and harmony of interest among service workers and users. On the contrary, it is obvious that we will inevitably be navigating between contradictory views and pressures which push and pull us in different directions.

But is this a problem or, rather, a condition of posing the right questions? Take, for instance, the incident in the interview I mentioned before. When the duty worker went off to seek the views of yet another team member, those third opinions would not automatically complement the second. Nor would the results necessarily please the waiting users. So nobody expected a neatly fitting jigsaw; the duty worker could eventually face conflicts and differences. What I'm arguing is this: for effective communication in any work-place, we always need a critical give and take, a push and pull. We need settings – if necessary protected settings – where people feel confident that they can be open and honest about their views, their doubts, and their feelings. Where they can own those views and feelings, as well as owning responsibility for their own power and own actions.

This is a safe place for people to say, 'I've got this problem and I don't know how to deal with it. I can't cope; give me some help here' (worker at Newcastle-upon-Tyne Family Service Unit, quoted in Stanton 1989: 320). Now, I'm sure that if I was saying this about a *family*'s communication, readers would wonder why I was wasting their time with the obvious. So consider why social services providers so often have one sort of model for healthy and effective communication among clients – inside families especially – and what seems altogether different for relationships among colleagues.

If it is altogether different, how can it affect the quality of communication with those who use services? It won't be surprising when I suggest that colleagues who have limited experience of plain speaking with one another, will be hindered when trying to be honest and clear with users. Especially if the prevailing culture of an agency is defensive and denying, won't staff find it hard to resist adopting this? When it becomes second nature to block and cover up, won't such habits inevitably seep and spill into relations with users?

At the extreme, how easy is it for a worker to be forthright and open with people outside their agency if they are afraid to speak up inside? Or when finding out what's going on means, as in one local authority 'department in deep distress', weighing up rumours (Centre for the Analysis of Social Policy: 1987). Even if a work-place isn't quite so secretive and disabling, those powerful 'force lines of organization' are still at work, shaping and colouring how staff behave. So you meet people who seem to be on bureaucratic autopilot, the way they say as little as possible, at length and with lots of jargon.

Sometimes these habits become so obvious and natural that you only notice when they're missing. That's why, when people in hierarchical jobs have dealings with a collaborative team, they typically complain that its members are rude and ill-mannered (Stanton 1989: 97). This usually means that such teams don't stand on ceremony. They are adopting an etiquette of *reference* (Who knows?) rather than the disabling habits of deference (Who's who?). They are often direct, honest and forthright; but then, aren't these exactly the qualities people who use agencies need if they are to have a clear and empowering relationship with an agency's staff?

Silent messages

There are other less direct ways in which agencies communicate with users, though these more silent and subtle messages often have just as much impact. For example, casual callers 'read' an agency through a wide range of signs and symbols, sometimes without realizing they are doing so. Is the waiting-room comfortable and cared for, or slovenly and ignored? Do staff keep to or ignore appointment times? Even the clothes which staff wear and the pictures on the wall carry meanings.

> The reception is busy, active; a lot of energy buzzing around; lots of information. Things that young people can take in very quickly. The general atmosphere has that sort of orientation. I think that's quite off-putting; some people feel a bit intimidated. It presents a certain image.
> (worker at the Islington Bus Company quoted by Stanton 1989: 364)

Sometimes there's nothing subtle about the message. I used to live near a (hierarchical) social work office where 'Reception' was a public corridor with a hatch. Clients were often left gazing at the top of a secretary's hairdo while she phoned her friends and family. It may seem that these niceties of manners are a long way from issues of empowerment. My point is that in organizational life everywhere such rules of behaviour reflect and interact with the values and social relations of an agency – including power relations. Conventions and manners aren't neutral. They serve to mark and confirm people's – usually unequal – status. Putting it another way, the fit we're examining is reflected in conversational and other social courtesies, including the courtesies offered people who use services.

Take, for instance, the division of space within an office. A typical hierarchical practice is for work-space to be divided up largely in line with people's power and status. As well as the boss getting the quietest, most comfortable room, his (and usually it is 'his') boundaries will be better protected. Admin. workers may intercept his callers; he may have a door, while other staff are over-looked in open-plan offices. And this is reinforced by the convention by which someone's right to intrude into a colleague's space is a measure of their superior position (Goffman 1971: 65; Derber 1983: 81). Conventions of deference also determine who can be kept waiting and whose summons overrides the day's schedule.

A parting of the ways?

Some readers, either working in or using social services agencies, may feel that I've been avoiding a core issue of power and empowerment as it now affects them. What if the interests of service providers and users are antagonistic? In practice, they ask, if staff have more power, won't clients have even less – and vice versa?

So, on the one hand, there are groups of users – elderly and disabled people are good examples – who are critical of agencies. For them, one attraction of consumerism is its apparent promise of more power: accountability to the 'customer'. They may ask whether a stronger, more collaborative workers' group would be even harder to confront and keep accountable. After all, groups can also be gangs, and there are staff teams who – from an outsiders' point of view, at least – seem to run very cosily for their own convenience and benefit.

On the other hand, service providers – and their trade unions – are currently worried about aspects of the over-empowerment of staff. This may take the form of intolerable stress and sometimes abuse from clients. Accepting that people using services are often oppressed rather than disadvantaged, workers are none the less fearful when some of the distress, pain and anger stemming from that oppression finds it way to the doors of 'helping' agencies. As incidents of violence towards staff go up, so do grilles and reinforced glass partitions. The challenge then is whether instead of a fit, there is finally, a parting of the ways, an *opposition* between the empowerment of the providers and the users of services.

Relieving the siege?

'I've deliberately put this challenge as strongly as it's been presented to me in discussions with service users and providers. I won't pretend there is a simple answer – a straightforward rebuttal. Perhaps one helpful observation is that this sort of 'siege mentality' is hardly a recent development. Nearly twenty years ago, at the inception of social services departments, Satyamurti observed workers' building defensive shields out of fear of control by clients. She argued that 'more co-operative work was a prerequisite for greater effectiveness' (1981: 199) and that such co-operation needed an atmosphere of mutual trust and respect (1981: 203).

In citing this study, I'm not saying things remain the same. My point is that there have actually been many strong, positive experiences of social services agencies changing and opening up. One of the important changes is a recognition that there is no watertight boundary between service providers and users. Workers are frequently users elsewhere – in health, say, or children's daycare, or in services for elderly people – whether for themselves or other family members. There has also been a welcome shift towards employing people with experience on the receiving end of services. These examples illustrate how 'users' are not a fixed group of people, but a fluid and changing category.

Valuing the knowledge of people using services is evidence of another positive development, away from feeling 'besieged by clients and potential clients' (Satyamurti 1981: 124). I've talked about building a culture among staff which respects an agency's users as citizens and as people with their own understandings and meanings. Such a culture recognizes that people are not the sum of their problems. They have strengths and resources, plans and hopes (de Graaf 1986).

A different, though complementary argument comes from research which views the primary problem as that stress and anxiety which users can bring to a 'helping' agency. But, even from this perspective, the agency and its staff are seen as carrying responsibility for their own interventions. So a shift in agency culture and structure can make the difference between meeting and relieving distress and anger, or blocking and even amplifying it (Menzies 1970).

Each of these points qualify a 'them' and 'us' view of agency services. They do not, though, settle the question of what happens when there is conflict and antagonism between the interests of providers and users. Clearly, there are times when mutual learning and persuasion seem to have run their course; when influence gives way to attempts at *control*. Exercising power and control in this sense means making other people do things they don't want to; what they perceive as being against their own interests (Lukes 1974). However, it would be wise not to pass too soon from this observation to the conclusion that the only remaining questions are 'Who's boss?', 'Who's got power over whom?' In particular, let's not jump too quickly to the agency barricades – as if, at this point, the only 'fit' that mattered was reinforced plate glass and better locks in 'Reception'. To understand why, let's look at some differing ideas and experience about agency 'openness'.

Opening up

As I've mentioned, at various times writers on social service agencies have proposed greater collective working as a means whereby staff may 'move out into the community and open themselves up to members of the public' (Parsloe 1981: 148). The notion is that groups of workers with greater internal strength are better able to manage the pressures and demands from 'outside'.

Metaphorically, having a tougher internal skeleton should enable them to cast off – or at least lower – their external shell. In some ways, the fit implied here is similar to that seen in democratic teams. One of the common threads linking a wide variety of collective and collaborative teams has been the aim of opening up to agencies' users and other local people. And one of the lessons (both for workers and outsiders) is just how difficult that is – especially when accompanied by vague and naive ideas about 'the community' and 'open door policies'. However, what we learn from such experiments in openness is not the necessity of battening down hatches and repelling boarders. Instead, the interesting developments have been in ways of *renegotiating* use of agency time, space and other resources (like staff skills) in the light of the needs and demands that users bring. And, at the same time, balancing these demands with those of staff as well. For they too have legitimate needs – in this case, for satisfying work and pleasant, safe working conditions.

Let me stress that by 'negotiation' I don't mean polite consensual chats. And by legitimate demands I certainly don't include physical aggression or verbal abuse.

> Maybe it's not a pressure in the sense of some organised campaign to get you to do something. But what it is, is people actually making demands on your time. . . For me it's about looking at the needs of the area and how we need to change.
>
> (worker at Newcastle-upon-Tyne Family Service Unit, quoted in Stanton 1989: 137)

I'm arguing that, whether among a team's members or in its relations to users, there is still a large distance between friendly persuasion and fear-provoking intimidation. And in this space – where people *are* exercising power – the fit I've described above still holds good.

How can that be? Well, recall what I've already said about the social relations aimed for among a democratic staff group. It isn't only being friendly, encouraging and nice to one another. There will be hard bargaining, and even arguments and rows. A healthy give and take includes getting and dishing-out criticism. In fact it invites and welcomes criticism. A collaborative organizational culture doesn't just mean giving support and mutual strength. It also entails the obligation to evaluate and demand quality from our colleagues and to have that demand made of us. Trust and mutual respect extend to telling each other those important home truths that will sting precisely because they come from people whose judgements we trust and value.

The aim then is a setting and culture where we accept and invite our colleagues' best criticism, disagreement and challenge. Indeed, when we would regard it as insulting if they did not offer their best criticism. Because it would be like saying, 'Well, I don't really expect anything better from you'. And if this permeates a team's dealings – becomes its natural 'common sense' – we can see how it would strengthen and support practitioners' who are trying to approach and deal with an agency's users in a similarly clear, honest and critical way. I'm not saying that it's automatic. Nor is it easy; what users say can also sting. If service providers invite best criticism from outside as well as inside their work-place they can expect complaints; with ill-informed and biased views, as well as useful challenges that help improve what they offer.

Finally . . .

Not a conclusion, but a last few comments for the sceptical readers I welcomed at the beginning of this chapter. Let's suppose that having read this far, they are – if not in full agreement with the ideas presented – at least ready to see them as a possible model. Here is a way of understanding some of the interaction between a staff group and the people who use its services.

How then, can we test this explanation, especially with a view to improving things? And isn't this a particularly bad time to try, given that our present government is committed to producing worse problems and deeper misery for the poorest and most oppressed people in our society?

On the first point, I've suggested that even a small group of staff or users – ideally, both in dialogue – can try making changes. The gap between fashionable empowerment rhetoric and agency practice can offer at minimum, some room to manoeuvre and maybe some resources for experiment. As for political timing . . . well, is there ever any choice? If '*How You Do It*' is really '*What You Get*' then failing to challenge a deferential and overpowering agency culture will, in effect, confirm and consolidate both providers' and users' lack of control over decisions affecting their lives.

References

Aninionwu, E. N. (1990) 'Community development approaches to sickle cell anaemia', in A. Watt (ed.) *Community Development in Health Education*, London: Health Education Authority.

Argyris, C. and Schön, D. (1978) *Organisational Learning: A Theory of Action Perspective*, Reading, Mass.: Addison-Wesley.

Beresford, P. and Croft, S. (1990 forthcoming) 'Involving people who use services', *Social Services Insight*.

Brenton, M. (1978) 'Worker participation and the social service agency', *British Journal of Social Work*, 8, 23: 289–300.

Centre for the Analysis of Social Policy (1987) *Review and Consolidation in Brent Social Services Department*, University of Bath.

de Graaf, M. (1986) 'Catching fish or liberating man: social development in Zimbabwe', *Journal of Social Development in Africa*, 1: 12–26.

Derber, C. (1983) *The Pursuit of Attention: Power and Individualism in Everyday Life*, New York: Oxford University Press.

Dobson, P. (1987) *An Exercise in Consultation – Residents Decide the Future of a Social Work and Community Work Agency*, MSc. thesis, University of Birmingham.

Freire, P. (1972) *Pedagogy of the Oppressed*, Harmondsworth: Penguin.

Gaventa, J. (1988) 'Participatory research in North America', *Convergence*, XXI, 2 and 3: 19–27.

Goffman, E. (1971) *Relations in Public*, Harmondsworth: Penguin.

Lukes, S. (1974) *Power: A Radical View*, London: Macmillan.

Menzies, I. E. P. (1970) *The Functioning of Social Systems as a Defence against Anxiety*, London: Tavistock.

Mitchell, G. (1989) 'Empowerment and opportunity', *Social Work Today* 16 March: 14.

Parsloe, P. (1981) *Social Services Area Teams*, London: Allen & Unwin.

Sacks, O. (1982 revised edn) *Awakenings*, London: Picador.

Satyamurti, C. (1981) *Occupational Survival*, Oxford: Basil Blackwell (though published in 1981, this research was carried out in 1970–2).

Stanton, A. (1983) *Collective Working in the Personal Social Services: A Study with Nine Agencies*, MSc. thesis, Cranfield Institute of Technology.

—— (1989) *Invitation To Self-Management*, London: Dab Hand Press.

Stevenson, O. and Parsloe, P. (1978) *Social Services Teams: The Practitioners' View*, London: HMSO.

Thomas, M. and Thomas, A. (1989) *Participative or Collective Working: A Characteristic of Social Economy Organisations?*, Milton Keynes: Co-operatives Research Unit, Open University.

van der Linden, J. (1989) *'Because as Women, We're in this Together': A Study of Women Working Collectively in Women's Aid*, Department of Sociology, University of Amsterdam.

11
Will women managers save social work?

Angela Everitt

This chapter considers the position of women in the social work labour-force. More particularly it examines the role of women within the management of social services departments and probation. Such consideration is particularly apposite at this time. The very concept of welfare is being rapidly redefined in the political, economic and social context of New Right individualism and family responsibility. Increased emphasis is placed upon social work as a form of social control, serving not only to maintain but also to extend inequality in a society already divided by gender, race and class. Accompanying such shifting paradigms in welfare are radical changes in its organizational form and methods of service delivery. In this, management has assumed an increasingly high profile. The use of performance indicators, tried and tested by City firms of management consultants and accountants, is symbolic of the move towards a vision of welfare consistent with an 'enterprise' economy: an economy and culture that depends on the family, and on women, for its servicing and support.

Women and men relate differently to social work. A clear majority of front-line workers in social services departments and the users of those services, both directly and indirectly, are female. Yet men predominate within management, training and policy-making (Dale and Foster 1986). Gender is central to any understanding of social work practice and organization. In the construction of the social work task, women are systematically disadvantaged as victims of domestic violence and abuse (Brownmiller 1975; Hanmer et al. 1989; Mama 1989; Pahl 1985); physical and mental stress (Davis et al. 1985; Graham 1984; Roberts 1981); and poverty (Carlen 1988; Glendinning and Millar 1987; Burden and Gottlieb 1987; Hanmer and Statham 1988). They are victimized as bearing responsibility for personal troubles as a consequence of being 'inadequate' mothers (Ash 1987; Calvert 1985;

Campbell 1988; Hanscombe and Forster 1982; Rich 1977); wives (Corea *et al.* 1985; Smart 1984); carers (Finch and Groves 1983; Hicks 1988; Leventon in this volume) and not behaving as good girls (Carlen and Worrell 1987; Hudson 1986). Welfare organizations reflect the positions of women in the private sphere and reinforce these. Women welfare workers inevitably become agents of a patriarchical state, simultaneously victimizing and victim-blaming.

Our thinking about welfare must be informed by notions of justice and equality (Baker in this volume, Chapter 13). The challenge is to develop and sustain such a discourse and the organizational forms and methods of service delivery that reflect these values. Feminists, through their theory and practice, have made visible the nature of patriarchy in welfare and its role in the oppression of women. They have also contributed to a clearer understanding of the marginalization of other groups. Their voices have added to the calls for more women to be promoted into management. As Hanmer and Statham argue, 'ultimately one of the changes must be a reduction in the number of men in senior management and the increase in the number of women' (Hanmer and Statham 1988: 108). It is a theme repeated in the social work press (Grimwood 1989; Lockley and Fawcett 1989). Management cannot be ignored by feminists. 'It is an important and strategical role and the site of power in every organizational setting. We must participate in it if women's priorities are ever to be equally represented and reflected in the structure of work' (Coyle 1989: 124). But will more women managers change the position for women workers and women clients? Are managers such as Allan (1989) correct when they assert that men have nothing to fear from working with and being managed by women?

Women in the work-force

Women make up 40 per cent of the UK work-force and evidence suggests that their participation in paid work is increasing: 67 per cent of the growth in the work-force between September 1983 and September 1988 was accounted for by women and it is anticipated that by the end of the century 44 per cent of the work-force will be women (*Employment Gazette* 1989a: 159–72). In welfare, women are particularly prominent. A survey of social services employment found 74 per cent of social workers and 90 per cent of welfare/social work assistants were women and that 'the growth in the profession in recent years has been weighted to females' (LACSAB and ADSS 1989b: 10). The survey was undertaken in the context of increasing concern about the number of vacancies in local authority social services departments and the need to develop effective employment and recruitment strategies at a time of increasing competition in the labour market for young workers. It recognized that 'the relatively high proportion of female employees is an important factor in considering recruitment and retention issues' (LACSAB and ADSS 1989b: 4). The report recommended that women-centred employment packages be developed which pay due attention to the need for refresher training, part-time contracts, job sharing and more flexible work patterns. Further it argued that

> child care arrangements such as nurseries, crèches and childminding support are options which social services are ideally equipped to provide . . . and that schemes such as these will gather force in other employment sectors and intensify competition for increasingly scarce labour supplies.
>
> (LACSAB and ADSS 1989a: 11)

What is not considered is the possible effect of gender inequality in retaining a committed female work-force. In relation to pay grades, for example, where the report did make suggestions for re-grading measures, such as the introduction of senior practitioner scales and accelerated promotion and progression schemes (LACSAB and ADSS 1989a: 45–7), no attention was paid to the fact that 'men are more likely to reach the social worker level 3 range or above' (LACSAB and ADSS 1989a: 17). 'Larger proportions of men than women undertake duties at level 3 or above – 73.3 per cent of full-time men, 61.7 per cent of full-time women, 80.0 per cent of part-time men, 73 per cent of part-time women' (LACSAB and ADSS 1989a: 19). Women only become visible in recruitment and employment strategies as 'working mothers, re-entrants to the labour market, those without full qualifications. People who could be coaxed into work by flexible part-time contracts' (LACSAB and ADSS 1989a: 48–9). A feminist employment package may look rather different from a women-centred one. It would not only focus on providing support and provision for women, but also challenge those mechanisms of patriarchy which assign to women responsibilities for nurture and care while maintaining their dependence on, and deference to, men.

The clustering of women in the lower levels of hierarchically organized social services departments and probation services is partly accounted for by the general rise in female employment. An additional factor has been the employers' concern to create a more 'flexible' and 'malleable' labour-force through the use of part-time and limited-term contracts, linked to an inevitable desire to reduce labour costs. A pattern of female part-time paid employment has emerged in the social services which dovetails neatly with pressures on women to undertake unpaid care, mothering and domestic work. Changes in the organizational form and delivery of social services occasioned by the development of packages of community care, involving as they must greater provision of domestic care and help, are likely to contribute to greater imbalance. Patch systems of delivery have laid the foundation for a new type of worker, hierarchically below the social worker. In their research, Hadley and Hatch noticed that these new workers 'were all women, between 30 and 60 years old. They have no formal training in social work, but have been selected for their sound common sense and experience' (Hadley and Hatch 1981: 154). People in such jobs have little opportunities for promotion, progression and professional development because of the seeming irrelevance for them of educational opportunities. While being attentive to the effect that this has on the position of women in work, it is also important to note that inequality is experienced not only through gender, but also through class. For example, training opportunities are being provided by one social services department in collaboration with a further education college and the WEA for redundant shipyard workers (who presumably do not have the caring common sense of women) to become 'Griffiths care workers'. Times are indeed changing, when workers' education becomes training in common sense!

At the other end of the scale, analysis of the work-force in social services and probation reveals that there are few women in the most senior positions in these organizations. In 1989, of 115 directors of social services in England and Wales, 11 were women. Of 53 chief probation officers, 5 were women. Of 12 directors of social work in Scotland, 2 were women (*Social Services Year Book, 1989/90*). All this will come as no surprise: it reflects a gender-segregated work-force that has operated consistently since the setting up of the social services and social work departments. For example, within probation the number of women chief probation officers has remained unchanged for a decade (Wells 1983: 6). Such vertical segregation has received considerable attention – being observed in all sectors of the labour market, including those seen as traditionally female: social work, health and education (see for example Walton 1975; Reid and Wormald 1982; Howe 1986).

In the past, things were different. The children's officers, the new chief officers of the local authority children's departments set up in 1948 following the recommendations of the Curtis Committee, were envisaged from the start as women – 'graduates, with social science qualifications, experience with children and with good administrative ability' (Packman 1975: 9). The key to understanding such a supposedly radical position in the context of women's employment lies in the conception of the job as personal care rather than as management. Packman draws attention to the Curtis Committee's conclusion that the essential qualifications for the job 'would be on the personal side. She should be genial and friendly in manner and able to set both children and adults at their ease' (Curtis Committee 1946: para 446). Packman continues:

> It was expected that, in all but large county areas, she would know all the children in her care personally. . . . In other words, Curtis seems to be suggesting, for most areas, a one-woman, personal social work service (though the term, as such, is nowhere used). The small scale of what was envisaged proved, in the event, grossly to underestimate the amount of work that would be involved and the number of subordinates required to carry it out.
>
> (Packman 1975: 9)

Appointment of such women did not always go smoothly. It was obviously felt to be against the grain to appoint women at such a level in local government. In Oxfordshire there were attempts not to give the children's officer the status of chief officer but to have her report to a male chief administrative officer. The county was overruled by the Home Office (Packman 1975: 17).

Twenty-five years on, the chief officers of the new social services departments, the 'Seebohm factories' which incorporated the children's departments, clearly required male qualities linked to managerialism and control. In 1977, 93 per cent of directors of social services were men (Howe 1986: 23). Male recruits from the welfare departments (imbued with Poor Law values of less eligibility) and from mental health sections of public health departments (based on the medical model) were deemed more appropriate for jobs as directors of social services than were the female children's officers – even though they were kind, pleasant and caring. Even though the children's departments were the most professionalized of the personal social services of the local authorities at that time, they rarely provided the top management.

Fearful women?

There is little information to draw on as to the politics of those women who became the new chief officers of the children's departments. Some indication of their background is given by Packman. She refers to a tutor from one of the newly established training courses in child care who 'recalls a candidate who presented references from Dame Myra Curtis herself and the Archbishop of Canterbury!' (Packman 1975: 11). Parker, in her study of Victorian women in public social service, suggests that, despite their choosing to enter public life often in place of marrying and performing their duties within the family, such women

> were not, of course, offending against conventional notions of sexual morality. They were mostly doing what could be regarded as women's work, though outside instead of inside their families. Their great achievement was the display of high ability, enterprise, determination and courage, qualities more commonly attributed to men. Their lives were practical proof that women could be exceptionally capable and skilled in the most responsible managerial and administrative jobs, in political argument and debate and in the analysis of social problems and social institutions.
>
> (Parker 1988: 3–4)

These were 'the pioneers of statutory welfare arrangements, and at the same time among the leaders of the movement of women out of private life into the public career, jobs and professions occupied by men' (Parker 1988: 1). From this we develop a picture of educated, self-confident 'ladies', having devout Christian beliefs and concern for injustice and deprivation. With families providing economic support, emotional care and a background in social and political debate, their sense of social obligation and public duty, and their drive to act on this, is evident. Some, like Florence Nightingale and Mary Carpenter, confined their public work to social and nursing care for the sick, destitute and children at risk: activities which clearly 'could be seen as a more or less respectable extension of women's familial responsibilities' (Parker 1988: 5). Others, like Beatrice Webb, engaged more in writing and social policy research and in pressure groups and political campaigns. The more these women became involved in social reform the more they aroused opposition and hostility. But, with only oblique references to their personal politics, we are left to wonder as to how radical these women really were in challenging the conventions, roles and behaviours socially ascribed for them as women. Did they only prove that women could do the job as well as men? Or did they redefine the very nature of the job to be done?

Through unearthing a history remarkably hidden from us, Jeffreys (1985) sets us thinking that the Curtis call for women to be the carers of children at risk could be understood in very different ways. Indeed this may have been the case for the women who took up these appointments, and by men who tried to block them. We all grow up to know the story of Florence Nightingale, the lady with the lamp caring for the wounded soldiers in the Crimean War. Parker develops a different picture: of a woman who grew up experiencing unease with the feminine accomplishments and socializing expected of her by her mother and sister. Who possessed

> such a sense of the destructive and intrusive character of family relationships and with so keen a desire for independent work . . . rejected marriage as a possible escape from the constrictions of home life.
>
> (Parker 1988: 97–8)

This rejection of marriage by Florence Nightingale and many of her contemporaries arose from an understanding of the power and control of men over women through marriage and hetereosexuality. These women struggled for the right of women to own their own bodies and 'saw it as necessary to devalue sexual activity between men and women' (Jeffreys 1985: 40).

> They saw the sexualization of woman limited her possibilities and exposed her to abuse. Prostitution, sexual abuse of children and sexual assault, were seen to be inextricably linked with man's view of woman as simply a sexual function and the notion that he could not survive without a sexual outlet.
>
> (Jeffreys 1985: 40)

Such women were arguing, through their writing and in organization together, that sexual relations with men, and motherhood, should be a matter of choice for women. They were exposing masculinity as fundamental to social problems:

> A determination to transform male sexual behaviour was a predominant theme of the constitutional and militant suffrage campaigners in the intense phase of feminist activity leading up to the First World War. When the vote became a major public issue after 1906 all the concerns which we have seen raised by earlier feminists in the area of sexuality came to the fore. These were the inequity of the double standard, and the effects of male sexual behaviour on women through prostitution, the white slave traffic and the sexual abuse of children. An issue which came into prominence particularly in this period was that of venereal disease. Whilst the vote was the focus of attention, issues of sexual behaviour were continually raised in the context of reasons why women needed the vote. Suffragists of all shades of opinion made it quite clear that they intended,

when the vote was gained, to be able to effect a total change in men's
sexual behaviour from a new position of strength.

(Jeffreys 1985: 44)

Those women seeking to expose the problems experienced by women and
children through prostitution, sexual abuse and incest, were radically confronting gender and race inequality. Many, through their own lives, were
showing that women do not need to service men in any way, and certainly not
sexually. They have been caricatured as spinsters and prudes. That many were
lesbians has remained hidden from history. The rise of scientific sexology and
of medical and psychoanalytic explanations of sexuality in the 1920s and
1930s dampened the understanding of sexuality and heterosexuality as social
and political forces. Compounded by an increasing devotion to motherhood
the discourse of children's departments was shaped. Within this discourse
there was little room for women managers to be anything other than nurturing,
caring and feminine. In addition any radical personal politics and subversive
activity would have remained hidden from our eyes. Women campaigning in
the 1880s and 1890s against the sexual abuse of children by men called for
women magistrates, doctors and women watchers or wardens at police
stations 'in order to prevent suffering from the possible vice, brutality, or
incompetency in illness of male officials' (National Vigilance Association
quoted in Jeffreys 1985: 61). The later call for children's officers to be women
may be similarly understood.

Powerful and powerless women

Many with power in organizations are increasingly eager for women to be
promoted into management. It solves the need to display themselves publicly as
equal opportunities employers and responds to the changing demographic
characteristics of the labour market. A critical analysis of the implementation
of equal opportunities legislation in relation to equality is demanded to ensure
that the feminist call for more women to enter management is not co-opted by
organizations anxious to display themselves as progressive and caring. To
promote women into management does not necessarily bring a change in
values and policies in the organization. Women can share the same values as
the men in management they replace. They can reinforce, or be used to
reinforce, those values, policies and processes which maintain women as
disadvantaged and oppressed in the public and private spheres. It is important
to reflect critically not only on the politics of women who may be promoted
into management but also on the political processes in organizations, mediated
through gender, class, race and femininity, that render some women powerful
and others powerless.

Large welfare organizations in both the statutory and voluntary sectors are
commonly hierarchical. Management is perceived to be undertaken by the few
at the top of the organizational pyramid, where people are paid more for the
job that they do. Gender inequality in pay and in managerial responsibility is
pervasive in such organizations. In this sense justice demands that more
women are promoted into management. However, while this may do

something to reduce the inequality of some women in relation to some men, it will do little to 'save' social work. The implications of the appointment of a New Right managerialist woman are clear. It would favourably alter the employment and income statistics relating to gender, and enhance the living standards of this particular woman, but it would do nothing to alter the patriarchal nature of welfare and its oppressive effect on women workers and clients.

Power operates formally and informally in organizations. Some decisions are made visibly through explicit and designated structures. Others emerge from the so-called informal organization: at parties and in pubs, in staff clubs and secret societies. Informal in this context quite wrongly suggests something ad hoc, haphazard and casual. The opposite is true. While the form of social intercourse and environment might appropriately be described as informal, the unwritten rules which determine who should be included, on what terms and upholding which values are as systematic as if they were written in a formal constitution. The informal organization supports and maintains formal decision-making structures and processes. It helps to ensure that policy outcomes are contained within acceptable boundaries. Key decisions are at best rubber-stamped, but more usually are assumed in the formal organization. More fundamentally, non-decisions are made: those decisions that leave issues off the formal agenda, that set up working parties in place of policy implementation programmes (should an unacceptable policy decision get through), that ensure that participatory processes in the formal organization include some while excluding others. Decision-making and non-decision-making (the very structuring of the agenda and processes for the making and implementing of decisions) (Bachrach and Baratz 1970) intermesh with predominant values and ideology (Lukes 1974). Thus, power in the organization operates publicly through hierarchical domination, but fundamentally through predominant values and mechanisms that maintain and reinforce class, race and gender divisions. Probably the most fundamental non-decision in some parts of social services and probation concerns the adoption of informal ways of working and processes of decision-making. Informality, a reaction to the structured and oppressive formality of large hierarchical bureaucracies, is thought to be more 'people-centred', less inhibitive and thus more participative. Practitioners' involvement in decision-making takes place in meetings that are not chaired, agenda'd or minuted; people drop in when they can and leave as soon as they can; ideas and plans are developed 'off the tops of heads' rather than through consideration of carefully informed papers. This culture of informality is not the same as the informal organization. But it is governed by the same implicit power relations unchecked through public procedures.

Thus 'structurelessness' becomes a way of masking power. . . . The rules of how decisions are made are known only to a few and awareness of power is curtailed by those who know the rules, as long as the structure of the group is informal. Those who do not know the rules and are not chosen for initiation must remain in confusion, or suffer from paranoid delusions that something is happening of which they are not quite aware.

(Freeman 1984: 6)

Crucial to gender relations within the work-place are questions of sexuality and sexual harassment. Elsewhere in this volume, the exercise of power through sexual harassment is further explored and such processes made more visible (Wise and Stanley in this volume, Chapter 2). Beyond vital questions of harassment attention must be paid to the fundamental 'relationship between power structures and the day-to-day negotiation and production of power' and 'connections between domination, sexuality and pleasure' (Pringle 1988: x). Heterosexuality, and masculinity and femininity, provide a means through which class, race and gender divisions are maintained. They are crucial to understanding the processes by which, through promotion into management, some women can become powerful; others can feel powerful, and yet be powerless; and the remainder, whether in management or on the shop-floor, feel and recognize their powerlessness. Women as managers are expected to conform to the stereotypical roles of mothers, carers and wives at the same time as being managers. Such roles are constructed heterosexually. Assertive but feminine women are tolerated so long as they continue to attend to the emotional and sexual needs of men. This is as important in relation to men who are hierarchically superior as to those lower in the pecking order. Thus, institutional racism and sexism interrelating with heterosexuality maintain the expectation that black and white women remain deferential to men, irrespective of hierarchical position. Femininity, with nurture and care, is exploited for its potential to facilitate social control: both the control of women and the control of men potentially in dispute with management.

> Femininity is constructed on the site vacated by masculinity, and this absence of maleness is manifested in two opposing sets of expectations, revolving around the socially ambiguous status of dependence. On the one hand, femininity is characterised by self-control and independence. Being a normal woman means coping, caring, nurturing and sacrificing self-interest to the needs of others. It also means being intuitively sensitive to those needs without them being actively spelt out. It means being more than a man, in order to embrace and support Man. On the other hand, femininity is characterised by lack of control and dependence. Being a normal woman means needing protection. It means being childlike, incapable, fragile and capricious. It is being less than man in order to serve and defer to Man.

(Carlen and Worrall 1987: 3)

The promotion of women as nurturers and carers fits with the organizations need for a human, equal opportunities face. Assertiveness training, Gucci briefcases, smartly feminine executive-style little numbers from the fashion houses and support networks: all these help women to fit. The literature on women in management concentrates on coping with the stress that arises from tokenism, discrimination, harassment and juggling the responsibilities at home as well as at work (Davidson and Cooper 1983; Groocock 1988). The handy hints on grooming for success, paying attention to appearance, body language, personal effectiveness in handling difficult situations assertively rather than aggressively, and saying 'No' without giving offence (Borland Hart 1980; Cannie 1979; Dunlop 1972; Fenn 1978; Hegarty 1976; Nelson 1979) all clearly conceptualize women as well fitted to the human relations school of management. Courses for women in management adopt the same approach, perhaps best encapsulated by a British Institute of Management two-day workshop on the Assertive Woman Manager designed to 'help women to use their power and authority as managers in ways that are effective, satisfying and not damaging to other people' (British Institute of Management 1989). The development of training and support networks for women in management needs to be understood in the context of current approaches to management.

Thinking about management

Two fundamental schools of management have informed management practice: the scientific, technical, rational ideology, promoted by the Harvard Business School (Taylor 1947), and the human relations ideology often associated with the Tavistock Institute (Mayo 1933). In the former, management is the province of experts schooled in the science of rational, logical, passionless analysis and decision-making. The human relations model calls also for experts but they should be informed by an understanding of human behaviour, motivation and attitude change. Within this approach it is argued that authority is more likely to be complied with and referred to if social as well as economic rewards and sanctions are applied. Control by top management, in both schools, was not questioned:

> If the human relations school's metaphor was the 'family' rather than the 'machine' of classical models, the organization was still thought to require a rational controller at its head. Writers on management practice and organization theory distinguished between the managers' logic of efficiency and the workers' logic of sentiment.

> (Kanter 1977: 24)

During the 1960s and 1970s theoretical analysis and evidence developed to reveal the hidden dimension of both schools: power (French and Raven 1959; Etzioni 1961; Kanter 1977). People in organizations became increasingly aware that both scientific and psychoanalytic models of management served to place management control firmly in the province of experts, thus ensuring that organizational decision-making and prioritizing remained technical and did not become political. Things were becoming dangerous: something was needed to stop the tide. Enterprise, supported and promoted through the training agency, has come to the rescue. The 'enterprise culture' combines enhanced professionalism of management with corporate identity and loyalty achieved through interpersonal and team skills development. It divorces power and responsibility. Teams of workers, be they NHS units, schools, or

Griffiths-style teams in social services, know that they are responsible for the continued effectiveness, even survival, of their service. Power is centralized.

Women are accorded a particular place in this humanized and enterprising organizational culture. Kanter suggests that despite the human relations approach

> adding what some have called a 'feminized' element to the old 'masculine ethic' . . . for most of the twentieth century a 'masculine ethic' of rationality dominated the spirit of managerialism and gave the manager role its defining image.
>
> (Kanter 1977: 25)

The new wave of enterprise incorporates women more firmly into management: after all, interpersonal skills are their very *raison d'être*. At the same time, equal opportunities requirements appear to be met. The human relations school of today combines management leadership qualities with personal effectiveness and self-development appropriate for the enterprise culture. Managers are given opportunity, through networks and training, to socialize together, to develop corporate cultures and to acquire personal skills for care and control in the pursuit of common purpose. Potential conflict is thwarted before it arises. Enterprise confirms the professionalization of a political activity and is rapidly sweeping into the public sector. Social work organizations are permeable to such change in that they are imbued with notions of people-centredness and profess skills in interpersonal relations. They have 'been built around the individual pathology model of practice and, therefore, . . . promote the traditional approaches of social work practice which maintain the status quo' (Gillman 1981: 1). The 'status quo' when Gillman was writing was bad enough. The collusion between such organizations and current government policy can be disastrous. Women trained and socialized to be enterprising, powerful women in their contribution of femininity to management effectiveness, will not save social work from patriarchy and New Right models of welfare.

Women as radical subversives don't fit within this paradigm. By accident some may find their way into management. Their ability to save social work will be curtailed by political processes in the organization designed to render them powerless. Kanter (1977) has described the processes of tokenism:

> Those women who were only few in number among male peers and often had 'only woman' status became tokens: symbols of how women can do, stand-ins for all women. Sometimes they had the advantages of those who are 'different' and thus were highly visible in a system where success is tied to becoming known. Sometimes they faced the loneliness of the outsider, of the stranger who intrudes upon an alien culture and may become self-estranged in the process of assimilation.
>
> (Kanter 1977: 207)

Tokenism operates to make women, and others in the minority in organizations, black people and people with disabilities, highly visible, but denies their individuality. They are stereotyped to behave as women should, as nurturers and carers, as appropriate lovers and mothers. They are noticed for their mistakes and for the ways they fail to match the appropriate model of woman in management. They are expected to perform as women should, to be gentle, compassionate, caring, and to leave the politics to the menfolk. Women as radical subversives will be matched against such models and against the good girls in the organization. They will be alienated from men and from other such women. The socialization in management training and networks brings with it not only cohesion, but also exclusion. The refusal or even inability to acquire and profess feminine accomplishments will lead to such women's becoming marginalized in the organization. They will be regarded as not proper managers because they are not proper women. Essentially because they, like some women before them, refuse to defer to men through femininity in heterosexually constructed organizations. Men and women, both hierarchically above and below them, will find ways to ignore such women by discrediting them.

One of the very problems with social work, with serious consequences for its ability to resist New Right changes in welfare, is that the power of management is not resisted or challenged. Practitioners lack autonomy. Gillman refers to 'the lack of confidence social workers have in their ability to be autonomous professionals' (Gillman 1981: 8). In 1959, Wootton criticized social workers for their paternalistic approach to clients (Wootton 1959). Thirty years later, the criticism could be extended. Daddy has become the manager: the social worker the mere messenger of 'what he knows best!' Daddy doesn't know best and neither, necessarily, would Mummy! Women in management won't make the difference, so long as the culture and traditions of these departments remain as they are. Too much is invested in management, too much is passively received from on high, too little in these departments is informed by an ongoing critical reflection and evaluation of practice. It is the responsibility of practitioners to provide evidence through their practice of the injustice of economic and social structure and policy, and the hardship and distress experienced by people as a result. It is vital that practitioners do not become comfortable in their bureaucratic organizations but act on their ethical responsibility to change the organization if it fails to meet the needs of its users (Resnick and Patti 1980, referred to by Gillman 1981: 12).

Reflection

There can be no conclusion. There are no simple strategies. It is dangerous, in its diversion, to suppose that the saving of social work will come through promoting women into management. To call for more women in management is open to exploitation. 'Good' employers will jump at it to demonstrate their human values. They will co-opt the 'natural' qualities of women in nurture and care to develop the style of management in interpersonal skills appropriate for the organization in consensus. Women will jump at it to pursue their personal careers, achieving status without real power. What is important to save social work is that those with the political values and determination to pursue change for equality assume power in the organization by acting autonomously in alliance with others. This may or may not mean being in the jobs formally prescribed as management. The power to change must not be assigned only to those with formal management positions. As policy is made through practice and not received passively from on high, so management must be similarly understood.

References

Allan, L. (1989) 'Women's vital role at work', *Employment Gazette*, March: 118–21.

Ash, A. (1987) *Father–Daughter Sexual Abuse: The Abuse of Paternal Authority*, Bangor: Department of Social Theory and Institutions, University College of North Wales.

Bachrach, P. and Baratz, M. S. (1970) *Power and Poverty, Theory and Practice*, New York: Oxford University Press.

Borland Hart, L. (1980) *Moving Up! Women and Leadership*, New York: Amacom.

British Institute of Management (1989) *Development Programme for Managers*, Corby, Northants: British Institute of Management Foundation.

Brook, E. and Davis, A. (eds) (1985) *Women, the Family and Social Work*, London: Tavistock.

Brownmiller, S. (1975) *Against Our Will: Men, Women and Rape*, Harmondsworth: Penguin.

Burden, D. S. and Gottlieb, N. (eds) (1987) *The Woman Client: Providing Human Services in a Changing World*, New York and London: Tavistock.

Calvert, J. (1985) 'Motherhood', in E. Brook and A. Davis (eds) *Women, the Family and Social Work*, London: Tavistock.

Campbell, B. (1988) *Unofficial Secrets, Child Sexual Abuse: The Cleveland Case*, London: Virago.

Cannie, J. K. (1979) *The Woman's Guide to Management Success: How to Win Power in the Real Organisational World*, Englewood Cliffs, NJ: Prentice-Hall.

Carlen, P. (1988) *Women, Crime and Poverty*, Milton Keynes: Open University Press.

Carlen, P. and Worrell, A. (eds) (1987) *Gender, Crime and Justice*, Milton Keynes: Open University Press.

Corea, G., Duelli Klein, R., Hanmer, J., Holmes, H. B., Hoskins, B. and Kishwar, M. (1985) *Man-Made Woman: How New Reproductive Technologies Affect Women*, London: Hutchinson.

Coyle, A. (1989) 'Women in Management: a suitable case for treatment?', *Feminist Review* 31, spring: 117–25.

Curtis Committee (1946) *Care of Children: Interdepartment Committee Report*, Curtis Report, Cmd 6922, London: HMSO.

Dale, J. and Foster, P. (1986) *Feminists and State Welfare*, London: Routledge & Kegan Paul.

Davidson, M. and Cooper, C. (1983) *Stress and the Woman Manager*, Oxford: Martin Robertson.

Davis, A., Llewelyn, S. and Parry, G. (1985) 'Women and Mental Health Towards an Understanding', in E. Brook and A. Davis (eds), *Women, the Family and Social Work*, London: Tavistock.

Dunlop, J. (1972) *Personal and Professional Success for Women*, Englewood Cliffs, NJ: Prentice-Hall.

Employment Gazette, (1989a) April, 159–72.

—— (1989b) March, 11.

Etzioni, A. (1961) *The Comparative Analysis of Complex Organizations*, New York: Free Press.

Fenn, M. (1978) *Making it in Management: A Behavioural Approach for Women Executives*, Englewood Cliffs, NJ: Prentice-Hall.

Finch, J. and Groves, D. (eds) (1983) *A Labour of Love: Women, Work and Caring*, London: Routledge & Kegan Paul.

Freeman, J. (1984) 'The tyranny of structurelessness', *Untying the Knot: Feminism, Anarchism and Organisation*, London: Dark Star Press and Rebel Press.

French, J. R. P. and Raven, B. (1959) 'The bases of social power' in D. Cartwright (ed.) *Studies in Social Power*, Ann Arbor, Mich.: University of Michigan, Institute for Social Research.

Gillman, M. (1981) *Integrating Family Therapy into Social Services Area Teams*, Birmingham: Charles Burns Clinic, unpublished mimeo.

Glendinning, C. and Millar, J. (eds) (1987) *Women and Poverty in Britain*, Brighton: Wheatsheaf.

Graham, H. (1984) *Women, Health and the Family*, Brighton: Harvester.

Grimwood, C. (1989) 'Training is the key to change', *Community Care* 31 August: i–ii.

Groocock, V. (1988) *Women Mean Business: A Success and Survival Guide for the Woman Executive*, London: Ebury.

Hadley, R. and Hatch, S. (1981) *Social Welfare and the Failure of the State: Centralised Social Services and Participatory Alternatives*, London: Allen & Unwin.

Hanmer, J. and Statham, D. (1988) *Women and Social Work: Towards a Women-Centred Practice*, London: Macmillan.

Hanmer, J., Radford, J. and Stanko, E. A. (1989) *Women, Policing, and Male Violence*, London: Routledge.

Hanscombe, G. E. and Forster, J. (1982) *Rocking the Cradle: Lesbian Mothers, a Challenge in Family Living*, London: Sheba.

Hegarty, E. J. (1976) *How to Succeed in Company Politics*, New York: McGraw-Hill.

Hicks, C. (1988) *Who Cares: Looking after People at Home*, London: Virago.

Howe, D. (1986) 'The segregation of women and their work in the personal social services', *Critical Social Policy* 15, spring: 21–35.

Hudson, A. (1986) 'Troublesome girls: towards alternative definitions and strategies', in *Girls in Trouble – Whose Problem? New Approaches to Work with Young Women for Social Work Agencies*, London: Rainer Foundation with CCETSW and the Adolescents Project.

Jeffreys, S. (1985) *The Spinster and her Enemies: Feminism and Sexuality 1880–1930*, London: Pandora.

Kanter, R. (1977) *Men and Women of the Corporation*, New York: Basic Books.

LACSAB and ADSS (Association of Directors of Social Services) (1989a) *Survey of Social Services Employment 1988, Report no. 1*, London: LACSAB and ADSS, May.

—— (1989b) *Survey of Social Services Employment 1988, Report no. 2, Key Results*, London: LACSAB and ADSS, May.

Lockley, J. and Fawcett, J. (1989) 'There is another way', *Community Care* 31 August: vi–vii.

Lukes, S. (1974) *Power: A Radical View*, London: Macmillan.

Mama, A. (1989) 'Violence against black women: gender, race, and state responses', *Feminist Review* 32, summer: 30–48.

Mayo, E. (1933) *The Human Problems of an Industrial Civilisation*, New York: Macmillan.

National Vigilance Association, *Committee Minutes*, 3 January 1889.

Nelson, R. (1979) *Success without Tears: A Woman's Guide to the Top*, London: Weidenfeld & Nicolson.

Packman, J. (1975) *The Child's Generation: Child Care Policy from Curtis to Houghton*, Oxford and London: Blackwell and Robertson.

Pahl, J. (ed.) (1985) *Private Violence and Public Policy: The Needs of Battered Women and the Response of the Public Services*, London: Routledge & Kegan Paul.

Parker, J. (1988) *Women and Welfare: Ten Victorian Women in Public Social Service*, London: Macmillan.

Pringle, R. (1988) *Secretaries Talk: Sexuality, Power and Work*, London: Verso.

Reid, I. and Wormald, E. (eds) (1982) *Sex Differences in Britain*, London: Grant McIntyre.

Resnick, H. and Patti, R. J. (1980) *Change from Within: Humanising Social Welfare Organisations*, Philadelphia: Temple University Press.

Rich, A. (1977) *Of Woman Born: Motherhood as Experience and Institution*, London: Virago.

Roberts, H. (ed.) (1981) *Women, Health and Reproduction*, London: Routledge & Kegan Paul.

Smart, C. (1984) *The Ties that Bind: Law, Marriage and the Reproduction of Patriarchal Relations*, London: Routledge & Kegan Paul.

Social Services Year Book, 1989/90 (1989) London: Longman.

Taylor, F. W. (1947) *Scientific Management*, New York: Harper & Row.

Walton, R. (1975) *Women in Social Work*, London: Routledge & Kegan Paul.

Wells, O. (1983) *Promotion and the Woman Probation Officer*, London: National Association of Probation Officers.

Wootton, B. (1959) 'Daddy knows best', *Twentieth Century*, October, winter: 248–61.

12
Which direction for assisted reproduction?

Eric Blyth

Involuntary childlessness is seen to strike at the very heart of self-esteem and adult identity. According to one recent medical authority:

> Probably no human affliction causes more distress than the inability to have children. . . . Today, infertility has reached epidemic proportions in America, Britain and Western Europe.
>
> (Newill 1986: xii)

Estimates indicate that between one in six and one in ten of the adult UK population of childbearing age may be involuntary childless (Mathieson 1986) although since such statistics tend to be extrapolated from the numbers attending for infertility treatment – primarily heterosexual couples – it is quite possibly an underestimate of the incidence of infertility in the whole population. In addition there are people for whom pregnancy and childbirth carry significant health risks, either for women themselves or for the children because of possible inherited genetic disabilities.

In recent years childless people have become increasingly vocal about their needs and have become better organized. Measures purporting to assist them achieve parenthood have assumed a greater technological profile and widescale publicity has accompanied the activities of entrepreneurial medical practitioners whose endeavours are underwritten by research institutions and the pharmaceutical industry. Technological developments in assisted reproduction (AR) and genetic research now hold the promise of parenthood for carriers of inherited illness and the virtual elimination of some forms of genetically transmitted disability.

However, developments in AR have not taken place in a vacuum. They have tested the limits of accepted legal, ethical and social systems in modern

societies. Conventional assumptions about 'the family' and family relationships, and about the relationship between individuals and society have been
challenged. New practices in child-creation have raised questions about how
far society should sanction and devote public resources to individuals'
attempts and wishes to become parents, and how far AR should be a matter of
private concern or subjected to state control.

At the same time, by successfully medicalizing relatively simple procedures
such as 'artificial' insemination, doctors have taken control of a substantial
share of AR services and look set to establish a state-legitimized professional
monopoly. For some, these developments have had less to do with AR than
with genetic engineering – a malevolent patriarchal plot to do away eventually
with women altogether (e.g. Spallone and Steinberg 1987). In Britain AR and
the related issue of embryo research have been the subject of a government-
appointed Committee of Inquiry chaired by Mary Warnock (DHSS 1984), a
subsequent DHSS White Paper (DHSS 1987), and a government Bill (HMSO
1989).

This chapter provides an outline of the nature of AR provision and a critique
of the debate concerning its future direction and regulation. Space limitations
will confine discussion for the most part to policies and practice in Britain.

The nature of AR services

Currently a range of services to assist infertile people exists. The principal
techniques are drug therapy, 'artificial' insemination (AI) and in vitro
fertilization (IVF). Winston (1986) provides a 'user-friendly' account of AR
services. Drug therapy is used to induce and regulate ovulation and improve
the quality of semen. AI involves depositing semen in the vagina close to the
cervix normally using a hypodermic syringe or other 'artificial' means.
Inseminated semen may come from the woman's partner or from a donor. IVF
is a process in which an egg is extracted from a woman and fertilized outside
the female body. IVF was developed primarily as a means of bypassing female
tubal disease which prevented fertilization taking place within the female
body. IVF may be accompanied by other procedures, notably Gamete
Intrafallopian Transfer (GIFT) and Embryo Transfer (ET). In GIFT egg and
semen are injected into the fallopian tube to enable fertilization to take place in
the woman's body rather than 'in vitro', while ET is the process by which an
embryo is placed in the uterus.

Surrogacy, the least technical of AR techniques and probably the longest-
established, describes the process by which a woman becomes pregnant and
carries a child which she will hand over to another person or couple at birth.
Conception is most usually achieved through artificial insemination of the
'commissioning father's' semen, although sexual intercourse between surrogate mother and commissioning father has been known to take place. More
rarely the surrogate has become pregnant following the use of donor semen or
following sexual intercourse with her male partner.

Commercial surrogacy, in which a fee is explicitly agreed with the birth
mother, is legalized in certain countries. It is currently outlawed in Britain,

although informal surrogacy is permitted here. Professional workers are rarely overtly involved in surrogacy arrangements, and the Warnock Committee recommended they should be legally prevented from actively assisting in the establishment of any surrogate pregnancy.

Provision of services

With the exception of commercial surrogacy AR services are not at present subject to statutory regulation in Britain and are provided on an ad-hoc basis through NHS facilities, private specialist clinics and hospitals, charitable organizations and self-help groups. Although no comprehensive information is available about the complete range of services some empirical studies have been completed (Mathieson 1986; Pfeffer and Quick 1987; Steinberg 1986). In addition the Medical Research Council and the Royal College of Obstetricians and Gynaecologists have jointly established a temporary Voluntary Licensing Authority (VLA) for Human In Vitro Fertilisation and Embryology. Since 1986 the VLA has produced annual reports about licensed IVF services.

Taken as a whole these sources of direct information indicate that infertility does not merit high priority within the NHS. As a consequence insufficient resources are channelled towards prevention, investigation and treatment. Even so a disproportionately high level of resources is allocated to high-cost, hi-tech treatment. Historically AR has evolved from mainstream practice in obstetrics and gynaecology while the specialized study of male infertility is virtually non-existent. As a consequence it is primarily women who are subject to invasive 'therapy.' while the problems of infertile men are largely ignored.

Robert Winston, one of the country's leading infertility practitioners, has indicted the quality of infertility services in Britain as

> scandalously poor. Women are given drugs to induce ovulation when they ovulate already; much tubal surgery is performed with instruments more suitable for sharpening pencils; infertile men are fobbed off with drugs which have no proven effect on sperm quality.
>
> (quoted in Feldman 1987: 33)

The geographical distribution of AR services is piecemeal and patchy. Those within the NHS are insufficiently 'user-friendly' and services are not always supported by adequate back-up facilities. Even basic services are rarely provided. It is common practice for men who are required to provide a semen sample to be handed a sterilized container, a supply of pornographic magazines and pointed in the direction of the Gents!

Even though recipients are required to pay for AR services provided by the NHS, many AI centres operate outside the NHS and most of the hi-tech services are provided in the private sector on a fee-paying basis. Access to services is largely dependent on the luck of geographical residence and the potential recipients' ability to pay, especially as infertility treatment is excluded from private medical insurance schemes.

Even paying a high price for treatment does not guarantee a successful outcome. Many private centres offer a relatively restricted range of services – usually the technologically sophisticated. Patients using such centres may be offered more technological and expensive forms of therapy when simpler and less expensive investigation and treatment procedures may have been more beneficial.

High rates of abortion and miscarriage accompany the more expensive, intrusive and hi-tech services, and success rates are extremely low. Some centres have inflated their claims of success, especially where continued viability depends on a regular supply of fee-paying customers. According to statistics provided by the VLA IVF success rates have shown marginal improvement in recent years, but are still no greater than one in ten:

Table 12.1   IVF live birth-rates (%)

1985	1986	1987
8.6	8.6	10.1

Source: MRC/RCOG 1988

Furthermore the multiple-pregnancy rate (MPR) is extremely high, so the actual number of people helped to become parents through IVF is not directly related to the number of IVF births. In 1987 the MPR for IVF was 22.4 per cent and for GIFT 24.7 per cent (MRC/RCOG 1989). Howie (1988) has identified the problems of multiple births following 'successful' IVF. These include premature births, early infancy death-rates in excess of 20 per cent, high levels of serious physical and mental handicap amongst survivors, resource problems in special care baby units – contributing to inadequate service delivery, and serious maternal health problems. Finally Howie identified the controversial practice of some doctors in resorting to 'selective reduction' (a medical euphemism for abortion) of surplus foetuses.

Evidence also exists of the iatrogenic consequences of less intrusive forms of intervention. The efficacy of some medication is in doubt. Hormones administered to facilitate post-coital examination may have the longer-term effect of acting as contraceptives, while the stress of investigation and treatment and regulation of sexual intercourse according to temperature charts can militate against the very behaviour it is designed to encourage. The effect of medication on semen appears to improve its quality under laboratory conditions yet has little proven impact on conception rates.

It is clear that infertile people are prepared to undergo extensive and intrusive investigation and treatment incurring high physical, emotional and financial cost in pursuit of parenthood. At the same time AR practitioners claim that their practice is primarily determined by consideration of the 'best interests' of the potential child rather than the needs or wishes of their adult patients. However, 'best interests' emerges as an essentially paternalistic concept designed to legitimize professional practice and is not infrequently

:elegated to subsidiary consideration. The dilemma posed by the 'best interests' principle is neatly summarized by Warnock:

> when we called on the good of the child as our justifying principle, we were as often as not attempting to prop ourselves up by clutching at something about to give way. . . . If we do make such judgements for the sake of the child we are hard put to it to support them by factual evidence. We are surreptitiously making *moral* judgements.
>
> (Warnock 1987: 20–1)

The child's 'best interests' can be considered in relation to the child's right to information about their genetic origins, the types of AR service made available and selection of potential recipients.

Under current British legislation adoptees have a statutory right of access to their birth records and information about their genetic origins when they attain the age of 18. In AR, however, the child's right to information about genetic origins and access to birth records is minimized. Furthermore, encouragement of duplicity and downright deceit to conceal the identity of the child's genetic father, including the mixing of donor's semen with husband's semen and destruction of clinical records, has been a hallmark of practice in AR.

The Royal College of Obstetricians and Gynaecologists still advises AID patients:

> Unless you reveal [AID conception] to your child, there is no reason for him or her ever to know that he or she was conceived by donor insemination.
>
> (RCOG 1987: 3)

Some practitioners have interpreted the intention of recipients to be open and above board about AID as a potential contra-indication for treatment (Saunders 1980).

Sandler (1987) manages to combine his insistence that the primary interest in AR must be the child's welfare with the argument against openness on the grounds that this would expose the 'father's' infertility, subject him to potential humiliation and undermine the father–child relationship. He speculates

> Telling children of their AID origin would surely have led to a much greater number of unhappy offspring than the very rare case of the child learning of his origin in an unplanned way.
>
> (Sandler 1987: 243)

The child's right to information about genetic origins is inevitably subsumed by the presumed need to safeguard donor anonymity, or to protect the feelings of infertile 'fathers'. Assumptions have been made that the removal of donor anonymity would exercise a draconian impact on the willingness of donors to continue to supply semen. However, evidence suggests that this would not necessarily occur and that donors are more likely to support openness and the possibility of being traced by their offspring than AID recipients themselves (Daniels 1987). Snowden and Snowden (1984) provide evidence that, as in adoption, parents of children born following AID can be successfully open with their children and the children themselves value their parents' honesty, experiencing few negative emotional consequences of being told. Conversely parents who maintained secrecy about their children's origins appear to have paid a high emotional price and those children who found out about their AID origins by less than direct means often expressed bitterness about their experiences.

The services and service providers

As assisted reproduction services have developed from obstetrics and gynae-cology the dominance of the medical profession should be hardly unexpected, in spite of the fact that those infertility techniques which have the most effective outcomes also tend to be the simplest to perform, requiring little in the way of clinical skills or knowledge, such as artificial insemination or surrogacy. Given the simplicity of the 'treatment' clinical expertise is not essential for AI, although the potential risk of AIDS following AID requires semen donors to be adequately tested for HIV antibodies as well as other sexually transmitted diseases. The medicalization of assisted reproduction needs to be seen as part of the wider process of medical aggrandisement and is based on social and political rather than merely technical and clinical factors. According to Snowden and Snowden (1984) the role of clinician in assisted reproduction is more properly regarded as that of 'honest broker' providing a cloak of respectability to practices which enjoy dubious social acceptance. In this context cautious and conservative practices are to be expected.

Consequently establishment disapproval of alternative DIY methods of self-insemination or surrogacy arrangements as undesirable and irresponsible are only to be expected since they permit bypassing formal control mechanisms (e.g. DHSS 1984; 1987). In Canada an official inquiry into AR concluded that all artificial insemination should be formally regulated to 'preclude unqualified persons from undertaking the procedure' (Ontario Law Reform Commission 1985: 30). The Commission argued that AI performed by 'unqualified' practitioners led to ostensibly unacceptable risks yet it conveniently ignored the (presumably acceptable but arguably greater) risks associated with much drug therapy and surgery performed by clinically qualified practitioners. It is salutary to remember that the four Australian women to contract HIV-3 antibodies following AI were patients at a reputable clinic and despite claims about the promotion of the 'best interests' of children AR clinicians still advocate the dubious practice of donor anonymity.

As already illustrated the cost of much assisted reproduction treatment serves to exclude the less financially well-off. While the Warnock Committee (DHSS 1984) recommended that everyone has a right to 'advice and investigation' of their infertility it explicitly prescribed restrictions on treat-ment to 'heterosexual couples living together in a stable relationship', even though it recognized that future marital stability and happiness were impossible to predict. It accepted that the state should not be in the business of deliberately creating single-parent families, although it did not critically examine the basis for discriminating against single people as potential parents. More generally the committee recommended that treatment could be withheld if there were 'valid' (but unspecified) reasons for believing that this would not be in the 'best interests' of the recipients or their immediate family, or the prospective child.

While accounts of clinical practice generally avoid discussion of selection criteria it is evident that, in the absence of centralized regulation, arbitrary and idiosyncratic criteria are employed. British AID centres routinely discriminate against poor applicants, those with disabilities and those of homosexual orientation (Steinberg 1986).

The major assumption supporting the utilization of social selection criteria in assisted reproduction is the primacy of the child's 'best interests' – that there is an ideal social environment for child-rearing and that there are essential parenting qualities, both of which can be identified prospectively. Clinicians have expended considerable effort in attempting to identify a psychogenic basis to infertility and there has been a traditional tendency to ascribe 'un-explained' infertility to psychological factors. Consequently part of the prac-titioner's task is to identify and exclude those who might be emotionally unsuitable.

However, neither empirical research nor clinical literature present substan-tive evidence that any psychogenic differences between fertile and infertile people are related to the cause rather than the consequences of infertility (Edelmann and Connolly 1986). Over time the reported incidence of psycho-genic infertility has decreased with improvements in diagnostic techniques.

If there is little evidence to support the psychogenic origins of infertility there is a widespread belief that infertility represents a 'psychological crisis'. Indeed the technical advances in this area have received substantial accolades on the basis that they have helped 'desperate' couples become parents.

Infertile people are obliged to demonstrate that their infertility has made some impact on their lives (or else they would be regarded as employing some repressive psychological mechanism), but they must not have allowed it to interfere 'too much' with their social and psychological functioning. 'Coming to terms with infertility' is a theme constantly referred to in adoption literature, although there is little evidence that practitioners utilize consensual under-standing of the term or can demonstrate its existence (Yingling 1987).

The British Agencies for Adoption and Fostering (BAAF 1987) argue that selection of potential recipients for assisted reproduction services is 'essential' to ensure their possession of the 'special qualities' required for successful 'artificial' parenthood. For BAAF these special qualities are intrinsically simi-lar to those pertaining to adoptive parenthood. The adoption lobby has been ready to identify the similarities between adoption and assisted reproduction – promoting its experience and expertise in devising selection criteria for poten-tial adopters in order to provide adequate and caring homes for children placed for adoption (e.g. BAAF 1984). Some medical practitioners received this advice with enthusiasm, for example Saunders (1980) endorses the use of modified adoption procedures which may have to be 'even more stringently applied' to prospective AI recipients.

However, the uncritical application of adoption practices to AR and the track record of adoption workers and agencies in their own field requires some further examination. Selecting appropriate adoptive parents and placing children with families through 'matching' procedures is now recognized as an insufficiently precise process. Indeed, there is now ready acceptance of the limitations in professional social workers' ability to predict 'good parents' and define with any degree of confidence what characteristics they should even be looking for, let alone try and find. In the light of the shortcomings of traditional selection methods in adoption, and recognition that 'there is no evidence that social workers have any proven expertise in the prediction of which adoptive parents are likely to provide a continuing, stable relationship and a secure family environment for an adopted child' (Howell and Ryburn 1987: 35), some adoption agencies have explicitly abandoned traditional practices of 'matching' and 'assessment' and developed a process of preparation and education to help applicants decide if adoption is right for them. Similar practices could be implemented in AR. However such apparently less restrictive perspectives equate recipients with 'couples', implying an insidious rejection of or a failure to acknowledge the parental aspirations of infertile single people.

Attitudes towards single or homosexual people as parents are largely based on dogma rather than argument – derived from traditional religious doctrine, psychoanalytic ideology, or downright patriarchical prejudice (Golombok and Rust 1986). In recent years the British government has waged a campaign against homosexuality, which it now devalues as a *'pretended* family relationship' (Local Government Act 1988).

Impartial evidence about single-parent and homosexual families is hard to come by, although researchers at the Institute of Psychiatry (Golombok *et al.* 1983; Golombok and Rust 1986) have in recent years considered the evidence concerning the psychosexual development of children reared in fatherless families. Their investigation refuted conventional stereotypes about lesbian families that they fail to provide children with a model of heterosexual relationships, perpetuate negative attitudes to men and impose pressure on children to adopt atypical sex roles. On the other hand the research supported the conclusion that the *major* disadvantages experienced by children living in lesbian and single-parent households derive from societal responses which subject them to prejudice and material disadvantage.

The development of policies in AR

In 1982 following emerging concerns about actual and potential developments in assisted reproduction the British government established a Committee of Inquiry into Human Fertilisation and Embryology chaired by Mary Warnock. The committee reported in 1984 (DHSS 1984) recommending legislation to permit some AR treatments and embryo research subject to regulatory control by an independent organization representing medical, scientific and lay interests. Following publication of this report the government initiated a consultation process with interested parties, prior to legislation. In advance of anticipated legislation establishing a statutory regulatory body for AR services the VLA (mentioned above) was set up. Centres licensed by the VLA are required to conform to specific guidelines, although some operate outside its remit. At the present time the RCOG maintains a list of private and NHS centres offering AID, although the Royal College undertakes no regulatory or inspectorial functions in relation to centres listed.

In 1985 in response to the highly publicized 'Baby Cotton' surrogacy case the government acted on one of the Warnock Committee's recommendations and introduced the Surrogacy Arrangements Act, which prohibited the operation of commercial surrogacy agencies. In 1987 the government published a White Paper, *Human Fertilisation and Embryology: A Framework for Legislation* (DHSS 1987), and laid a Bill before Parliament in November 1989. In the mean time the VLA decided to emphasize the point that it was only intended as a stop-gap measure by redesignating itself the Interim Licensing Authority (MRC/RCOG 1989).

Given that numerous problems with AR services have been identified, how far do the regulatory proposals recognize these and attempt to tackle them?

The major plank of the proposals is the establishment of an 'independent' Statutory Licensing Authority the Human Fertilisation and Embryology Authority (HFEA). The HFEA will have responsibility for regulating and licensing treatments and research involving human embryos, treatments involving the use of donated human eggs or sperm, storage of human gametes or embryos and use of diagnostic tests involving cross-species fertilization. In addition the HFEA will have responsibility for advising ministers, providing reports to Parliament and guidance on 'good practice', maintaining a register of information about gamete and embryo donations and resulting births. In fulfilling its responsibilities the HFEA will have powers of inspection and will be able to impose (so far unspecified) licensing criteria. Despite proposals that membership of the HFEA will represent medical, scientific and lay interests it will serve to confirm the control over AR services that the medical establishment has already achieved. Given that the MRC and RCOG have successfully pre-empted legislation by establishing the ILA this body and its sponsoring organizations will have at least five years' experience behind them and will be in a uniquely strong position to influence the composition and direction of a statutory body.

The pre-eminence of formally regulated AR services will be further promoted by the proposal that unlicensed practice should be subject to criminal sanctions. This means that procedures such as AID, which are currently totally unregulated, will become the exclusive prerogative of licensed practitioners. Self-help AID would be criminalized even though policing such practice would be totally impractical. Ironically, if not inconsistently, the government recognized this dilemma in relation to surrogacy. The Bill proposes that commercial surrogacy should continue to be prohibited. However, since private and non-commercial surrogacy cannot be successfully eradicated, they will be permitted in law but are not to be encouraged. Currently professional involvement in surrogacy arrangements is discouraged – a practice which may well serve to prevent those contemplating surrogacy from obtaining necessary medical and legal information and treatment or the opportunity to discuss in detail the possible consequences of their actions. Indeed it was this vacuum which created the climate for the emergence of a self-help organization, Childlessness Overcome Through Surrogacy (COTS). However, although there is a positive disincentive for professionals to become involved in surrogacy before the event, it is a different matter afterwards, for social workers at least. Current guidance to Social Services Departments (DHSS 1985) reminds local authorities of their responsibility to ensure that the child born as the result of a surrogacy arrangement will not be 'at risk'. Such a responsibility requires social services departments to investigate all known cases of surrogacy. It could be argued that the interests of all parties might be better served if official intervention were to take place at an earlier stage rather than following the child's birth, especially if legal and emotional complications arise, such as the birth mother's changing her mind about parting with her child. The Ontario Law Reform Commission (1985) took the view that it was indeed preferable if surrogacy were to be subject to legal sanction and control. Currently the British government appears not to have made up its mind completely on surrogacy and indicates that the HFEA will be required to keep the question of surrogacy under review. The White Paper envisages the possibility that, at some future stage, non-commercial surrogacy services could be brought within the remit of the HFEA.

The Bill requires all licensed infertility and donor centres to make counselling services available to potential AR recipients. Counselling should be distinguished from discussions with the practitioner about specifically medical treatment and should be provided by someone ('preferably' qualified) other than the medical practitioner responsible for AR treatment. Apart from this neither the Bill nor the White Paper gives no further guidance on the required qualities of counsellors. Effective counselling should provide potential AR recipients with the opportunity to discuss the nature of the range of AR treatments available and their legal, social and emotional implications. At the present time where counselling is available, it tends to be provided by social workers, nurses, psychologists and members of self-help groups. Determining whether any one group is best placed to offer counselling is not my consideration here, although in the run-up to legislation competing claims from various lobbies will no doubt be made. Social work, with its experience of adoption and child care practice, has a very definite role to play. What is clear is that whoever provides counselling will need to be aware of the wide range of medical, legal, social and psychological implications of AR.

The Bill does not oblige recipients of AR treatment to avail themselves of counselling opportunities so undergoing counselling cannot be made a criterion of selection for treatment. However, by driving underground certain AR practices as a result of formal regulation some people will be denied the opportunity of receiving counselling.

The White Paper ruled against the establishment of formal statutory procedures to assess suitability for AR treatment although it will require the HFEA to take account of centres' procedures for deciding whether to offer treatment to 'particular couples'. I have earlier shown that current selection on social grounds is at best idiosyncratic, at worst blatantly discriminatory. The Bill offers no safeguards that discrimination against certain groups, those who cannot afford high-cost private treatment, those with disabilities, homosexuals, single people, and those who appear not to possess the required 'special qualities' will not be perpetuated. Given that social workers employed in AR settings are likely to find themselves in the thick of policy decisions about selection criteria they will need to examine their own assumptions about children's 'best interests'. Like everyone else, social workers are subjected to dominant ideologies which portray the normality and extol the virtues of the conventional nuclear family. However, they must also bear in mind the explicit exhortation to develop anti-discriminatory practice, whether in terms of age, race, gender, sexual orientation or disability (CCETSW 1989). They will need to question how far the operation of some selection procedures for assisted reproduction, ostensibly in the pursuit of the child's 'best interests' is consistent with such requirements.

One inevitable consequence of having formally regulated AR services utilizing rigid selection criteria is that some people will fail to be selected. It is axiomatic that there is no effective barrier to parenthood for those sufficiently determined or with adequate financial resources. Non-marital sexual relationships, private surrogacy, purchasing babies from the Third World and even baby-stealing present themselves as potential alternatives: it is hard to see how such developments best serve the interests of children. Those who advocate both the state control and regulation of all assisted reproduction services and the application of formal selection criteria need to recognize both the impracticality of effectively policing such a system and the consequences that follow from it.

Finally the Bill will require the HFEA to maintain a confidential record of births following donations and details identifying donors. However, parents registering the birth of a child will not be obliged to disclose whether the child was born following gamete or embryo donation and although children so born will have a right of access to this knowledge at the age of 18, they will probably only receive *non-identifying* information about the donor. The nature of this information is yet to be prescribed. The White Paper recognizes the potential spuriousness of the argument that removal of donor anonymity would drastically curtail supplies of donated semen yet the Bill has failed to take the opportunity to challenge current medical practice and will allow the perpetuation of deception. The White Paper avoided a positive stand by lamely acknowledging that attitudes towards donor anonymity and the child's right to identifying information about the donor may change in the future. Even though future changes concerning access to information about genetic origins could be made retro-active this will do little for those already born following AR techniques whose links with their genetic past have already been irretrievably destroyed as a result of the deliberate destruction of records.

Conclusion

The proposals contained in the Bill fall far short of adequately addressing a number of significant issues: the protection of children's rights, the abolition of discriminatory practices, the development of more humane AR services and greater emphasis on preventive work and identifying the causes of infertility. These are areas in which social workers, as well as others committed to progress in AR, can make a potential contribution.

Superficially convincing claims that practice is inherently derived from children's 'best interests' principles or that such interests will necessarily be safeguarded should be treated with circumspection. Rather the idea of children's rights should be substituted for the paternalistic concept of 'best interests' and all such claims should be rigorously checked and challenged, if need be, to ensure that 'the welfare of the child' is not being used to disguise coercive or discriminatory practice. While I earlier expressed a measure of scepticism about the relevance of some adoption practice for AR, there are clear parallels in relation to rights of access to information about genetic origins. Similarly there are lessons to be learned from the development of the more progressive practices of 'selecting' prospective adopters and consumer accounts of their experiences of the adoption process.

Social workers have had considerable experience of working in non-social work settings, hospitals, schools, prisons, etc. and of contributing to the development of humane service-delivery. While it is evident that consumer satisfaction is higher with AR services in the private rather than NHS sector (Pfeffer and Quick 1987) there is also a need for more humane provision in both sectors. Those infertile people who utilize private AR services (and not exclusively the very rich) do so primarily because of the inadequacy of NHS provision rather than on ideological grounds; NHS charges tend to price the very poor out of an AR service altogether. While social workers are unlikely to experience difficulty in urging improvements in NHS facilities for infertile people their potential role in private health care may be more ethically challenging. However, if the private sector continues to be responsible for a major proportion of AR services (and there seems little reason to presume this will not be the case) this challenge must be faced.

AR services in this country will soon be subject to formal regulation. Social work's contribution to AR has hitherto been conspicuously less significant than it might be. However, the experience and expertise of social work can contribute to the vital examination of current practice, the assumptions which underpin it and the development of improved future services.

References

BAAF (British Agencies for Adoption and Fostering) (1984) *AID and After*, London: BAAF.
—— (1987) *Response to DHSS Consultation Paper: Legislation on Human Infertility Services and Embryo Research, December 1986*, London: BAAF.
CCETSW (Central Council for Education and Training in Social Work) (1989) *Statement of Requirements for Qualification in Social Work*, London: CCETSW.
Daniels, K. R. (1987) 'Semen donors in New Zealand: their characteristics and attitudes', *Clinical Reproduction and Fertility*, 5: 177–90.
DHSS (1984) *Report of the Committee of Enquiry into Human Fertilisation and Embryology*, Warnock Report, Cmnd 9414, London: HMSO.

—— (1985) *Responsibilities of Local Authority Social Services Departments in Surrogacy Cases*, LAC(85)12 HC(85)21, London: HMSO.

—— (1987) *Human Fertilisation and Embryology: A Framework for Legislation*, Cm 259, London: HMSO.

Edelmann, R. J. and Connolly, K. J. (1986) 'Psychological aspects of infertility', *British Journal of Medical Psychology* 59: 209–19.

Feldman, R. (1987) 'The politics of the new reproductive technologies', *Critical Social Policy* 7, 1: 21–39.

Golombok, S. and Rust, J. (1986) 'The Warnock Report and single women: what about the children?' *Journal of Medical Ethics* 12, 4: 182–6.

Golombok, S., Spencer, A. and Rutter, M. (1983) 'Children in single-parent and lesbian households: psychosexual and psychiatric appraisal', *Journal of Psychiatry and Psychology* 24: 551–72.

HMSO (1989) *Human Fertilisation and Embryology Bill*, London: HMSO.

Howell, D. and Ryburn, M. (1987) 'New Zealand: new ways to choose adopters', *Adoption and Fostering* 11, 4: 38–41.

Howie, P. (1988) 'Selective reduction in multiple pregnancy', *British Medical Journal* 297, 6,646: 433–4.

Local Government Act (1988) Section 28. Chapter 9. London: HMSO.

Mathieson, D. (1986) *Infertility Services in the NHS: What's Going On?*, London: House of Commons.

MRC/RCOG (Medical Research Council and Royal College of Obstetricians and Gynaecologists) (1988) *The Third Report of the Voluntary Licensing Authority for Human In Vitro Fertilisation and Embryology*, London: MRC/RCOG.

—— (1989) *The Fourth Report of the Voluntary Licensing Authority for Human In Vitro Fertilisation and Embryology*, London: MRC/RCOG.

Newill, R. (1986) 'Preface', in J. Bellina and J. Wilson (eds) *The Fertility Handbook: A Positive and Practical Guide*, Harmondsworth: Penguin.

Ontario Law Reform Commission (1985) *Report on Human Artificial Reproduction and Related Matters*, Ministry of the Attorney General, Ontario.

Pfeffer, N. and Quick, A. (1987) *Infertility Services: A Desperate Case*, London: Greater London Association of Community Health Councils.

RCOG (Royal College of Obstetricians and Gynaecologists) (1987) *Artificial Insemination*, London: RCOG.

Sandler, B. (1987) 'Donor insemination: more facts and less fantasies', *British Journal of Sexual Medicine* 14, 9: 243–4.

Saunders, D. (1980) 'Assessment of the infertile couple for AID', in C. Wood, J. Leeton and G. Kovacs (eds) *Artificial Insemination by Donor*, Melbourne: Brown Prior Anderson.

Snowden, R. and Snowden, E. M. (1984) *The Gift of a Child*, London: Allen & Unwin.

Spallone, P. and Steinberg, D. L. (eds) (1987) *Made to Order: The Myth of Reproductive and Genetic Progress*, Oxford: Pergamon Press.

Steinberg, D. L. (1986) 'Research in progress: a report on policies of access to AID as a medical treatment in the UK', *Women's Studies International Forum* 9, 5: 551–4.

Warnock, M. (1987) 'Ethics, decision-making and social policy', *Community Care* 685: 18–23.

Winston, R. (1986) *Infertility: A Sympathetic Approach*, London: Martin Dunitz.

Yingling, D. (1987) 'The high stakes of motherhood', *Guardian* 16 September: 13.

13
Your arguments
for equality

John Baker

Are you depressed and angry about the destruction of the welfare state and the rampant contempt for equality which has accompanied it? I am, too. Reversing the tide won't be easy, but one of the things we can do to help is to reassert and reformulate the case for equality itself. Equality, however, is a complicated idea. Its expression, defence and implementation depend on a co-operative project involving people with many types of experience. This chapter is addressed to welfare workers as participants in that project. In it, I ask you for your contributions to the case for equality: to clarifying its central principles, to reinforcing the arguments in its favour, and to developing the practical policies necessary for its implementation.

Clarifying the central principles of equality

Equality has been defined in various ways. My own view is that it is helpful to think of it under several basic headings. First, there is the principle that everyone has the right to the satisfaction of their basic needs. Egalitarians reject the idea that some should live in luxury while others face utter deprivation. Instead, they look forward to a society in which everyone has not just a bearable, but a satisfying, fulfilling life. Second, egalitarians stand for equal respect. They reject any form of degrading treatment or circumstances, as well as the patronizing attitudes of the privileged and the deference which they foster. Egalitarians look towards a society in which everyone has an equal social status, and in which people relate to each other on the basis of fellow-feeling or community, not hierarchy.

Egalitarians also believe in economic and political equality. They call for much more equality in income and wealth, both within societies and between them, as well as for democratic control of production and access to decent work for everyone who wants it. They value the formal political rights of voting, free speech, and so on, but for them political equality means equal power, and thus a wide-ranging and imaginative extension of democratic participation. Finally, egalitarians stand for sexual, racial, ethnic and religious equality, rejecting the ways in which some people are treated worse than others because of gender, skin colour, culture, or any other irrelevant difference.

One of the contributions welfare workers can make to egalitarianism is to help to clarify and defend the central concepts in which these principles are expressed. To illustrate, I want to look in particular at the ideas of need and respect, and at the meaning of sexual, racial, and ethnic equality.

Needs

The idea of need is a central, justifying concept in welfare work, but explaining what needs are raises serious problems. Most accounts start by distinguishing 'instrumental' needs from 'intrinsic' needs. Instrumental needs are things someone requires for some particular purpose, like needing a can opener to open a tin of beans. Intrinsic needs are things without which a person would suffer harm. But harm of what kind? Some authors think that this can be defined very generally, as damage to the interests which all human beings have in survival and personal autonomy (Plant *et al.* 1980; Wiggins 1985). Others take a more socially relative approach. Braybrooke (1987: 48) relates need to what people in a particular society require for performing the basic roles of parent, householder, worker and citizen, while Walzer (1983: ch. 3) defines need and harm by reference to the particular priorities of each society. Miller's account (1976: ch. 4) is even more relativized: needs consist in what is essential to each individual's plan of life.

Accounts such as these raise various problems which threaten the very idea of need. In particular, the disputability of what counts as harm has made some people argue that political thinking would be much better off by avoiding the concept of need altogether (Barry 1965: 47–9). Others seize on the idea of social relativity to suggest that need has no moral force above the level of mere subsistence, and that more extensive claims of need only reflect a conventional 'rising minimum' as societies get richer (Rosen 1977). As welfare workers, you are in constant contact with people's needs. Can you use your experience to help to refute these objections?

It is easy for a theorist, remote from real cases of need, to raise doubts about the idea of harm, and to suggest that need is endlessly disputable. But welfare workers are continually dealing with needs which nobody could dispute. It is indisputable, for instance, that a woman who has suffered violent attacks from her husband needs not only some kind of protection but also help in coming to terms with very conflicting feelings and beliefs. These are not, for most women, survival needs: it is all too evident that many women have survived lives in violent households. But their description as needs does not depend on contentious claims about what actually harms people. Nor are these needs cases of the so-called rising minimum – something which people are thought to need only in affluent societies. Social and economic changes may have influenced the possibility of women effectively articulating these needs, but prosperity didn't invent them. So even if needs are sometimes disputable, there are cases in which they are perfectly clear. From your own experience, you can surely make a list of many other cases of indisputable need, and thus help to defend need as a central principle of social policy.

To deal with the second problem about need, social relativity, it helps to distinguish between 'conventional' and 'real' needs (cf. Braybrooke 1987: 81–111). A sense of need is merely conventional when people in a society have simply come to expect something as part of a normal life. By contrast, the way a society is organized may make it necessary to use certain socially specific means as the only way to satisfy certain indisputable needs. In that case there is a real, though relativized, need. For example, there is a widespread belief in Britain and Ireland that people need meat. The existence of many healthy vegetarians shows that this is a merely conventional view. Contrast this with the need to be able to read and write. That is not something which everyone in every society has always needed, but it really is needed in Britain and Ireland today because society is so structured that life is intolerably difficult for the illiterate. Obviously there is a process by which conventional needs can turn into real needs, or even vice versa, and there are intermediate cases. But this doesn't undermine the distinction altogether. Now when the opponents of equality try to discredit the idea of need, they talk as though every socially relative need is a matter of mere convention. You who work with the needy can help to rebut that attack, by showing just how necessary many things are for preventing real harm.

Respect

A second key egalitarian idea is respect. But what is it to respect someone? Perhaps the most famous philosophical account comes from the eighteenth-century philosopher Kant: 'Act in such a way that you always treat humanity . . . never simply as a means, but always at the same time as an end' (Kant 1785: 91; see also Williams 1962; Lukes 1977). A fine sentiment, but (it might be argued) far too abstract and subjective a notion to relate to the legislative and institutional issues which politics is about (Charvet 1969). If respect is to play an important role in the idea of a good society, it has to be grounded in everyday experience. It also has to be shown to have a clear, objective application to questions of social and political policy.

As welfare workers you can defend the concreteness of respect by describing clear cases in your own experience. Consider, for instance, the following newspaper report:

> The Labour Court has recommended that a woman who was dismissed by Kildare Street and University Club, Dublin, should receive the equivalent of two weeks' wages and be provided with a reference in more favourable terms. . . . She washed dishes, prepared cheese and made tea and coffee. A representative of the club said that she was a bad time-keeper, tended to be idle and displayed no interest in her work.
>
> (*Irish Times* 1989)

The sheer contempt displayed by the club's representative in this report is palpable, but far from unusual; in your experience, you can doubtless cite many similar cases. It is from these real-life examples that the idea of a society based on mutual respect gets its force.

But is the idea of mutual respect too subjective, too personal, to be the aim of a political movement? We can see from the example that even if what ultimately matters is interpersonal attitudes of respect, it is still possible to change the way people treat each other. Thus, even if individual employers have contempt for their workers, they can still be required to operate in a context which refuses to institutionalize this contempt and thereby to condone it socially. This change of context can also help to change attitudes themselves.

Lack of respect doesn't have to be deliberate. It is often the result of an unexamined failure to take other people's interests seriously. A good example is the traditional lack of wheelchair access to public buildings. It is not as if architects and planners sat down and deliberately chose to exclude disabled people; it is precisely the failure even to consider their needs which counts as a form of disrespect. By thinking of other examples, with a view towards analysing and understanding the various ways institutional arrangements can express this lack of consideration, you can help to show that respect is not too personal or subjective to form the basis for radical social policies.

Sexual, racial, ethnic and religious equality

A third set of principles important to equality falls under the heading of sexual, racial, ethnic and religious equality. These ideas, though clearly important, raise many problems of interpretation; perhaps the most central is the question of the distinction between different treatment and unequal treatment (Barry 1965: ch. 7). For instance, our language treats men and women differently in many ways (Strainchamps 1971; R. Baker 1979). Is it a mere difference, or is it an inequality, that women are colloquially referred to using terms for domesticated animals, or that English uses gender-specific pronouns in the third person singular? The key issue is whether such differences in treatment can be demonstrated to increase or decrease inequalities of wealth, status, power and opportunity between men and women.

Many issues of social policy present serious difficulties of this kind. The most intractable cases are multi-faceted, so that different treatment is egalitarian in some respects and anti-egalitarian in others. A widely discussed example concerns interference in the practices of minority cultures. Non-interference seems not only to respect ethnic equality, but also sometimes to reinforce inegalitarian customs. Whether this conflict within egalitarianism is inevitable, and, if so, how to resolve it, depend very much on a detailed understanding of particular cultures, including an informed view of the internal importance of their allegedly inegalitarian features. Welfare workers can be well placed to explain such issues, since you are often concerned with the ways in which both majority intolerance and minority practices can lead to suffering and despair.

These are only some of the ways in which welfare workers can help to clarify and defend the central ideas of egalitarianism. In each case, these ideas have a real social relevance – that is what makes them so important. But unless their relevance is constantly reasserted and verified by our own experience, they can become empty phrases to which everyone does lip-service while behaving exactly as they please.

Reinforcing the arguments for equality

In my view, arguing for equality occurs in two stages. The first stage sets out the basic case for equality, based on the ideas of need, respect and community. The second stage involves rebutting the common arguments against equality, often by showing that the very ideas which anti-egalitarians put forward can be used to provide positive support for equality itself. I have in mind, in particular, the belief in equal opportunity as an alternative to full equality; the suggestion that the privileged deserve their privileges and that the deprived deserve their deprivation; the arguments that equality would destroy freedom and that inequality provides incentives which benefit everyone; and the conviction that equality is in any case impossible. I cannot summarize all of these arguments here (for a fuller treatment, see J. Baker 1987). Instead, I want to suggest some ways in which welfare workers can contribute to their success.

The basic case for equality is fairly simple. If you are concerned about the needs of others, if you believe in basic human dignity and respect, and if you value a sense of community, then you ought to care about equality. This is partly a matter of understanding clearly how these ideas are related conceptually to the principles of equality, but it is also because inequality leads in fact to frustrated needs, assaults on human dignity, and divided communities. At least, that's the theory. What you can do is to provide as much evidence for the theory as anyone can.

Being in constant contact with people in need, you can see, more clearly than most, how inequality prevents these needs from being satisfied. You can explain, in a concrete way, how inequalities reinforce each other so that some people are cushioned against ever falling into serious need while others are so badly off in every way – economically, politically, socially, educationally, physically and emotionally – that their voices never get heard, their interests never get taken seriously, and their needs are never met. A classic example is the case of a homeless person who cannot get a home because she has no job and cannot get a job because she has no home. Because she has no job she has a very low income, but because she has no permanent home she has unusually high expenses. As she has nowhere to cook, her diet is poor and she is prone to illness; her mental life is full of anxiety and depression. Not being settled, she does not even count politically, and certainly hasn't the organizational resources of long-time residents. This is, of course, simply an image, perhaps even a stereotype. What welfare workers can provide is as many actual examples as anyone can ask for in demonstrating the interaction between need and inequality.

Anti-egalitarians like to think that it is possible for a society to sustain respect for others and a sense of community even if there are major inequalities of wealth, power and status (Lucas 1977: 264–70). Some of them even claim that our own society is a case in point. No one engaged in welfare work can believe that. You are vividly aware of the contempt shown towards the poor and powerless, often by welfare bureaucracies themselves, and of the sense of alienation and social division at the bottom end of all the social scales. It is only to be expected that the well-heeled will try to deceive themselves into thinking that everyone in western societies has a respected place as a member of a single community. You can help to shatter that self-deception, both by articulating the facts about degradation and alienation and by encouraging the unprivileged to find their own voices and to make their own claims for respect and for full membership of society. And because you can see the interconnection between these wrongs and the huge inequalities which create the gulf between the rich and the poor, the powerful and the powerless, you can press home the argument that only an egalitarian society can create a real sense of mutual respect and concern.

So much for the basic case for equality. But what about those who argue that full equality is unnecessary, if only we had equal opportunity (Friedman 1962: 195)? Well, it is natural enough for welfare workers to press for greater equality of opportunity, and especially for programmes of positive action and preferential treatment (Wasserstrom 1980). But there are a lot of problems with equal opportunity which we shouldn't lose sight of (Schaar 1967). One of the most serious is the degree to which major inequalities of condition make real equal opportunity impossible. That is a statement of fact, for which welfare workers have all the evidence anyone needs. You see, year in and year out, the effects of poverty and powerlessness on the ability of people to gain the skills and qualifications they need to compete in a supposedly equal opportunity society. You can challenge the believers in equal opportunity with concrete cases of children whose prospects in life were sealed from before they were even born, of adults whose lack of opportunity is the direct result of lifetimes of social deprivation. How could all that be changed except by a real equality which made equal opportunity redundant?

Another objection to equality is the idea that some people deserve to be better off than others, because they've been so diligent or clever or resourceful (see Miller 1976: chs 3 and 6). But if anyone believes that the rich deserve their privileges because of hard work, they must surely have no idea of the work done by the worst paid. If they are sympathetic to the stress and responsibility of corporate executives, they must surely have no idea of the stress and responsibility of unemployed parents trying to raise their children. Anti-egalitarians also claim that the captains of industry and of high finance make more of a contribution to society than cleaners, child-minders and cooks. That view is problematic in many ways, but particularly in its central value judgement about who does most for society. You are in a position to question that judgement – to ask what the captains of industry have done to help those most in need; to stand up for the contributions made by ordinary people to their families and local communities; to defend the contributions made by the social services themselves. Finally, there is the widely held view that the poor deserve their poverty, because they are feckless, lazy and unreliable. Sensational stories in the tabloids about 'dole scroungers' and 'problem families' reinforce that image. You can prove just how false it is, by matching every sensational case with countless examples of enforced poverty. Your detailed knowledge of poverty, unemployment and lack of opportunity is absolutely essential in winning the case against the idea of deserved inequality.

In the past twenty years or so, anti-egalitarians have returned with a vengeance to a venerable line of argument: that equality would destroy freedom (Lucas 1977: 270–3; Nozick 1974). We might well ask, particularly in contemporary Britain how strong a commitment to freedom is exhibited by government restrictions on broadcasting and publication, on the rights of trade unionists, and on the powers of local governments. But more fundamentally, we can ask about the effects of inequality itself on the freedoms of the worst off (Norman 1987: ch. 7). As welfare workers, you are confronted every day with those effects. You see how narrowly circumscribed are the choices of the poor, the needy, the disabled, how little scope they have for developing their capacities, for exercising their democratic rights as citizens, even for choosing between brand X and brand Y in the local supermarket. You have observed the way the worst-off members of society are treated by the police, the courts, the schools – as well as by the social services. That knowledge needs to be shared, to become common knowledge, if the issue of freedom for all is to get a fair hearing. Only then will people begin to see that the freedoms championed by the right – freedoms of self-development, of property ownership, of consumer choice, of democratic participation – are systematically thwarted in an unequal society.

The opponents of equality are not always so blind to the interests of the disadvantaged. One of their favourite arguments, in fact, is that inequality is actually good for people, because it creates incentives. The efforts drawn forth by high salaries at the top of the scale create benefits for everyone (Rawls 1972: 78 and 315). It is a nice theory, but is it true? Welfare workers who have dealt with poverty and deprivation for ten, twenty or thirty years have seen various incentive policies come and go, with the rich sometimes benefiting by hundreds of thousands of pounds. What have these policies done for the poor? Has prosperity trickled down? If the incentives allegedly generated by greater inequality were really justified, their effects on the lives of the worst off would surely have been more visible. Meanwhile, the bad effects of inequality remain and are intensified. The frustration, depression, envy and lack of self-esteem which inequality engenders are among the all-too-visible costs which the incentive argument ignores. As welfare workers, you can explain vividly and compellingly how these arise from inequality, as well as describing how little effect incentive policies have had on the lives of the worst off. In doing so, you are making vitally important points about the true costs and negligible benefits of inequality.

A final argument against equality claims that equality is impossible; that human nature is too competitive for advantage, too eager for domination and superiority. Against this argument, egalitarians have always maintained two things: first, that it exaggerates the degree to which equality requires people to be nice to each other, and second, that it ignores the effects of social structures on people's attitudes and values. Equality does not expect people to be angels. On the contrary, egalitarians often point out that equality would be in the self-interest of the great majority of citizens. But an egalitarian society would also encourage and reinforce different attitudes and values. In welfare work, you are constantly reminded of the way people's characters are affected by their social circumstances and by the broader structure of society. That immersion course in social psychology is worth any number of textbooks in showing how malleable human nature is. It provides yet another kind of knowledge which needs to be deployed against the view that human nature makes equality impossible.

In this section, I have considered a selection of arguments for and against equality, and have tried to show how your own experience as welfare workers can contribute to the egalitarian case. The selection is not exhaustive; there are many other arguments to analyse and to answer. But I hope these examples have shown that the case for equality is not an abstract philosophers' game to which lived experience is irrelevant. It depends, time and again, on basic facts about everyday life – facts which you are particularly well placed to reassert.

Developing egalitarian institutions

Equality is more than a set of principles. It is a vision of an alternative society, based on and developing those principles. That means thinking seriously about how the principles of equality can be implemented through appropriately constructed social institutions. There are undoubtedly many areas in which your special experience can be invaluable in this respect. To illustrate, let us look at the principles of need, respect and democracy.

The work of existing welfare bureaucracies is widely supposed to be based on need. But anyone who works within them knows that they are far from perfect, that legislation and organizational practices sometimes prevent them from meeting needs effectively or even from recognizing the needs that are there. An egalitarian society would certainly have to include institutions designed to satisfy needs; the experience of welfare workers, as well as that of the users of welfare services, will be absolutely vital in replacing existing structures by new and sometimes radically different ones. You need to tell the rest of us what you think is wrong with services as they stand and how they could be more effectively organized. We have to know how much of their work is concerned with patching up damage done by current inequalities and how much would still be necessary in a more equal society. There will be questions in an egalitarian society about integrated and specialized services, about decentralization, about forms of provision, about the treatment of offenders, all of which we ought to be thinking and talking about now. There is always a temptation to concentrate on short-term reforms; this is only a plea for some visionary thinking as well.

All of these questions raise a strongly related issue, namely how a society committed to satisfying needs can simultaneously treat every one of its members with respect (cf. Downie and Telfer 1980). For there is probably no better example of how institutions can foster disrespect and contempt than classic welfare bureaucracies and residential institutions. What can welfare workers teach us about the design of systems to avoid such effects? How, in particular, can the major institutions for planning an economy according to need be constructed so as to avoid the belittling effects of current bureaucracies?

Surely a part of the answer to these problems lies in the idea of democracy? The paternalism and oppression typical of classic welfare systems necessarily depend on such systems being organized in undemocratic ways. In the classic welfare bureaucracy, power rests firmly at the top of the organizational pyramid. That has got to change, not just in welfare work but throughout society (Norman 1987: ch. 8). Some welfare organizations, particularly those in the grant-aided 'voluntary' sector, have already experienced such changes, and should already be able to contribute to the effective design of participatory work-places. But welfare work is also by its very nature a social service which involves more than just worker-management, and an increasing number of welfare services include their users in key decisions, based on a principle of democratic control by everyone involved (Beresford and Croft 1986). As in any democracy, this must surely create serious conflicts and organizational difficulties; as in any new initiative, it must also make for mistakes and for learning by trial and error. The question of how to empower the users of welfare services while respecting the employment rights and personal integrity of welfare workers has wide-ranging ramifications for the design of a democratic economy. Many welfare workers are already at the frontier of these issues and you need to share your experiences and reflections about them.

Conclusion

In this chapter I have not tried to tell you as welfare workers how to be egalitarians in your work. That is something on which your own reflections will have much more bearing than anything I could say. What I have tried to do is to encourage you to tell the rest of us how your work can contribute to the development of a new vision of society: how it can help us to clarify key ideas, how it can further the arguments for equality, and how it can lead to the development of new forms of institutions based on egalitarian principles. It seems particularly appropriate to address these questions to people whose work often generates strong personal and political tensions between privilege and deprivation. For equality will not be brought into being by academic theorizing or by government think-tanks. It will come, if at all, out of the lived experience of people like you.

Acknowledgements

I am grateful to Gabriel Kiely for his helpful comments and suggestions.

References

Baker, J. (1987) *Arguing for Equality*, London: Verso.

Baker, R. (1979) ' "Pricks" and "Chicks": a plea for "Persons" ', in S. Bishop and M. Weinzweig (eds) *Philosophy and Women*, Belmont, Calif: Wadsworth.

Barry, B. (1965) *Political Argument*, London: Routledge & Kegan Paul.

Beresford, P. and Croft, S. (1986) *Whose Welfare?*, Brighton: Lewis Cohen Urban Studies Centre.

Braybrooke, D. (1987) *Meeting Needs*, Princeton, NJ: Princeton University Press.

Charvet, J. (1969) 'The idea of equality as a substantive principle', *Political Studies* 17, 1: 1–13.

Downie, R. S. and Telfer, E. (1980) *Caring and Curing*, London: Methuen.

Friedman, M. (1962) *Capitalism and Freedom*, Chicago, Ill: University of Chicago Press.

Irish Times (1989) 'Court ruling on reference', 17 January, p. 2.

Kant, I. (1785) *Groundwork to a Metaphysic of Morals* in H. J. Paton (ed.) (1948) *The Moral Law*, London: Hutchinson.

Lucas, J. R. (1977) 'Against equality again', *Philosophy* 52, 201: 255–80.

Lukes, S. (1977) 'Socialism and equality', in S. Lukes, *Essays in Social Theory*, London: Macmillan.

Miller, D. (1976) *Social Justice*, Oxford University Press.

Norman, R. (1987) *Free and Equal*, Oxford University Press.

Nozick, R. (1974) *Anarchy, State, and Utopia*, Oxford: Blackwell.

Plant, R., Lesser, H. and Taylor-Gooby, P. (1980) *Political Philosophy and Social Welfare*, London: Routledge & Kegan Paul.

Rawls, J. (1972) *A Theory of Justice*, Oxford University Press.

Rosen, F. (1977) 'Basic Needs and Justice', *Mind*, 86, 341: 88–94.

Schaar, J. (1967) 'Equality of opportunity, and beyond' in J. R. Pennock and J. Chapman (eds) *Nomos IX: Equality*, New York: Atherton.

Strainchamps, E. (1971) 'Our sexist language', in V. Gornick and B. Moran (eds) *Woman in Sexist Society*, New York: Basic Books.

Walzer, M. (1983) *Spheres of Justice*, Oxford: Blackwell.

Wasserstrom, R. A. (1980) 'Preferential treatment', in R. A. Wasserstrom, *Philosophy and Social Issues*, Notre Dame, Ind: University of Notre Dame Press.

Wiggins, D. (1985) 'Claims of need', in T. Honderich (ed.) *Morality and Objectivity*, London: Routledge & Kegan Paul.

Williams, B. (1962) 'The idea of equality', in P. Laslett and W. G. Runciman (eds) *Philosophy, Politics and Society: Second Series*, Oxford: Blackwell.

Wollheim, R. (1975) 'Needs, desires, and moral turpitude', in R. S. Peters (ed.) *Nature and Conduct*, London: Macmillan.

14
The realities of caring: an inside view

Sandra Leventon

Carers have been with us from time immemorial, as have their needs and their crises and emotions. Florence Nightingale, promoted for so many years as the paragon of patience, cared first for her father and then for her mother for seven years, at the end of which she expressed relief that her 'morally inescapable' domestic duties were now over and she could get back to her own interests and life. A carer in 1986 expressed the same feelings to me when, after eight years of caring for his mother, he asked for help to 'get back into life'. Thackeray in *Vanity Fair* wrote of Amelia's life as 'Ceaseless slavery meeting with no reward' – not an inappropriate description of the situation of some of today's so-called 'informal' care-givers.

In 1981 I became one of the millions of care-givers who try to cope 'Behind Closed Doors', as the Equal Opportunities Commission (EOC 1980) so aptly entitled one of the first surveys of the group. I know now that there was no way I could have been totally prepared for the situations and the stresses that have arisen over the past nine years of caring for a severely disabled elderly person with several degenerative diseases. However, the experience of those years has convinced me that there are ways of alleviating the strains, the isolation and the dangers of caring at home. I was fortunate in being able to use skills from my 'past life' (as I am prone to call it because it seems so divorced from the effort of surviving the current one), to examine, to analyse and to identify ways of alleviating the problems which have arisen.

Emotions experienced during caring cover a wide and intense range, whether one is nursing someone terminally ill with cancer for a few weeks or months or one is trying to make a chronically sick friend or relative's life more comfortable, enjoyable and positive for a number of years. Some of these emotions are par for the course: to watch someone for whom one cares greatly – dare one say love – in extreme pain is beyond description. As one of my friends, Brenda, put it (and I bow to her experience of twenty-six years of caring): 'When my mother has a pain, I have a pain'. Guilt seems to be another consistent experience. But for me anger has been present also and, in speaking with other carers, I find I am not alone in this.

The anger stems from the lack of recognition of the degree of the so-called 'burden of caring', the contribution we are making to both social welfare policy and the economic situation. The first reliable national survey (Green 1988) of how many carers there are in the country was not done until 1985 and reveals that carers considerably outnumber mothers of 'normal' children under 16 years of age. Yet health visitors whose primary role is an educative and preventive one rarely have carers as their priority group; more usually, their priorities lie with the under-5s.

Informal Carers (Green 1988: Sections 2.2 and 2.6) – and how we hate that adjective – revealed that there are 6 million people contributing some degree of care to either a relative or friend at home. About 14 per cent of all adults are involved in caring but, given the larger female population, most carers are women. What has changed since 1976 when Invalid Care Allowance (ICA), the only benefit in the social security system for carers, was introduced, is that instead of the typical carer being a single, unmarried, middle-aged woman caring for an elderly parent, the majority of female carers are married. Whatever the demographic or other reasons for this change, it still took a three-year campaign and a case at the European Court for ICA to be extended to married women.

The likelihood of being a carer increases to a peak in middle age, for both men and women, with the highest incidence to be found in the age group 45 to 64: three times as many as in the under-30s age group. Overall 15 per cent of women were identified as carers and 12 per cent of men: about 3.5 million women compared to 2.5 million men. The proportion of women to men carers in the 45–64 age grouping differs substantially, with almost 25 per cent of women in that age grouping being carers compared with 16 per cent of men.

Differences also arise when one looks at the number of hours spent caring. In the group doing at least twenty hours a week (24 per cent), most of them are women. Six out of every ten in that group are doing more than fifty hours per week, so the question arises about the other family commitments of married women in that group, let alone what time they have for their own interests and 'life'. One carer expressed this visually as the Indian goddess with five pairs of hands – one pair being pulled by the person needing care, another pair by her husband and marriage, yet another by her children, the fourth by the career and interests she had once had and the last pair tearing out her own hair.

It is a 'job for life' in many instances or at least a long-term commitment. Having invested nine years of my life in this 'job', I am one of the 25 per cent who have been involved for between five and ten years. Another 18 per cent have been looking after the same person for more than ten years. It becomes a way of life which has equally long-term effects on one's own health, employment prospects and even one's own old age. Yet campaigns to attract women back to employment are concentrated on mothers of young children, not on older women who want to 'get back into life', after their caring responsibilities end. In encouraging employers to look at ways to encourage women back to work, much is being made of flexible working hours to fit in with school or crèche facilities. We have yet to see similar incentives for the older group involved in caring for elderly or disabled people.

A new and vigorous campaign to draw attention to the needs of carers was begun in the early 1980s by the newly formed Association of Carers (AoC), and they, in turn, were building on the work of the National Council for Carers and their Elderly Dependants (NCCED – previously the National Council for Single Women and their Elderly Dependants). While not totally in competition for membership (the NCCED's title indicates the limitations), discussions on merger came to fruition in 1988 with the formation of the Carers' National Association. Together with Contact-a-Family, a third but separate voluntary organization concentrating on the needs of families with children with disabilities, the campaign is being moved forward to keep the needs of carers on the agenda. In 1989 they began a programme to find the 'hidden' carers – those whose needs were unknown to either statutory or voluntary agencies – between 50 and 70 per cent (Green 1988: Section 5.2).

The individual situation in a household influences the way in which delivery of services are wanted, but the basic needs of carers are the same. One of the first research projects on carers, sponsored by the AoC in 1984 (Bonny 1984), identified the areas of need as being information, respite, training, education and assessment and aids to living and caring, as well as financial and emotional support.

When information on local services is made available to them, carers often say 'If only I'd known that before'. Even with the advantage of working for some twenty years previously in social education, and with a wealth of information about how local services were managed, structured and obtained, I had extreme difficulty in determining just who was responsible for what, coming to terms with the extreme fragmentation of the origins and delivery of services and, equally important, determining what was *not* available. If, for example, one takes the subject of what Heinz Woolff calls the 'Tools for Living' (Woolff 1979a; 1979b) (or in our case, tools for caring), how was I supposed to know that in the area where I live everything in and around the bed is supplied by the district nursing service but all other equipment comes from social services? In the best areas, such 'tools' come from a store run jointly by health and social services and a carer does not have to expend precious energy trying to find the right number to ring. What makes me most angry is that providing such information is probably the cheapest service to deliver; in our local CARERS region where we have been producing packs and booklets of this nature ourselves, they have become 'best-sellers' amongst the professionals as well.

We need regular time off – what a DHSS film of 1986 calls *Time to be Me* and L. S. Lowry, another famous carer, called the need to 'let off steam (Rohde 1979: 136): time to do the everyday things that others take for granted, like shopping, attending to our own health needs, catching up on sleep and even spending time in, in the true meaning of the word, recreation. Unfortunately, for some service deliverers the word 'respite' has come to mean residential accommodation – usually beds in elderly people's homes or nursing homes or hospitals for a fortnight – and, as one district nurse defined the term, for when the carer cannot cope any more. When a group of carers discussed this recently, we decided that we wanted to do away with the word itself because it had acquired such crisis connotations.

What we need is 'respite'; what we want is 'the next shift coming in to take over' and we want that regularly and as of right, not when we cannot go on any longer. And it makes economic sense: the more 'respite' we get, the longer we can carry on caring. In no other job is there an expectation that the person carrying the main responsibility will do so for 168 hours a week – and live on the job in many cases. Yet that is the amount of time for which a carer, responding to the daily living needs of a person, every day and night in the week, is 'on duty'.

Respite can take many forms: day care for the person needing assistance gives the carer time for his or her own life; so, too, does employment. The oldest carer in my area is 86, caring for her middle-aged son, who recently got his first job. She *chose* to use that respite from her family domestic caring role to volunteer to do a session at the local CAB because she had done that many years before and found it a most positive experience. What is wanted is a variety of flexible services which can suit the many different household and family situations. What we do not want is only one way in which to get respite. Most damaging is the lack of opportunity to express our wishes in this respect or systems which bring us into conflict with the wishes of those whom we are helping.

So, a majority of carers are fearful of offers of residential care and this is not without reason for carers of elderly confused people: confusion has been proven to increase after a stay in a residential establishment. This is not necessarily a reflection on the quality of residential care but often the result of having to cope with strange environments and different regimes. Frequently too, for those who are not confused but who are placed in homes where many people are, there is the stress of seeing people in their own age grouping in such a painful condition. Yet this frequently happens given the shortage of residential places and the incidence of confusion amongst the 75+ age group.

For my own part, my mother's condition has now reached the stage where leaving her own home so that I can get a longer break takes on the colouring of a sacrifice on her part. But it does not even coincide with my wishes. A residential home means that I can go away only when a bed is available. If there is no bed available in the one local authority respite facility, then I have to survey the private sector for a suitable and available place. Short-term beds are not a viable economic proposition for businesses, which rely on keeping their beds filled for as much of the time as possible. Added to that, even with such Department of Social Security assistance as is available (so-called 'board and lodgings' payments for those eligible for income support), I may also have to contribute financially around £60 per week. Our preference is for help to come into the house to take over my duties while I am away – 'in-house respite'.

Since November 1988, financial help has been available for such respite for people, who receive Attendance Allowance and are eligible for Income

Support, through the Independent Living Fund (ILF), set up as a result of protestations when the domestic assistance addition (an 'add-on' to the supplementary benefit system) was abolished in April 1988. The government is contributing £5 million per year to the scheme for five years. The specific term for ILF was at the insistence of the disability organizations, who consider application to a charity to be degrading as compared to a benefit by right. In that there is no right of appeal against decisions of the Fund, this attitude is understandable and the future of the Fund forms part of the review of the position of people with disabilities.

Whatever the uncomfortable connotations of going 'begging' in this manner, I have found that it has given me regular, reliable breaks in an acceptable form for the first time in nine years. The Fund pays for my mother to hire a 'carer' from an agency for the whole time I am away and covers the cost bar the amount of the Attendance Allowance. This has become more important as I have grown older and the caring tasks have become more exhausting. I am now unable to continue for periods longer than eight or nine weeks. The pattern that best suits me is of short breaks of five or six days, every eight weeks, rather than the opportunity of two weeks every six months. And most helpful is the knowledge that there is choice in the system for both of us.

We need training to undertake our caring tasks with confidence and so that we do not endanger the health of those for whom we are trying to care. We need educating about the diseases with which we have to cope, especially education which will warn us of symptoms to expect and help us prepare for some of the more frightening behavioural problems. We need to understand about the importance of diet and of exercise: what use is a surgeon's skill to save a man's life, if his wife is not told the dangerous effect on his recovery if he stays in bed? We need to be taught simple first aid and the correct way to lift or move people so that we do not cause pain, and we need education as to the nature and effect of the drugs which some of us are expected to dispense every day.

Not everyone is suitable for the task and yet very few people seem to be given the choice of whether to take on the role of carer or not, let alone being assessed for the ability to undertake it. Discussions with prospective carers seem to be the exception rather than the norm. There are, of course, situations where the recognition that someone needs assistance with daily living is gradual. This is particularly true of elderly people but there are still too many situations where assessment of the carer is ignored. Assumptions are made that a person, usually a female, will take on the tasks involved. The 'Have you got a daughter?' syndrome has been replaced by 'Is there anyone who can look after you?', especially where discharge from hospital after some trauma is involved. In the best areas, after say a stroke or immobilizing illness, the patient is assessed as to the level of his or her capabilities but it is still rare for the prospective carer, that is, the person who has been named by the patient anxious to get home, to be brought into those discussions.

Even those of us who are prone to asking for and demanding information about the illness, treatment and prognosis of our relatives and friends find that such probings are not always welcomed by the professionals. Recently my enquiries about new medication for my mother brought this response from the sister on the ward: 'Why do you want to know?'

My view about the need for training, education and assessment for carers is that it is an ethical question. There is rightly considerable concern that people are cared for in residential homes without any approved standards and opportunities for inspection by individuals known to be unqualified, or even unsuitable. Yet that is also the position every day of the week in thousands of situations involving care in the home.

Twenty-six organizations have come together under the title 'Caring Costs' to improve the financial position of caring households. The 'cost' refers to both personal loss of income to a carer on giving up or not being able to undertake paid work, and to the expense of caring at home. Loss of income is hardly compensated for realistically by the Invalid Care Allowance, although that is its intention. It is not a payment for caring but a poverty benefit and is at such a level that, in some households, the main source of income is the social security benefits of the person being cared for. Caring for someone at home increases the outgoings in a household, not only in relation to obvious items like extra heating and lighting but also in wear and tear and equipment. Yet not only is this situation not recognized by the social security system but also, since 1987, changes which have taken place in the areas of taxation, unemployment benefits and elsewhere have actually withdrawn what small financial recognition there was previously.

Another slogan, suggested by a carer, is that 'caring can damage your health'. She was referring not only to the long hours, the loss of sleep and the emotional stress but also to the dangers which exist for physical damage simply because we are not aware of the 'tools for living' which could prevent such damage. The technology exists but is rarely offered until, as with respite, crisis occurs. A carer needs to be taught how to avoid back damage by correct methods of lifting a person into bed or out of the chair but, in many situations, provision of appropriate equipment would make such skills unnecessary, as well as making life more comfortable, independent and dignified for the person needing the help. A carer damaged in this manner does not have grounds for an industrial injury claim.

Above all, we need help to gain some insight and understanding of the emotions that arise in the intense climate of caring for someone whom one loves (or hates), catering to their most intimate needs, crossing sexual taboos, acting as parent to one's own parent or becoming nurse to one's partner. Taking on such a life-style for so many years can have a long-term debilitating effect. If your day is dictated totally by someone else's needs, over a long period, the temptation is to under-value yourself. From the time at which I rise to the time at which I can go to bed – and even how much sleep I can get – my life is dictated by the needs of another, my mother. It is a slow but insidious danger which can happen even to the most secure of carers. 'Is it all right if I . . .' can become too frequent a question for comfort sometimes and is a warning.

Caring responsibilities are to be found in all social class and income groups but there is no doubt that caring in a household which has sufficient income to pay for adaptations like stair lifts and additional purpose-built bathrooms, for help to share the care, for private consultations with personnel who hold necessary information and skills, as well as the obvious necessities like heating and special clothing, makes an enormous difference. It is my belief, based on these last ten years, that about 80 per cent of the stresses of caring can be alleviated, if not eliminated. What money cannot do is to eliminate all the effect of the emotions experienced.

Some of the emotions arise from the other needs discussed above – lack of sleep can lead to exhaustion which affect how the carer responds to the demands of the job as well as the behaviour of the person needing the help. It is a cycle which is difficult to break when guilt results from those responses. If your energy supplies are low, then the constant and repetitive questioning of a demented person becomes intolerable, sometimes to the point of a physical response by the carer just to get some peace.

Some emotions are part of the desire to care. Caring for a husband in the final stages of multiple sclerosis not only is physically demanding to a point beyond true understanding for those of us not in that situation but also is emotionally exhausting in that one is simultaneously grieving. Motivations for caring are complex – love, duty, martyrdom, security, power – all are tested if the person for whom we are caring undergoes a change in personality as a result of the illness, sometimes out of all recognition to the person we once knew or enjoyed being with. Then we are truly bereaved, yet we are still undertaking the physical care. Giving up caring can be the most difficult decision for a carer to make, since often the carer has become emotionally dependent in turn upon the cared-for person. And for those who want to be relieved of their caring responsibilities, too often the appropriate facility to enable them to do so is not available.

Given the impossible conditions which are manifest in caring at home the question then arises of why it has taken so long for carers themselves to become demanding and why the services, while showing a definite improvement in some areas in recent years, are still so dangerously missing the target in their delivery response. I do not believe that the term 'dangerous' is over-dramatic in this context since there is evidence that tragedies have arisen where the lack of relevant and appropriate intervention by services has led to, at the best, the break down of the carer's health (surveys reveal over 60 per cent of carers in ill-health) and, at the worst, incidents of abuse, suicide and murder, of either the carer or the cared-for person. A large number of carers now have sufficient anger aroused that they are not prepared to wait until public outcry about such situations leads to action, as it did with child abuse, because like that topic, we might be presented with yet more inappropriate responses.

Indeed, there is already talk of an elderly 'at risk' register. What does not seem to be recognized is that all carers and households, where caring is a major factor, present an 'at risk' situation. Given the level of stress present in so many of the situations, whatever the origin of that stress – relationships, impossible hours and environment in which to operate, conflicts and pressure from other sources – 'at risk' is inherent. We are all liable to what, in other circumstances, would be unthinkable behaviour, and some of the accounts now available of carers talking about their feelings and experiences confirm such a generalist statement (Briggs and Oliver 1985: 64).

Recognition is a key word – recognition of the needs mentioned before; recognition that this is a job which we do and which society needs us to do since it has been estimated that we are contributing between £15 billion and £24 billion each year by undertaking these tasks (Family Policy Studies Centre 1988: 1); recognition that, in so doing, we are not just another client group presenting impossible demands on diminishing resources; recognition that we have separate, and sometimes conflicting, interests from the people we are caring for; and, above all, recognition that sometimes we need help to acknowledge that we are individuals separate from those whose immense daily living needs are in danger of subsuming our own identities. This means that, for the service deliverers, there are conflicts in their attempts to help us. Julia Twigg, looking at the way in which social care agencies conceptualize their relationship with carers, came to the conclusion that because carers occupy this ambiguous position of sometimes being client and sometimes colleague (within the community care framework) this in turn leads to an ambiguous response from the services (Twigg 1989). In addition, because those services are predominantly structured around the dependent person, rather than the carer, this has important consequences for the delivery of services and their evaluation.

As a carer, I would state this more strongly. It is positively degrading, and harmful, to be labelled a carer of an elderly person, or of a stroke patient, or of a handicapped child. A carer's identity is as a carer, making a valid contribution to a care system. Carers should be seen to exist by virtue of their own roles, not by the label of the disease or age of the people being cared for. A carer is a carer is a carer and our wishes are different because of ourselves, not because of the situation of the person we are assisting.

In addition to being seen as co-workers or co-clients, carers are also named as 'resources' (Twigg 1989). Being seen as a resource can mean services are not appropriate or simply do not appear. Those labelled as coping may not have ready access to a social worker; files are closed and check-up visits never made, despite the fact that caring is a dynamic and volatile situation with new problems arising, suddenly as well as gradually, from changes in the health and age of both carer and dependant.

Being regarded as a co-worker would be more acceptable in that it would be a means of recognizing the contribution that we make to community care policy. The review of community care undertaken by Griffiths (1988) did manage to identify clearly 'informal' carers and, even more pleasingly, used the adjective only once or twice. The term 'informal' can be seen as a degrading description for a group of 6 million people without whom social service and health budgets would have to be increased overnight by some 25 per cent. Griffiths also highlighted policy issues which are crucial if the realities of caring and carers are to be truly recognized. Not least of these is the involvement of carers, and those needing the care where this is feasible, in the development of individual care packages.

However, during the time which elapsed between the publication of the

Griffiths Report and the announcement of a White Paper, our initial excitement once more turned to bitterness and, as with other small pieces of 'recognition', doubt has set in that any action will ever be taken on the scale recommended.

When looking at the different responses to the recommendation of Griffiths that the agent for such packages of care should be the local authorities, as a carer, I have to admit to being indifferent, conditional on that agent actually being able to deliver the services. As a carer, I would welcome a donkey in a duffle coat who could deliver the services needed efficiently and sensitively and it would not matter to me whether the 'donkey' came from the local authority, the health service or a voluntary agency.

The same contradictory view of carers identified by Twigg (1989) amongst service deliverers seems to be present amongst policy-makers, at both local and national level. Greater acknowledgement has come over the past ten years, albeit too late for many and too little for others. However, the will to construct policies to enable appropriate and flexible services to exist seems to be slower than slow. Only a handful of local authorities have carers' co-ordinators or support workers (social workers are sometimes commended for their valuable work with carers while having to do such work on their own time) and most still structure their policies around disability or age. Nor are health authorities exempt from this approach. A recent report (Webb 1987: 18–21) revealed over seventy different titles of post in answer to the question about who was responsible for carers in their area. Most were named by their managers in the response because of their focus on elderly people, or mentally ill people, or the young disabled, or whatever.

At national level, this contradictory approach appears even more blatant. The Department of Health advocated, over a period of three years, a more pointed and sensitive approach to the needs of carers, including funding three demonstration districts to develop support services which could be models for other areas. During that same period of time, other government departments have taken steps which have wiped out what little manifestations of recognition did exist in their areas of responsibility.

The review of the social security system in 1986 rejected recommendations from numerous sources that carers should be eligible for similar premiums as elderly and disabled people on the grounds of necessity. The response was that they (carers) have no greater financial need than other fit, unemployed people of the same age.

Since 1988, people who have been in receipt of the Invalid Care Allowance for more than two years are no longer eligible to receive unemployment benefit once their caring responsibilities cease. The Dependant's Tax Allowance was abolished by the Chancellor of the Exchequer in 1988 – one of the few things that recognized that caring costs. Another similar step comes with the introduction of the community charge. Previously, rate relief – a reduction in the rateable value of the house – was available to those households where changes had been made to enable a person to be cared for at home. For example, since the front living-room in our house can no longer be used as such but is a bedroom for my mother, a £30 reduction is made on the rateable value.

Under the community charge system, which is no longer property based, this goes.

Elderly and disabled people living in residential accommodation are exempt from the community charge, but people in the same groupings being cared for at home, by the family taking on the very responsibility that current government philosophy promotes, have to pay either the full rate or at the least 20 per cent. This compounds the gross differential between the financial support available for those who cannot or do not care for dependent people at home and those who do. Being told what a grand job one is doing is no compensation for such realities which, far from rewarding those who take on their responsibilities in this way, seem to penalize them.

Carers themselves, however are not without a touch of these same contradictions: self-recognition is an important step in taking a pride in what one is doing, yet too many carers, particularly women, still accept that what they are doing is part of their domestic role. The high content of domestic tasks involved in caring at home, like washing, cleaning up, cooking and so on, encourages this attitude amongst women for whom it is seen as an extension of a role previously performed. A related view is noticeable amongst parents of children with special needs in that they may see themselves first as parents, rather than as carers. Indeed, a frequent discussion point is whether the name 'carer' is a positive one.

Those same parents begin to change their views when they themselves identify differences between themselves and parents of, say, adolescents of the same age as their children but who are not in need of special care and are seeking to leave home and gain independence. At that point, they seek contact with other carers and not just parents of children of the same age. Some of the most perceptive accounts of family life, including the effects on other children in the family, in current literature on carers comes from this group (Hicks 1988: 108–37; Briggs and Oliver 1985: 11–15; 24–30; 69–78).

Ten years ago there was little in the way of written material either about carers or for carers. This is no longer the case. Some of the vast range is the result of the market recognition of the current interest in health matters; others are related to medical research and specific diseases or illnesses. There are a number of 'handbooks', giving information and hints to carers like *Caring at Home*, commissioned by the King's Fund Carers Project (Kohner 1988). Some are essential reading while others, owing to the jargon used, the way in which they are organized or their layout, bear no relation to the reality of caring. Local information handbooks are increasing but again are sometimes being produced without reference to the consumer view. A fourth section does constitute a form of recognition of carers and their needs – *Who Cares?* (Hicks 1988) is one of a welcome spate of books of interviews with carers or first-hand accounts of their experiences. Such books do help other carers to identify their own personal needs and feelings and combat the isolation and alienation of individual carers but there may be a need to limit such 'How does it feel?' books. Some carers feel that too much of this approach is merely a substitute for action. There is not a dissimilar approach to research – that the time has come to put an end to researching the needs of carers and concentrate on putting the research to use. As one carer put it, 'I've been consulted enough: it's time for some action now.'

The action referred to by that carer may be different from the action sought by another, even one in a similar position. We come to caring from different motivations, through different life experiences and with different levels of relationships with the people for whom we care. We cope in different ways because of these different approaches. While our needs are the same, the ways in which we want those needs to be met may be very different. But one thing remains constant: we want choice. Not only in the major question of whether we want to take on the role of caring but also in the nature and amount of the care that we give, and in when and in what manner we give up our caring responsibilities.

The consensus is that caring changes your life, both in the present and in the future. Not all is gloom and doom – I have had an opportunity not open to many adults of a continued close relationship with a parent, brought closer perhaps because of the mutual need to retain a positive approach to life in difficult circumstances. Others have written of the 'joy of caring'. The problem is that whether the 'joy' remains uppermost and that period of one's life is a growth period or one which lays down bitterness and damage for the future is not always within one's own control. The extent of recognition of the realities of caring and the help that is needed is somewhat of a lottery in terms of local and national policy and there are gross differences of response, both of quality and quantity, regarding support services available to help those who care for friends or family within the community.

References

Bonny, S. (1984) *Who Cares in Southwark*, London: Carers' National Association.
Briggs, A. and Oliver, J. (1985) *Caring: Experiences of Looking after Disabled Relatives*, London: Routledge & Kegan Paul.
EOC (Equal Opportunities Commission) (1980) *The Experience of Caring for Elderly and Handicapped Dependants*, Manchester: EOC.
Family Policy Studies Centre (1989) *Bulletin*, winter, London: FPSC.
Green, H. (1988) *Informal Carers*, General Household Survey OPCS, London: HMSO.
Griffiths Report (1988) *Community Care: Agenda for Action*, London: HMSO.
Hicks, C. (1988) *Who Cares? Looking After People at Home*, London: Virago.
Kohner, N. (1988) *Caring at Home*, Cambridge: National Extension College.
Rohde, S. (1987 edn) *A Private View of L. S. Lowry*, London: Methuen.
Twigg, J. (1989) 'Models of carers: how do social care agencies conceptualise their relationship with informal carers?' *Journal of Social Policy* 18, 1: 53–66.
Webb, I. (1987) *People Who Care*, Report on Carer Provision in England and Wales, London: Co-operative Women's Guild.
Woolff, H. (1979a) 'Tools for Living', *Action Magazine*, National Fund for Research into Crippling Diseases no 26: 26–32.
—— (1979b) 'Tools for Living: a blueprint for a major new industry', in J. Bray and S. Wright (eds) (1980) *The Use of Technology in the Care of the Elderly and Disabled*, London: Pinter.

Useful addresses

Carers' National Association, 29 Chilworth Mews, London W2 3RG tel: 01-724-7776.
King's Fund Carer's Project, King's Fund Centre, 126 Albert Street, London NW1 7NF.
Caring Costs Campaign, c/o 29 Chilworth Mews, London W2 3RG.

15
A small light: reflections on contemporary group work in social welfare

Jenny Lumley and
Nano McCaughan

The wintry haw is burning out of season,
crab of the thorn, a small light for small people,
wanting no more from them but that they keep
the wick of self-respect from dying out,
not having to blind them with illumination.

(Seamus Heaney, 'The Haw Lantern')

Social work and social welfare in the UK have had an ambivalent and changing relation to the use of group work as a method of practice. This has been influenced by contemporary and dominant theories connected with helping people as well as the current structure by which welfare workers are organized. In the late nineteenth and early twentieth centuries, casework with individuals and families began to be organized into a planful method and to hold a valuable place, for example in the Charity Organisation Society. At the same time the settlement movement and Workers' Educational Association (WEA) influenced the growth of local groups concerned with education and self-help because of the concern about neighbourhood and community development. Later the advent of and spreading influence of psychoanalytic thinking, particularly on social work training from the 1930s to the 1960s, created a separation between social welfare workers and neighbourhood or community workers. Psychoanalytic thinking was not so easily transferred to group work, based as it is on the experiential inner world of the individual. By the 1960s group theories were developed from a psychoanalytic base by Bion (1969), Foulkes (1975) and others.

Workers have to harness methods developed by group psychotherapists to theories of small group psychology which were not directed predominantly at problems generated by the social context – poverty, housing needs, knowledge about welfare benefit rights and so on.

> The leadership method employed by this approach was mostly passive, and the techniques used were non-directive, relying largely on the interpretation of here and now phenomena occurring in the group, or to here and then interpretation of material shared by individual members.
>
> (Triseliotis 1988: 11)

Many welfare workers were fearful of organizing groups because of the assumed complexity of group processes, and the dissatisfaction experienced by members who could not see the relevance to their day-to-day problems. On the other hand, community work developed along a different theoretical and methodological base, using interactionist and social education models, helping people in disadvantaged areas to define social needs, organize, campaign and understand better how to tackle local and national power structures. This led to a growth of consumer-led voluntary self-help organizations such as Gingerbread, MENCAP and Contact a Family. In the 1970s the reorganization of social work and social welfare staff into large generic departments allowed a better appreciation of the necessity of working both on inner concerns as well as on the social context. For example, in the case of young people separated from their families and joining another, or elderly people faced with growing physical dependence and frequently the loss of a cherished partner.

Humanistic psychology provided other variants of psychotherapy which seemed less mystifying: Rogerian encounter groups, transactional analysis in groups, structured experiential learning. There has accordingly followed an expansion of more time limited and task-centred group work as a legitimate method of achieving the aims of the personal social services and voluntary organizations. Such group work is practitioner- rather than management-led, and is more modest and limited in its purposes than that with a psychoanalytic derivation. Welfare workers appear now to have more confidence to build their models and draw on an eclectic range of methods. 'Group work currently is an all-encompassing description of activities which vary from group therapy and social group work to social action, self-help and consciousness-raising' (Preston-Shoot 1987: 2).

In the late 1980s social welfare takes place in a sociopolitical atmosphere which seems less promising to the traditional users of our social welfare services than in the optimistic climates of the 1960s and 1970s. Contemporary group work therefore has an emphasis on concepts such as 'empowerment', 'self-advocacy' and 'mutual support': an attempt to redress the balance and allow disadvantaged groups to discover and use their collective voice.

What follows below is an identification of current dominant themes worked on in groups with some examples. This is an attempt to provide a typology but in no way could each theme be said to be distinct or unique.

Healing and restoration

Individuals, in a variety of circumstances, seek the support of others to help re-establish and affirm their identity. Circumstances as diverse as the loss of a partner or parent, being involved in a tragedy such as a train crash, or being a vulnerable member of a family where sexual or physical abuse has taken place can provide the focus for group work intervention. It is increasingly used as we become more aware of the long-term negative effects of avoiding grief and of the processes which lead back to acceptance and integration of the toxic experiences. Self-help organizations such as CRUSE, which caters for those recently bereaved, include social workers in the facilitating role. Other short-term groups take place in hospitals, parishes, residential homes for older people, child guidance clinics and family centres. These may focus on the grief experience; promote the necessary 'talking about the experience', facilitate mutual support, and normalize the strong and natural feelings of bereavement.

Transitions

Contemporary social policy and social phenomena such as the increasing divorce rate are creating the necessity for many people to make traumatic life changes. These would include the large-scale move of patients from some long-stay mental health or mental handicap institutions to life in the community – that is with families, into hostels or small group homes. Other transitions might be becoming adopted as an older child; becoming a step-parent and having to amalgamate two families; or being housed in a new housing estate distant from one's local community as a young single parent. These events are the experience of a very sizeable minority of citizens. Group work is intended to help people prepare for, make sense of and learn to use opportunities in the new situation.

This form of group work makes use of a wide variety of education methods designated 'life skills and social skills'. They can range from physical or personal care of oneself, practical domestic skills such as shopping, cooking, washing which institutionalized people have no chance to practise. They also focus on more abstract aspects of personal growth: being self-confident, learning to make friends without overwhelming others with one's personal needs, joining and making use of community leisure or informal educational activities. The company of similar others can help to make the learning interesting and enjoyable and relieve individual anxieties about being different or inferior.

Empowering

It is an increasing practice for workers in social welfare to use their own training and life skills to empower others, not to dominate or increase their dependency and lack of self-esteem, *vis-à-vis* professionals or 'experts'. Feedback from users of social welfare agencies in the past and evaluation of service results may lead to painful insights such as were summarized in the campaign poster of a society campaigning for people with disabilities: 'His greatest handicap could be your attitude'. A literature is developing to enable professionals to examine and change their attitudes (see for example Hollins and Grimes 1988; Ernst and Goodison 1981). This reflects a growing climate of opinion in the social welfare world that partnership should be the relationship between worker and client, coupled with the realization that most people, however disadvantaged, have great potential for developing their skills and are easily helped to become aware of their wants and goals. Part of this group work would be consciousness-raising and to that end it is crucial to have available 'competent' models from the group member population rather than from professionals alone.

Groups working on the empowerment theme would be exploring training needs, sharing information freely, examining differences and being prepared to acknowledge what the workers and the organization have to learn. Additionally, they will be exploring their experience of the realities of power and oppression, and aiding members in tackling inequalities both intra group and between group members and individuals or agencies in their context. Some group work would be especially structured to identify and train citizen advocates for those who will need an additional voice or support.

Consumer rights

In the late 1980s there was clear evidence that many individuals and families are growing relatively poorer. Consumer rights groups have started up sponsored by social welfare workers and by voluntary agencies such as CAB. Parents of children undergoing care proceedings by local authorities are becoming more conscious of their legal rights and the activities of organizations such as the Family Rights Group has drawn considerable attention to certain abuses. Concern regarding New Right consumerist ideologies and the recognition by the left of the necessity for local accountability has led to some group intervention with the consumers of the personal social services. This is perhaps more appropriately developed by voluntary organizations, especially as it challenges the power or competence of central or local government policies and services. There are a growing number of group projects focusing on issues such as welfare rights, disability access, fuel poverty, inadequate housing or state-owned provision. This work often includes local campaigns as well as information-giving, encouragement and training.

Humanizing institutions

As more staff in the field of residential and day-care settings have access to training in human relationship skills in addition to care or craft skills, the institution itself as well as discrete parts of it can become targets of change. For example, bringing a home for young adults into line with 'normalization' principles, requires changes in perception, attitudes and behaviour of each member of staff and residents, as well as changes in the building or location, or in the way in which local community resources are used. Arguably, it is no longer considered sufficient in most service provision to run day centres as mini work production units. Group work focusing on social skills, using leisure activities, and working with citizen applicants is becoming a part of programmes.

Social control

This category refers to groups formed with persons to whom the agency has a statutory authority to engage in social work, or probation work which is expected to lead to a change in attitudes or behaviour. People in these groups are most commonly parents whose child care is considered to be below the current norm, leading to risks for the children of physical, sexual or emotional abuse; or offenders whose behaviour has lead to court appearances and who are in danger of receiving custodial sentences for further offences.

Group work might operate on the principle that physical abuse of children was connected with the tensions and frustrations of poor housing, unemployment and poverty. The aims would therefore be to help parents improve their living situations in practical ways. A number of projects, mainly in clinical settings, strive to offer therapeutic change to families where child sexual abuse has occurred by offering different group work to the various actors in the situation; perpetrators, spouses and victims. Groups with a more focused 'teaching' aim (of better parental skills) are run in social services department area teams to assess, monitor and support the parents of children on the Abuse Register. Brown and Seymour (1983) describe the widespread use of initial assessment groups for clients of a probation service who have been put on probation.

The context of group work

Training for the practice of group work in social work and social welfare strikes the specialist as a rather hit-and-miss affair. The individual and family context of helping, advice-giving and counselling has always provided more training opportunities than work with groups. Most basic courses preparing and forming people to support those deemed to be in need of professional facilitation in order to lead satisfactory lives has included a respectable proportion of knowledge and skill development, individual psycho-social development theories, assessment skills, individual counselling skills, reactions towards asking for and receiving help, and the use of the helping relationship. Group workers have not been so well served. While most courses provide a sequence on work with groups, this can be as little as four sessions on a one- or two-year course. Time devoted to teaching psychology and sociology far outweighs that of social psychology or group dynamics theories. There are a notable few exceptions, usually when there is a committed and experienced group worker on the academic staff, where courses may offer as much as three or four terms' teaching coupled with good practice opportunities. Teaching about the technical aspects of the social worker's role, for example children and family law, necessarily diminishes the time available for developing practice methods.

Following a little experience of basic training, most interested group workers have to piece together their own professional development from in-service or other short courses, usually either introductory and general or focusing on a specialist theme – either a particular method (task centred) or a particular user group (reminiscence work with elderly people). Here and there in a few regions experienced practitioners have collaborated to organize more substantial but inevitably part-time training courses. Other training opportunities available have come from institutions wishing to promote a particular conceptual base that may act as a core knowledge and value background to their work. Examples are the group relations conferences run by the Tavistock Institute of Human Relations, the Grubb Institute of Behavioural Studies or the Institute of Psychoanalysis' foundation courses. Such courses provide an introduction to a training in group psychotherapy or analysis, or an exploration and method of studying group processes in organizations. They are not specifically designed for social group workers who have to make their own choices and applications of what experiences and theories to use in their work.

There is no association as yet of social group workers, not a consensus that this might be a valuable object to strive to establish. Consequently there is no body of committed teachers and practitioners to help develop curriculum, comment on standards of practice and training needs and promote a method through research and publications. One reason for this is that it is not yet clearly decided in the social work profession whether group work should be an essential core method used by every social worker, or remain a specialist option. Another reason is the interdisciplinary nature of much of the work. The first specialist UK journal *Groupwork* was established in 1988 and may go some way to provide a central focus around which other opportunities may be organized.

There are, however, a variety of local networks through which practitioners can get in touch with each other by informal communications, attending short courses, or through the Group Relations Training Association or other networking organizations. This has meant that there are local sources of creativity, support and consultation which have to be explored by practitioners with some initiative.

One example of a type of ad-hoc development has been in an area of London, where through the activities of an independent group work consultant, several local authority social services departments appointed a group work adviser to a newly created post, to work across the different client divisions. The staff appointed formed a support group for themselves and through their discussions about developments and about the problems they were experiencing, began to share activities – running joint introductory courses and specialist workshops; identifying gaps of knowledge or skill in the organizations which were hindering group work developments. One such gap was the unfamiliarity of many middle managers with group work practice and therefore their resistance to promoting it or attempting to support progress through the supervision of staff engaged in it. This led to joint workshops to support these key people. These had a demonstrable impact on the numbers of projects developed and also on team development.

Identifying and training staff who can offer supervision to people planning to set up groups is a key factor in any consistent development, whether the group workers are staff or volunteers. Many volunteers cannot afford to finance their training and may be reliant on the perception of organizations to discern the importance of their contribution, and the need for reflection and subsequent increased understanding and response.

There are many citizens with special knowledge and experience, such as parents of children with disabilities, foster parents, step-parents or cancer survivors who can and do form groups to support similar others. The support can often be disrupted or remain limited unless they too can have opportunities to deepen their self-awareness in group facilitation, learn about different outcomes of stress, cope with the power and strength of feelings arising in groups, accept and work with the inevitable projections that come the leader's way in a group, and be sensitive to the need of individuals to end their work or indeed the group itself to dissolve, and not to feel rejected or incompetent because of that.

Understanding how we function in groups should be a key dimension and valued skill in any organization. Without training and consultancy and the opportunity to study and reflect on their own behaviour, and that of the day-to-day group life they experience, staff (or volunteers) find it hard to be objective, and tend to use such mechanisms as scape-goating, projection of blame, dependency or confusion. The demands of the individual's egos can then easily swamp the collective work of groups.

Personnel in social welfare organizations often take for granted that the wants of a local community (which are usually first expressed as individual requests) have to be responded to individually, or in some formal service delivery model. Therefore it is unlikely that there are many organizations that have a consistent way of identifying and researching the possibilities for group work. For example, if 200 parents, inevitably mainly women, were to ask for a day nursery place over the course of a year, staff would probably only deplore the shortage of places and believe that there was only the option available of offering a waiting-list place. Agency staff tend to think of service delivery models rather than community development, and respond to demands which exceed resources with evasion and guilt rather than creatively and inventively. Some support with child care is undoubtedly better than none for those who request it. The Pre-school Playgroups Association was developed with a self-help motivation around this issue. Some staff in family centres run by voluntary organizations have also demonstrated that there are a variety of ways of contributing help with the burdensome aspects of child care without necessarily establishing day nurseries run by professionals (Phelan 1983).

In organizations where group work becomes established and valued, it is interesting to note the possibilities for effecting change in the values and practice of other staff. It becomes possible, for example, for teams to think of resources such as 'holding' groups – offering an immediate place in a rolling programme of group work for applicants who would have to wait for an individual service. Examples of this could be a group for children having difficulties at school and young people leaving care. Teams can be enabled to pay more attention to their own processes and be more open to work as a group in improving their communication and other work processes. Participation at meetings will improve and individual staff members begin to take more responsibility for the ownership of collective goals. Additionally, teams of workers who arrange to spend a regular session reflecting on their work processes tend to value the opportunities inherent in group work and therefore to take the necessary steps to develop group work projects for consumers.

Given the policy and subsequent practice developments of the 1980s – the rights of users to have a say in the management of institutions such as day care, family and neighbourhood centres, the move to small group homes from large institutions for those who need special living arrangements, group living, the attempt to humanize the large units which have to exist until they can be replaced, the change from providing mini work production units for people with disabilities, to an enriched programme of education, independence preparation and social skills – small group work is particularly appropriate as a method. Some training is currently provided on basic professional preparation courses, and post-qualification training opportunities are patchily available. However, for a more consistent development of good practice, experience indicates that it is essential to have some senior role in organizations to co-ordinate the training, planning, practice support and evaluation of work with groups. This could be held by a specialist method adviser or consultant, or a training officer or manager with a developmental remit.

Training methods

One of the hallmarks of social group work is the belief in, and commitment to, using action methods of learning. The growth of groups with the aim of improving social life skills was supported by a variety of literature suggesting action methods for using with these groups (Scally and Hopson 1979; Brandes and Phillips 1978; Priestly and MaGuire 1985). Contemporary educational experiences concerning effective ways to assist adults to learn offer useful concepts that clearly fit in with the practice values employed by groupworkers for many years. Kolb *et al.*'s (1981) experiential learning cycle is one of several models that demonstrate the value of the 'action' or the doing in the learning cycle. Group workers and group members continue to modify, improve, invent and improvise action methods. Workers have become more experienced at matching the activity to the phase of the group's development. Handy suggests we live in an age of 'discontinuous change'. One way of surviving and managing such a change is 'upside-down thinking' (Handy 1989). Many of the inventions of the action methods have come from such 'upside-down thinking'. To manage the new ways of the future, he suggests, we need to look at things in different ways: 'upside-down thinking wonders what magic it is that determines that forty hours spread over five days should be the working week for most people' (Handy 1989: 21).

Role play, for example, can be used to try to gain insight into new or different situations. Sculpting can be used to explore the nature of relationships in a group; who is close to whom, who is seen to be powerful or excluded.

Murals of all kinds can be used to demonstrate the norms and cultures of a particular group. Collages are used to enable the group to make a statement about an issue or an experience. For example, a women's group may work on a mural about their experience as women. Trust exercises can assist in 'bonding' the group, and there are a range of exercises designed to explore issues of touch, personal space and dependence. Other action methods are used to assist in an exploration of values and beliefs, for example, setting five- and ten-year plans for yourself, planning one week of your life as if it was your last, writing your own epitaph or obituary. Exercises to agree priorities of all kinds sharpen the mind into discovering what beliefs are really important. Groups become very imaginative in designing exercises for themselves, and this leads to many more 'group specific' action methods being used. For example, a group of adults with a learning difficulty who live in a home met to work on bereavements that they had all experienced. They spend each group session for a while visiting each other's childhood homes, which revived many memories and led to some very rich sharing and support.

Co-working is an issue that has attracted considerable interest and attention over the last few years. In the experience of the authors, most workers favour a co-working model and the majority of groups are co-led. The advantages are seen as benefiting both workers and group members. Because the nature of the work is changing, due in part to the recommendations of child abuse reports, there has of necessity been a move towards more co-working across the disciplines. Personnel from health, education and the police have to be involved together in many instances and this has fostered a greater understanding of roles and tasks. Additionally, the self-help ethos has led to a move towards co-working with non-professionals. Both the pleasures and the perils have been clearly set out by Hodge (1985). High on the list of pleasure for many workers is the opportunity that co-working offers for consultation, support, feedback and a sharing of both achievements and pressure. For the group co-working effectively can demonstrate how two adults can interact, have differences and generally enrich leadership resources.

The perils or potential disturbance include slipping into competitive relationships, the loss of competence of one worker, or succumbing to powerful splitting techniques.

Contemporary practice issues

Racism

There is growing awareness and concern that many of our social institutions, because of their history and nature, are oppressive to most minority groups. This presents group workers with considerable challenges. Many workers are now examining the ways in which the planning and management of the groups with which they are working are merely preserving the status quo. Increasingly workers are being reminded that all too often their practice does not take account of issues of class, gender, race and ethnicity. A current analysis suggests that contemporary social work gives the impression that these issues are being taken account of; in fact the evidence is that they are not (Dominelli 1988: 2). There is other evidence which demonstrates the prevalence of racism despite considerable efforts to address the issues. Examples include the fact that black children are grossly over-represented in the 'in care' population and also in the prison population (Commission for Racial Equality 1988).

One area of group work that is coming under considerable scrutiny concerns the whole area of pre-group planning. Here it seems that some activities that were thought to be good practice now look to be increasingly suspect. For example, numbers of both black and multi-racial groups are run by white workers. Notions about structure, programming, venues and refreshments, setting objectives, are based largely and often unconsciously on white cultural perspectives; exercises are all too often drawn from literature written by authors from white cultures. Well-intentioned events are offered to group members particularly in multi-racial groups where increased understanding can be gained and where differences can be positively framed. However 'racial inequality has not disappeared because white people understand better customs, traditions and religious activities of other ethnic minority groups' (Dominelli 1988: 2). One of the challenges appears to be how workers and their agencies can make group work opportunities more widely available. Imaginative approaches need to be made which do not prescribe for, and therefore oppress, the very groups who should have equal access to this resource. There are a number of initiatives where groups are run for people from the same race which give an opportunity to make space for a specialist perspective, for example, issues of race as they apply to being Asian women. In some instances, the groups may be able to organize some change in the agency. There is much to learn about the appropriate use of such groups: 'same race groups have advantages in many circumstances, and only experience (and our mistakes) can help build the confidence to know when and how to set up such groups' (Muston and Weinstein 1988: 35).

Disabilities

Similar assumptions are also being challenged by staff working with people who have disabilities. One of the preoccupying concerns held by group workers in the field of disability is the culture clash between the experience within the groups (where the aims would include full participation, taking opportunities and sharing the power) and the experience in the world outside. The wider society would often provide painful reminders of the handicapping effect of attitudes and behaviour that still excludes disabled people from social and cultural life.

Full participation in the basic units of society – family, social groups and community – is the essence of human experience. . . . In reality disabled persons are often denied the opportunities of full participation in the activities of the socio-cultural system of which they are a part. This deprivation comes about through physical and social barriers that have evolved from ignorance, indifference and fear.

(World Programme of Action Concerning Disabled Persons 1983)

Growing awareness about this has meant that group workers have had to examine their role very carefully in the light of consumer feedback. Some people with disabilities are clear that they wish to join existing groups. People with a disability are also women, may be bereaved, may wish to improve social skills or parenting skills, may wish to join a campaign group, or wish to clarify their rights and benefits. The notion of having a group for people with a disability may simply provide further stigmatizing. However, there is valid justification for working with some groups that are specifically for disabled people.

One group was set up for diabetic adolescents with the aim of helping them to manage the difficulties of self-injection of insulin. The group members felt that they had got an enormous amount of confidence and support from each other. One voluntary organization invited the siblings of disabled young people to share together their experiences of living in families with a disabled member. This group was felt to be very successful in that it gave a voice to young people whose previous experience had often been that they were ignored by the professionals involved. Another group offered recently disabled people, wheelchair users, an opportunity to discuss and share concerns. They provided a strong support group, advising each other on the overwhelmingly complex array of information and opportunities. Workers with these groups are having to take account of any work that needs to be done with the relevant systems outside the groups. It has also meant that the focus of the work at some point in the groups has to be on assisting members to develop strategies to manage those oppressive events faced every day by people with disabilities. Managing how to be 'receiver of others' curiosity and naivete, be an object of others' sadness and sorrow, to constantly be seeking a means to replenish exhausted internal resources; to experience wrath and rejection at not fitting the stereotypical norm' (Quinn 1989: 3).

Gender

The gender dimension is a further consideration to add to the factors currently challenging the group worker. There is a struggle to make women visible, both as clients, as workers, and to work towards non-sexist women-centred practice (Hanmer and Statham 1988).

One attempt that group workers in many settings have made towards that has been to establish women's groups to explore issues of being women. This is a shift from the 'parent' or 'mother and toddler' groups where the focus remained on the parenting role. Women's groups have sprung up in many organizations, often working on how non-sexist practices can be encouraged. Women alone cannot make all the changes, however, and there is evidence that men's groups are also growing. Workers running groups in family programmes are making increasing attempts at attracting men to join the groups.

Residential establishments are offering separate groups for men and women to explore issues of gender and how they are being managed in the institution.

Thus, there appears to be a revival in group work which may be in part linked to these new challenges facing group workers. There also appears to be growing recognition that 'service delivery and service system issues are important and should not be separated from issues of service effectiveness themselves' (Ephross and Vassil 1988: 9). Enhanced understanding about how these issues affect us all – both consumers and deliverers of the service is perhaps leading to a greater use of small group situations. Thus we find that in teams, in work groups and client groups attempts are being made to tackle the issues.

A review of the social welfare journals suggests that one area of expansion has been groups around the theme of child abuse, for children, parents and abusers. One significant conclusion in a review of articles concerning group work in this area suggests

> group work can be employed creatively in the core interactions of statutory social work. . . . It can be a major method in its own right, perhaps used as a preventative measure with parents of children 'at risk' or used as an additional therapeutic tool in work with parents and children where separation has had to be legally enforced.
>
> (McCaughan 1988: 79)

One encouraging indication here is that in some places at least, group work is experienced less as a peripheral and somewhat marginalized activity, and more as a potentially core method. As such it is obviously more appropriate for some people at some points in their life.

It might seem that because of the changes in society and the subsequent issues we face, that welfare organizations should be essentially concerned with providing group work services. However, the infrastructures of some organizations, particularly the personal social services, require on the whole that the services are delivered to one person or family and the accountability invested in one worker. Because of the bureaucratic nature of these organizations, they cannot easily facilitate a more pro-active response, nor do these structures support easily the notion of serving several consumers at the same time. The structures positively militate against any more collaborative practice and it is because of this that many potentially skilled group workers lose heart. Several authors have demonstrated the importance of group workers having the skills to 'manage' these structural issues (Douglas 1976; Brown 1979).

Conclusion

In writing this paper, we realized how stimulating it had been to group work practice, to work with and respond to the many changes that face us in contemporary Britain. There is an encouraging sense that group work in some instances played a part in some of the changes and is now taking the initiative in many places in shaping some of the responses. We would wish to avoid making exaggerated claims for the effectiveness of group work in changing social policy. However, in informal evaluations most clients express satisfaction with their group experiences. It seemed to us that Seamus Heaney's poem, quoted at the beginning of this chapter, reflected the core values that most group workers would wish to adhere to.

Acknowledgement

We are grateful to Faber and Faber for allowing us to quote from 'The Haw Lantern'.

References

Balgopal, P. R. and Vassil, T. V. (1983) *Groups in Social Work: An Ecological Perspective*, New York: Columbia University Press.

Bion, W. R. (1969) *Experience in Groups and Other Papers*, London: Tavistock.

Brandes, D. and Phillips, H. (1978) *Gamesters' Handbook*, London: Hutchinson.

Brown, A. (1979) *Groupwork*, London: Heinemann.

Brown, A. and Seymour, A. (1983) *Intake Groups for Clients*, University of Bristol, School of Advanced Urban Studies.

Commission for Racial Equality (1988) *Annual Report, 1987*, London: CRE.

Dominelli, L. (1988) *Anti-Racist Social Work*, London: Macmillan Education.

Douglas, T. (1976) *Groupwork Practice*, London: Tavistock.

Ephross, P. H. and Vassil, T. V. (1988) *Groups that Work*, New York: Columbia University Press.

Ernst, S. and Goodison, L. (1981) *In Our Own Hands*, London: Women's Press.

Foulkes, S. H. (1975) *Group Psychoanalytic Psychotherapy: Method and Principles*, London: Gordon & Breach.

Handy, C. (1989) *The Age of Unreason*, London: Business Books.

Hanmer, J. and Statham, D. (1988) *Women and Social Work: Towards a Women-Centred Practice*, London: Macmillan Education.

Heap, K. (1977) *Group Theory for Social Workers*, Oxford: Pergamon Press.

Hodge, F. J. B. (1985) *Planning for Co-Leadership*, Newcastle-upon-Tyne: Groupvine.

Hollins, S. and Grimes, N. (1988) *Going Somewhere*, London: Society for Promoting Christian Knowledge.

Kolb, D., Rubin, I. and MacIntyre, J. N. (1981) *Organisational Psychology: An Experimental Approach*, Englewood Cliffs, NJ: Prentice-Hall.

McCaughan, N. (1988) 'Swimming upstream: a survey of recent articles on social groupwork', in *Groupwork* 1, 1: 77–89, London: Whiting & Birch.

Muston, R. and Weinstein, J. (1988) 'Race and Group Work – Some Experiences in Practice and Training', *Groupwork*, 1, 1: 30–40.

Oliver, M. (1983) *Social Work with Disabled People*, London: Macmillan Press.

Phelan, J. (1983) *Family Centres*, London: The Children's Society.

Preston-Shoot, M. (1987) *Effective Groupwork*, London: Macmillan.

Priestley, M. and MaGuire, J. (1985) *Learning to Help*, London: Tavistock.

Quinn, G. (1988) 'The demands of being different', unpublished paper.

Scally, M. and Hopson, B. (1979) *Life Skills Teaching in Schools and Colleges*, University of Leeds.

Schwartz, W. and Zalba, S. (1971) *The Practice of Groupwork*, New York: Columbia University Press.

Triseliotis, J. (1988) *Groupwork in Adoption*, London: Batsford.

World Programme of Action Concerning Disabled Persons (1983) in *A Decade of Disabled Persons*, United Nations (1983 to 1992), available from UN Information Centre, Buckingham Gate, London.

16
Future of social work education: recovering from *Care for Tomorrow*

Phyllida Parsloe

It was only a short time ago (1987) that the Central Council for Education and Training in Social Work (CCETSW) submitted its plans to the government for the future of social work education in a document called *Care for Tomorrow* (CCETSW 1987). Looking back even this little distance it seems incomprehensible that anyone could have thought that the Thatcher government would have agreed to plans which not only involved expenditure of £40 million but also meant lengthening social work education to a minimum of three years and raising it to degree level. Such plans would be unlikely to find favour with a government set on reducing public spending especially in the service sector, which holds that welfare should be a residual activity, and which, with some justification, sees social workers as supporters at least of a liberal democratic, if not a socialist, view of society.

Yet the Council, supported by a wide range of service and educational organizations, not only agreed to present the plan but also appeared to be reasonably optimistic about the government's response. This is hard to understand and as someone who was a Council member at the time I have personal, as well as political, reasons for wanting an explanation. My suspicion is that all those involved were so heartily sick of the seemingly endless review of social work education, which had been going on since 1983, that we colluded in a false consensus under the spirited, and apparently confident, leadership provided by a new Chair and a new Director of Council. Certainly looking back on the Council meetings I believe we were the subject of 'group think' (Janis 1972). This was most evident at the point at which Council received what at first sight, and now with hindsight, seemed to be a negative letter from the minister. Somehow we were convinced that the words were not really a true indication of his intentions, that he was just warning us of the case we needed to make rather than signalling future rejection. During the coffee break I, among others, expressed my scepticism of this interpretation but like others in the meeting I kept silent and even began to feel optimistic.

What the Council got were some promises for future years which by the nature of public expenditure have to remain vague, and a more definite statement that funding for the purpose of extending one-year postgraduate courses to two years would be made available. This was for the future; immediately the Council was offered money to spend in a very short time-span on upgrading and increasing practice placements, developing partnerships between agencies and educational institutions and a small amount to support developments in social care.

The Council accepted the money offered by the government, although not without some debate. By this time Council had passed a motion stating that both the Certificate of Qualification in Social Work (CQSW) and the Certificate of Social Service (CSS) were equivalent qualifications in social work. This was a major decision and reflected the strength of the employer interests on Council which Jones explored in the last issue of this *Yearbook* (Jones 1989). It was also one which created major questions for social work education. It would have been one thing to have two routes to a new social work qualification as proposed in *Care for Tomorrow*, quite another to say that two forms of training, originally designed for different purposes, should now qualify people for the same job. The decision was taken before the rejection of *Care for Tomorrow*, at a Council meeting at which, on reflection, unity appeared to be more important than any other consideration.

Given that decision it may seem strange that the Council was prepared to take money to increase the length of training for students who have spent three years doing a social science degree followed by an additional year on a postgraduate social work course which in some instances gives them both a CQSW and a masters degree. One might have thought that the courses most in need of lengthening were the two-year non-graduate CQSW programmes and the CSS schemes. Increasing the postgraduate courses without a similar increase in non-graduate and CSS schemes creates a strange situation, especially for educational establishments which offer both types of courses. It appears to suggest that social science degrees are of little value in social work. Perhaps this is what is intended and, if so, it is certainly in accord with a general scepticism about the relevance of theory which permeates much of the social service scene.

Upgrading – as it is called – of one-year postgraduate programmes is to take place by 1995 and a number of such courses are to change each year. This is the plan, but since it depends upon other changes, particularly those concerning the funding of universities and polytechnics and their students, the Council finds itself, once again, planning in an arena where it has little power to affect crucial decisions. Recent events have made this even more obvious. Fees which undergraduates pay from 1989 are to be nearer to the real cost, apparently in order to create a market in student places by allowing institutions to enrol students above the quota number for which they get funding in addition to fees. More recently the Universities Funding Council has announced that it intends to introduce a number of fee bands to which different subjects are allocated and that institutions will be asked to make bids at whatever price they wish per student against a fixed maximum. If the original plans are enacted, undergraduate social work courses will be in the lowest fee band. At present the plans refer only to undergraduates but the principle of the market will presumably be extended later to non-graduates and postgraduates. The likely outcome of these changes appears to be a worsening of staff–student ratios. What is required, if standards are to be protected, is for institutions to get together and bid at a common and realistic level; given the past record on collaboration this seems unlikely and the fear is that competition will prove the enemy of quality.

Returning to CCETSW, money for one-year courses is to come in the longer term but the Council accepted the offer of more immediate funds for encouraging partnerships in programme planning, developing practice placements and the registration of practice teachers and their agencies. Taking this money caused organizational problems for the Council. In a very short time the money had to be spent; the changes it was to achieve had to take effect at local level but the Council only had local committee structures in Northern Ireland, Scotland and Wales – what are now in government parlance to be called the territories. In England there were regional offices of Council staff but no regional committees. Faced with this and with considerable pressure from employers and educators to have a say in how the money was to be spent, the Council set up Interim Planning Groups, each chaired by a Council member and with a membership appointed from local practitioners, employers and educators. The remit for these groups was never entirely clear, at least not to the members, but there was a tendency for them to want to take on an executive role and see themselves as responsible for the future of social work education in their area. In the event they were short-lived since Council abolished them in the spring of 1989.

While the Interim Planning Groups perhaps posed an unwelcome threat to the national role of the Council they were instrumental in setting up subgroupings of educators and employers in which planning for the new jointly run programmes began.

In April 1989 this process was strengthened by Council taking the final decisions about the regulations needed to introduce a new award, to be called the Diploma in Social Work (DipSW). Programmes leading to the award can be proposed only by a partnership of at least one employing agency and one educational institution; they may offer a college-based or an agency-based route and the Council's role, it is said, will be to assess output rather than programme content.

While the attention of social work educators and Council has been focused upon recovering from *Care for Tomorrow* the social care sector has been moving ahead quickly. The Welfare Industry lead body is established and sets of competencies for the four levels of the National Council of Vocational Qualifications (NCVQ) are being agreed. NCVQ and the Diploma in Social Work are not yet linked together although routes from the one to the other are to be created for some staff. The question of NCVQ moving into level 5, the level of professional qualifications, is much in the air and seems to have the support of government, perhaps because it could bring professional bodies more under employer control. For social work this may be the final logic of the process which has moved CQSW into the employers' arena. What may also be occurring is a return of the history of CQSW and CSS. Once again those who work in residential and day care, and especially with elderly people, may be given a different kind or level of qualification from those who work in the field. Level 3 or 4 for the former, level 5 or DipSW for the latter.

The introduction of a new word 'competencies' into the jargon of social work should not pass without comment. Apart from its inherent ugliness it seems an inappropriate word to describe activities which involve knowledge and skills used in accordance with a value base. Social work, and social care, unlike plumbing for example, are not value-free activities and what is more they can only be carried out in interaction with users. We must hope that those who are establishing the competencies for social care are ingenious enough to develop tests for such complex activities.

Where are we now?

With all the activity of the last few years it is easy to forget the reasons why the Central Council originally embarked on a review of qualifying training. In 1983 the Council stated that it had decided to review its policies relating to qualifying training: 'Its purpose was to consider whether the policies carefully developed over the decade remained relevant or should be modified to meet the needs of the next decade' (CCETSW 1983: 3).

At the time the review was resisted by social work educators who made formal protests through the Social Work Education Committee of the Joint University Council, arguing that many of their courses were already under threat of staff cuts or even closures and all available energy was needed to deal with these challenges. Their case failed to persuade the Council and it was the view of employers, and especially the Standing Conference of Chairmen of CSS Schemes, which carried the day. Their reasons for wanting a review were made clear in the early stages of the process. They were critical of CQSW courses because of the alleged gap between what was taught on such programmes and the actual job of being a social worker. By contrast CSS students, who were both employees and students at the same time, were said to fit more easily into the organizational structures and to suffer less, if at all, from culture shock when returning to full-time employment after qualifying. At the time there was no research in social work to substantiate these views although research in other fields, such as teaching and engineering, certainly suggested that the transition from student to worker was a difficult one (see for example Bolam 1982). More recently work by Thomas (1988) suggests that people on CSS schemes see themselves primarily as employees and do not consider either joining a scheme or leaving it as a break in the continuity of their experience. Those on a CQSW course, by contrast, regard themselves as students and on qualifying need a period in which to assume the role of employee and professional.

Behind criticisms of relevance lie issues of control and of commitment. Jones (1989) suggests that the Association of Directors of Social Services (ADSS) was critical of CQSW courses at least partly because they did not control them in the way they did CSS schemes. This led not only to a belief that CQSW provided a less relevant programme but also to a reluctance to commit staff time to CQSW students. As local authorities suffered increasingly from cuts some became more and more reluctant to provide practice placements for CQSW courses or to accept responsibility for the standards of those they did offer. This was not everywhere the case and even where there were problems many of the individual practice teachers remained committed and enthusiastic. However, by 1988 the situation had deteriorated to the extent that in some areas a considerable proportion of students did not start their placements on the first day because no placement had yet been found for them.

Relevance, power and commitment were issues in the debate which tended to drive a wedge between CQSW and CSS protagonists. Other reasons for the review united them. There was general agreement that social work education had suffered from a knowledge explosion and that the minimum time needed to acquire the knowledge and skills demanded of a qualified worker was three not two years. There was also a measure of agreement about what constituted social work and that it now embraced a wider range of activities than had been generally accepted in 1975 when CSS schemes were launched. While there is still a debate about exactly which staff in residential and day care establishments require a social work qualification it is now agreed that some at least are doing social work and that a CSS has qualified them to do this work.

During the review, although not at its start, another criticism of social work education emerged: its failure to deal with issues of discrimination and, in particular, with racial discrimination. How then have the new arrangements for social work education dealt with these aspects which gave rise to the need for a review and what problems remain?

Control and commitment

Let us start by considering the question of control and commitment. While it is too early to be clear exactly how the new requirements will operate, what is certain is that there has been a considerable shift in power from educational establishments to agencies so far as the college-based route to the DipSW is concerned. The Council will approve only those courses which are submitted in partnership, will itself appoint external examiners and theoretical work will not be assessed *per se* but only for its contribution to practice. This is likely to create difficulties for universities and some polytechnics. It seems probable that they will continue to insist that they appoint external examiners if they are giving an award (in addition to the DipSW) and that a more extensive knowledge of underlying theories may be required than that demanded by CCETSW. How these two assessment and examining systems are to relate to each other without imposing a double burden on students is yet to be decided. The danger, for those who believe that the users of social services benefit from the fact that some social work education takes place in higher education and particularly in universities, is that such establishments will find it more convenient to dispense with social work education than to take on the complex negotiations required to make the new system work. While Council has expressed its wish to maintain university-based education for social work its actions in this and other areas could well be interpreted as an intention to make sure that universities reject social work education. Such an interpretation is strengthened by the widely accepted view that social workers and their managers are by and large anti-academic and, unlike other professional groups such as psychologists and lawyers, pay scant attention to the development of research.

The power shift may, however, have the effect of developing a real commitment by agencies to the provision and standard of practice placements. Registration of agencies, or parts of them, and of practice teachers should ensure a basic minimum standard of teaching for all students although it is difficult to see how standards and quantity can be addressed at the same time. At present the question of placements is being used by agencies as a bargaining counter for additional resources and progress seems unlikely until those financial questions are resolved.

Relevance

The question of the relevance of social work education has several different aspects and is complicated by the fact that there is no clarity about what is really meant by relevant training. For the purposes of this discussion I shall consider the following aspects: first, the confidence of newly qualified workers and the relationship between specialization in training and confidence on the job, second, the structures for providing social work education, third, the expanding nature of social work and its boundaries and, finally, the contribution which research into adult learning can make to the relevance debate.

Confidence and specialization

One of the complaints levelled at CQSW courses, and where they are compared unfavourably with CSS schemes, is that they do not produce students who are competent and confident enough to get on with the job. One reason suggested for this difference is that a CQSW course is required to provide a general introduction to social work practice. This means that in two years it must address all client groups, all social work methods and all settings. CSS schemes on the other hand are job related and, although students undertake a common unit, their learning is orientated to a particular setting and client group. Later in the general and the special units their learning is specifically related to their job.

The DipSW attempts to strike a middle position. All students are to acquire the core knowledge and skills of social work and are then to demonstrate that they can apply these in a particular area of practice. They must also acquire some specialist knowledge in this area. This resembles the current experience of many CQSW students, since on most courses it is possible, in effect, to develop a specialism by a judicious choice of study, placements and essay topics. The change then, for college-based routes may be to formalize existing practice and move a little in the direction of specialization, although we should note this is not the word used by CCETSW regulations, which manage to dodge both the word and the issues it raises. For employment-based programmes the shift is in the opposite direction towards more core teaching and here a very great change will be required. The DipSW requirements may thus have the effect of giving more students an area in which they feel confident and therefore improve their initial competence in their first job after qualification. What they do not do is help to solve the generic-specialist tension. But perhaps CCETSW cannot be blamed for that since the situation in agencies is confusing and there is no general pattern. While some agencies are moving towards at least partial specialization, usually by separating fieldwork with children and families from that with all other groups, others, by moving towards patch-based field teams or the establishment of resource centres where field, residential, domiciliary and day care services are provided by a team of workers seem to be going in the opposite direction towards genericism. Social work has not solved the question of how to develop specialization and the DipSW will not help. What is needed is an investment in post-qualifying education since real specialization must take place alongside experience. Neither the Council nor employers nor social workers themselves have taken post-qualification training seriously. The Council intends to introduce a post-qualification award but has not yet faced the questions of funding and how to establish adequate standards in the modular format which has been agreed. The locus of social work in local government, the lack of any viable professional organization, an anti-intellectual tradition and a Council without adequate funds, have combined to make post-qualifying training a matter for lip service and it is not clear that a new award will alter this. Without it the issue of specialization cannot be addressed, let alone solved and users of social services will, in general, continue to receive only a basic service.

The structures for social work education

The new DipSW will be achieved through programmes provided in partnership by educational and employer interests. The thinking seems to have been that CSS schemes dealt better with the issue of relevance than did CQSW courses and the reason for this was the joint management structures which CSS schemes had and which CQSW courses lacked. This is no more than an assumption and it may well be that the difference, if there is one, depends upon some other factor such as the role of the learner and not upon management structures. We shall not know that until well after 1995, when the new programmes have been in operation for a number of years.

However, it is at least possible that the Council has lost an opportunity to address the structural problems which really influence relevance. If one looks at other professional groups there are two, nursing and medicine, where, whatever the complaints are, they are not of lack of relevance or of a disjunction between training and the job. My own view is that medicine in particular offers a model which social work would have done well to emulate.

(I am not of course referring to what is often called the medical model of doctor–patient relationships but only to the way medical education is structured in a real partnership between universities and the NHS.) It provides a structure where students do real work of increasing responsibility, where teachers retain a responsibility for practice and where practitioners provide teaching, all in an ambience where research is expected and respected. It appears to address most of the problems which affect social work education. But maybe by the time the Council came to review training it was too late for a major change since the courses were established in higher education and practice was concentrated in local government, which has no traditions of educational partnership.

Expanding the definition of social work

The arguments for extending social work training to three years have been lost and for the foreseeable future British social work will have only a two-year training.

This raises very considerable problems, some of which were intensified by the way in which the Council conducted its campaign for *Care for Tomorrow*. This consisted not only of saying that the view of what was social work had expanded and that this and other factors had led to a great increase in the knowledge a qualified worker should have, but also of joining with the critics and 'rubbishing' existing social work education. This is a dangerous tactic and a deadly one if you lose the argument and that is what happened. So the Council was faced with having stated publicly that social work education was inadequate and with having failed to obtain a longer training period. The tactic then adopted has been to take the requirements for a newly qualified worker which were part of the three-year *Care for Tomorrow* package and rework them into what it is thought (hoped) can be achieved in two years. It is really unknown whether they can be achieved and in any case the Council would have difficulty in suggesting that the new standard is adequate, given its continuing commitment to a three-year minimum.

What this tactic has certainly not done is to address the problem of overload in basic training or reduce the expectations which employers are likely to have of newly qualified workers. The situation is at least as bad as it was when the review started and probably worse, since demands upon social service staff have increased greatly since 1983.

The failure to achieve a three-year training has other potentially serious implications of which we have become aware since the European directive on diplomas was issued. This states that professional qualifications, based upon either at least three years' training or those required to enter a particular job, are to be acceptable in all countries of the European Community (EC) from 1992. Social work in Britain fails both tests. Training is not three years long for all entrants nor is it always necessary to have a qualification before taking up a social work post. The effect of this is that British social workers will not be able to work as qualified social workers in other countries of the EC although social workers in all other countries meet the diploma test. This may not affect a great many people directly but it is a blow to the standing of British social work and social work education that the DipSW will not be accepted as a qualification by the EC. Britain, which has always been a leader in the European social work scene, now cannot even claim membership of the qualified club.

The Central Council hopes to alter this situation before 1992 but it is not clear what the options are. Some social workers in Britain do meet the three-year test and probation officers may meet both the length test (if their probationary year is included) and the test of requirement. It may or may not be possible to argue that some British social workers meet the criteria of the directive while others do not but this has yet to be explored. On the face of it the directive refers to the general situation and not to particular groups.

Another issue which has arisen during the review period and has come to a head since the publication of the Green Paper *Punishment, Custody and the Community* (Home Office 1988) concerns another kind of expansion of social work. In general the wider view of social work which embraces residential and day care has caused few difficulties. It is generally accepted that work in such settings is based upon the same values, knowledge and skills as work in more traditional social work settings. The Green Paper however brings to a head the somewhat uneasy balance which social work maintains between care and control. It has long been held that social work involves social control and that it was not just in the probation service that clients were controlled by social workers; the control exercised by local authority social workers is at least as extensive, and probably more so, especially in relation to children at risk and to those in care. Control might include punishment and still be acceptable within the values espoused by social workers provided that the intention of the punishment was the good of the individual. What would probably be rejected by most social workers would be punishment which was intended as retribution or to deter others from similar behaviour.

The Green Paper suggested that probation should be involved, to a much greater extent than before, in activities such as tagging which seem questionable ways for one human being to treat another. They are of doubtful benefit to the individual and seem to contain elements of retribution and general deterrence. By going beyond measures designed to help the individual alter his or her offending behaviour and by confusing the controlling aspects of punishment with those designed to alter the behaviour of people, other than the person on whom the sentence is inflicted, the Green Paper raised again the question of where social work ends.

The debate continues. Many probation authorities and the National Association of Probation Officers have rejected the idea of probation officers as agents of retribution and general deterrence. Some social work courses have taken a similar line and for them the issues have been brought to a head by a Home Office review of courses with probation options (Coleman 1989). This review is another indication of the power of employers, since CCETSW staff apparently agreed to the Home Office undertaking a review of the 'probation aspects' of CQSW courses. It is said that the Minister personally selected a social anthropologist, David Coleman, to undertake the review, accompanied by a senior probation officer. The review dealt only with what Coleman considered to be the probation-related aspects of the CQSW courses concerned. He seemed able to make a distinction, which the courses do not, between what students had to learn to become social workers and what they need to be probation officers.

The report of the review was issued in July 1989. It recommends two possible ways of re-allocating Home Office sponsorships based upon the recruitment needs of the services in different geographical areas and the quality of courses. The latter are apparently judged by the amount of time they spend on what Coleman considered were probation-specific teaching, on staff interest, experience and research in probation-related matters and on the courses' attitudes towards the 'new approaches in probation'. This is defined by Coleman as consisting of

1 offence centred treatment, confrontation and behaviour modification
2 issues of punishment and rehabilitation
3 the assessment of effectiveness both at the level of the outcome of probation service activities and of individual performance
4 the changing role of the probation service in the criminal justice system.

(Coleman 1989: 6)

At the time of writing, responses to the report are still awaited. For courses whose sponsorship are recommended for removal the report may be a threat to their immediate existence but all would be wise to regard it as a threat at least to their independence. Coleman drafts his report in terms of 'the lever' which sponsorships give the Service on training courses 'and which should be used more systematically to influence course content and methods'. There is no mention of employer–educational partnerships, although presumably Coleman was aware of the Central Council's policy. Levers and partnership belong to different leagues of human interactions but it is quite clear that Coleman is wanting a radical shift in power towards the Home Office and one which he suggests should be policed by the Probation Inspectorate. It is interesting that what is suggested is central control but this was probably essential if the values Coleman espouses are to be put into effect since his report suggests that the Service itself has not, in the words of the Cheshire Service, 'resolved its central dilemma of being a rehabilitative and caring service as opposed to a containing and overtly controlling service' (Coleman 1989: 19). This can be put more starkly. Is probation to offer social work to offenders so that they can confront and, if they so decide, change their offending behaviour or are probation officers to become the agents of punishment in the community? (See Allan, Chapter 3, in this volume.)

Together the Green Paper and the Coleman Report will have raised the question for social work educators as to how far they are willing to act as agents of the Home Office in training students for probation work which, at least in part, seems to fall outside the accepted boundaries of social work. These events put a different meaning into the question of the relevance of training for the job. Social work training may not be relevant for some jobs because these jobs cannot be considered to be social work.

Theories of adult learning

A different aspect of relevance relates to the research findings that transfer of skills and knowledge for training to the job depends in part upon the way in which training assists students to learn. Research into adult education (see for example Gardiner 1988) suggests that adults learn, at what has been called a deep level, where three conditions exist:

1 They learn in relation to problems which they consider real and important;
2 They learn with peers;
3 They learn when they control the content and pace of their own learning.

Deep learning means making knowledge one's own in a way which renders it usable in different situations from those in which it may first have been acquired. It is contrasted with surface learning, which is the kind of learning we all undertake in order to pass some specific test. Once passed the information is lost since it has served its purpose.

Looking at the conditions for deep learning it is apparent that the traditional CQSW social work courses fail to provide much if any of these conditions. Most courses are subject or topic rather than problem-led; students learn only in part from and with each other and have relatively little control over their own learning. CSS schemes come out of this comparison better in so far as the concurrent employment and learning allows for a closer relationship between what is learnt in class and what is done on the job. Some CSS students can bring problems from work directly into the classroom. They may have no more opportunity for peer learning than their CQSW contemporaries but the individualized study contracts and the availability of study supervisors should provide the opportunity for greater control over the content and pace of learning.

Despite the fact that CSS comes out better, even it has a considerable way to go towards a model of learning based on the research findings. Such a model does exist, although not in the United Kingdom and not in social work education. It is the problem-led model adopted for medical education at some universities including McMaster in Canada, and Newcastle in Australia (see for example Pallie and Brain 1978; Engel 1983).

In this model students work in peer groups with a staff facilitator on a series of problems. The problems are selected with the assistance of the local medical practitioners and a student who works through the whole series will have covered the same areas of knowledge and skills as are taught in traditional medical education. The difference is that the student will cover the areas because he or she wants to know in order to address the problem confronting the group. What a student learns and when he or she learns it are determined by the individual in consultation with the peer group. Staff act as facilitators of the groups' enquiry and as resource persons, but they only assume the latter role at the request of the students. By this method students acquire knowledge but much more important perhaps they acquire a method of problem-solving which will serve them throughout their professional life. They will not learn in one way during training and then have to find a new way of addressing the problems of practice.

This model seems to offer what may be a more suitable form for social work education and Bristol University Social Work Department will be changing to it in 1990. The traditional subject and methods teaching sequences will stop and staff will become facilitators for student learning.

To date the Department's experience of running experimental units, of what is being called Enquiry and Action-led Learning, have been positive. Students have found them stimulating and our fear that they might use problems to avoid getting a grasp of the relevant literature and research has not materialized. Staff too have enjoyed acting as facilitators although some are still concerned about the change being asked of them. What opposition there is comes from the field where some managers do not believe that students will, for example, learn child care law unless a lecture is provided on the topic.

The hope is that such a programme will prove relevant to the demands of practice and produce social workers who know how to approach problems. To the extent that the complaints about lack of relevance rest upon a failure by social work courses to teach problem-solving this method should contribute to relevance. What it may also do is produce students who know how to question accepted ideas and the ways of the establishment. If any of the employer's criticisms are based upon a view that basic grade workers should accept the dictates of the bureaucracy without question then they will like the products of this new form of training even less than they like the present output.

Expanding into anti-discriminatory practice

Social work education could well have been criticized for its failure to recognize the position of various disadvantaged groups in British society. There was a marked change in the last five years especially with regard to race and to a lesser extent towards gender. It is true that social work education may not yet have moved far enough and also that the advance is patchy. Nevertheless it is obvious that there has been change. The Council's new regulations are specific about requirements for all students to demonstrate a capacity to work in a multi-racial society and to take issue with discrimination. The Council has appointed a black perspectives committee which, in the last year of the 1986–9 Council, was beginning to promote anti-racist strategies. Courses have moved from racism awareness to anti-racism and students are proving to be a powerful force in changing the practice of courses, schemes, and in some instances employers.

Other forms of discrimination have received less attention. Some programmes pay attention to issues of gender but there is little Council initiative in this area and almost none at all in relation to discrimination against elderly people or those with a disability. Even more serious is the total lack of concern about what might be seen as social work's own particular form of discrimination – that against clients. We have yet to tackle what might be called clientism; the attitude of mind which sees those who are clients of the social services as different and less worthy than other people. It is an attitude which has its roots in our society's Protestant ethic that to need or to seek help is essentially shameful. Social work is for stigmatized people, and social workers and social work educators are not entirely free from this attitude themselves. Take a look at most social services or probation department waiting-rooms and you will not think that they cater for a highly regarded group. Social work educators may unwittingly have contributed to clientism by their attempts to make their teaching relevant. If all or most examples in sociology and psychology teaching are drawn from clients of the social services it is little wonder that students, many already imbued with the Protestant ethic, begin to see clients as different. Perhaps social work education could give some of the attention it is now focusing on race and gender to the stigmatized client. It is particularly important at a time when government policy interprets social need as social pathology.

Conclusions

This has been a gloomy account. At a time when the values of social work most need to be promoted, social work education is in a weak state. It has been subjected to a long and enfeebling review and has emerged from it having gained little. The future lies in the balance which can be developed in the educator–employer partnerships. One scenario is of an employer take-over with the logical result that social work education will be largely in-service and closely tied into the NCVQ framework, where employment competencies are the desired end. The other is of a partnership in which the strengths of employers and of educators come together to design and run programmes which produce competent practitioners with a desire to further their knowledge and skills and where the relationship between theory and practice is seen as invigorating and stimulating the development of each, rather than as a battle-ground for snipers.

References

Bolam, R. (1982) *Inservice education and training of teachers*, Paris: OECD.

CCETSW (1983) *Review of Qualifying Training Policies*, Paper 20, London: CCETSW.

—— (1987) *Care for Tomorrow*, London: CCETSW.

Coleman, D. A. (1989) *Home Office Review of Probation Training*, London: Home Office.

Engel, E. C. (1983) *The Undergraduate Programme 1980–83* vol. 2, Faculty of Medicine, University of Newcastle, New South Wales, Australia.

Gardiner, D. (1988) 'Improving students' learning – setting an agenda for quality in the 1990s', *Issues in Social Work Education* 8, 1: 3–10.

Home Office (1988) *Punishment, Custody and the Community*, Cm 424, London: HMSO.

Janis, I. L. (1972) *Victims of Group Think*, Boston, Mass: Houghton Mifflin.

Jones, C. (1989) 'The end of the road? Issues in social work education', in P. Carter, T. Jeffs and M. Smith (eds) *Social Work and Social Welfare Yearbook*, Milton Keynes: Open University Press.

Pallie, W. and Brain, E. (1978) 'Modules in morphology for self study: a system for learning in an undergraduate medical programme', *Medical Education* 12, 107–13.

Thomas, M. (1988) Personal communication based on research comparing a CSS scheme and a CQSW course.